Don Shiach

Prose
and
Poetry

The Reading
of the Text

CAMBRIDGE
UNIVERSITY PRESS

Published by the Press Syndicate of the University of Cambridge
The Pitt Building, Trumpington Street, Cambridge CB2 1RP
40 West 20th Street, New York, NY 10011-4211, USA
10 Stamford Road, Oakleigh, Melbourne 3166, Australia

© Cambridge University Press 1996

First published 1996

Printed in Great Britain by Scotprint, Musselburgh, Scotland

A catalogue record for this book is available from the British Library

ISBN 0 521 498945   801.95   Sth

Prepared for publication by Paren & Stacey Editorial Consultants
Designed and typeset by Geoffrey & Marion H Wadsley

Notice to teachers
It is illegal to reproduce any part of this work in material form (including photo-copying and electronic storage) except under the following circumstances:
(i) where you are abiding by a licence granted to your school or institution by the Copyright Licensing Agency;
(ii) where no such licence exists, or where you wish to exceed the terms of a licence, and you have gained the written permission of Cambridge University Press;
(iii) where you are allowed to reproduce without permission under the provisions of Chapter 3 of the Copyright, Designs and Patents Act 1988.

MHW

Contents

PART A   PROSE

1 The uses of prose

2 The text in context

6   The distinctive features of poetry

7   More about the language of poetry

8   Who writes poetry?

9 Poetry and genre

10 Further poems for appreciation and comparison

Prose

The word 'prose', like many other English words, has a Latin derivation: *prosa*, which means a direct form of discourse, either oral or written, used in everyday communication. Yet, however direct, everyday and functional prose may be in many of its uses, it can also be indirect, decorative, flamboyant and 'poetic'. Indeed, the distinction between what is prose and what is poetry is often difficult to define.

Nevertheless, it is still useful to analyse what we call 'prose' and what we define as 'poetry' separately, if we bear in mind that these are essentially artificial categories. Prose and poetry may be seen as particular ways of arranging language, but they are not entirely separate from one another. They share characteristics, but prose in general arranges language within different types of discourse and within different compartments of genre from poetry. As readers, when we identify a written text as prose rather than poetry, we have different expectations about the kind of language use that is being practised.

1   The uses of prose

In this unit we are studying a wide variety of uses of prose. The given texts range from what appears to be the purely functional communication of information to the creation of a short literary form; from prose that seeks to persuade to spoken language that is affected by ritual and 'hallowed' surroundings; from the 'objective and scientific' to the highly personal. One issue that will emerge in discussion is whether language use can ever be 'neutral'.

1.1   The use of language in conveying information

Faced with the world in all its aspects, human beings have developed language systems that employ words to differentiate one thing from another. In this way we can describe the world for ourselves, and for others. For example, the word 'cat' in English differentiates one small four-legged animal from other animals, say, from a 'dog'. But the use of the word 'cat' to describe that particular animal could be said to be purely arbitrary; in a different language system, say in French, the equivalent word is 'chat'. Each language has its own way of imposing divisions between the infinite variety of things and ideas that constitute our experience of the world. The word 'cat' has evolved and been accepted as the term in English to describe that particular animal, but its use is only a means of describing the animal, it is not the cat itself. By using the word 'cat' to describe a particular type of domestic pet, we are trying to capture the 'reality' of a cat. Language often defines 'reality' for us, but if we accept the idea that words impose arbitrary divisions between things and ideas, we may have to reassess that 'reality', by re-examining the language we use.

When language aims to communicate precise information, it strives to erase any 'grey' areas of interpretation or 'meaning'. Words are intended to mean what they say, no more, no less. For example, in written agreements between people, the language usage is very formal and appropriate to the **context**. The context is the real, external situation in which any language use is taking place. The type of language used in legal agreements belongs to a particular code, a specific range of signs in the form of words which needs to be decoded. Below is an extract from a contract between a writer and a publisher, which lays down in exact terms what the agreement between the two parties is.

AGREEMENT	made this 17th day of September 1996 BETWEEN Leslie Adams, 146 Writers Alley, Gresham GR3 4FF (hereinafter called 'the Author') AND Educational Publishing Ltd., Waterloo House, Maypole Road, Lanchester ORV 5YY (hereinafter called 'the Publishers') Whereby it is mutually agreed as follows: the Author is writing a literary work entitled 'How to Write A Best-Seller', hereinafter called 'the work', comprising not less than 50,000 words and no more than 60,000.
DELIVERY OF TYPESCRIPT	Two copies of the completed typescript shall be delivered to the Publishers not later than the thirty-first of May, 1997, and the Publishers shall, under the imprint of Educational Publishing Ltd., produce and publish the work, unless prevented by circumstances beyond their control. Should the author fail to deliver the typescript in a form acceptable to the publishers within a month of the prescribed date, the Publishers will be within their rights to decline to publish the said work.
ROYALTIES	The Publishers undertake to pay to the author the following royalties or percentages calculated on the Publishers' net receipts in respect of volume or sheet sales during the legal term of this agreement: a) an advance of £2000 (two thousand pounds) on account of future royalties, payable as to half on signature of this contract by both parties and half on the date of publication. b) a royalty of 10% (ten per cent) of the monies received by the Publisher on all the copies of the work sold.
ACCOUNTS	An exact royalty account shall be calculated annually to the last day of March and settled in the month of July following.
COMPETING PUBLICATIONS	The Author undertakes not to write or publish any other book on the same subject which may reasonably be regarded as likely to compete with or affect adversely the sale of the work.
OPTION	The Author agrees to give to the Publishers the first refusal (including the first opportunity to read and consider for publication) of the Author's next work suitable for publication in book form.

Group discussion

- Working in pairs, read through the terms of the contract carefully and decide what meaning is produced for you by the language in each of the five sections.
- Words and their associations are an essential part of their meaning. For example, the words 'Top Twenty' derive their meaning mostly because of their association with the pop music industry. 'No Entry' is easily understood because of the associations with traffic signs. Each sphere of activity has some kind of 'code' of language that users and 'receivers' have to understand.

  Make a list of any words and phrases from the contract that derive meaning from their close association with the sphere of activity (writing and publishing) described.

- A *register* is a particular variation of language defined by its specific use. Register defines three main aspects: mode, field, tenor. The *mode* can be written or spoken, the *field* defines the specialist area in which the language is being employed, and the *tenor* is the tone and manner. Discuss the register of the above contract and decide on its mode, field and tenor.

Writing ☞

Draw up a simple contract which requires you to provide a service of some kind to a company or business. The contract should be divided into sections with headings ('Services to be provided', 'Salary', Conditions of work'). Each party to the contract should be given a particular title, for example, 'the adviser', 'the employee'. The tone and language should be formal.

If you prefer, you may write a parody of such a contract.

GLOSSARY

Context: the real external situation in which language is being used. For example, an analysis of the kind of spoken language used by a game show host on television would have to be discussed in terms of that particular context: a 'popular' programme on television watched by millions of people.

Register: a register is a variety of language differentiated by its specific use. For example, an article in a scientific journal would belong to a particular register: in the written *mode*, in the scientific *field* and using a formal manner *(tenor)* full of technical jargon.

1.2 Conveying information: semantic field

Words, then, derive their meaning partly from the context in which they are used. We cited the phrase 'Top Twenty' in the previous section. That phrase derives its meaning from the context of popular music and its associations. The words have certain **connotations** (pop charts, competition, perhaps a certain glamour). The associations words have and their connotations (emotional or other overtones) are important aspects of their meaning.

In addition, individual words acquire a part of their meaning from other words of a similar kind. We can call this the **semantic field** in which words operate. To illustrate the concept of semantic field, look at this extract from a holiday brochure.

From **£17** per night

ARIZONA
If you knew it, you'd do it.

GRAND CANYON AREA

HOLIDAY INN FLAGSTAFF

Moderate First Class
This hotel is perfectly positioned to enjoy historic Flagstaff, located in the shadow of the magnificent San Francisco Peaks, as well as an ideal base from which to explore the region's treasures including the magnificent Grand Canyon & Oak Creek Canyon. The Holiday Inn has excellent facilities including a swimming pool and jacuzzi. Guest rooms are tastefully decorated and have private facilities and colour TV.
  ★ Humphreys Restaurant & Lounge
  ★ Heated swimming pool
  ★ Jacuzzi
  ★ Guest laundry

HOLIDAY INN FLAGSTAFF Code: 328	Twin prices per person per night	3rd/4th Adult Price	Children Free*
January–April November–December	£21	£3	
May–October	£29	£3	17

LAKE POWELL

WAHWEAP LODGE & MARINA

First Class
The Wahweap Lodge offers a superb location right on the shores of the beautiful Lake Powell. Spacious and comfortable air-conditioned rooms all feature phone, colour TV and patio or balcony. Boat tours and fishing guides

on Lake Powell can be arranged from the property's own marina. A great place from which to explore the soaring canyons and sparkling waters of this great recreation area.
  ★ 2 Restaurants
  ★ Outdoor swimming pool
  ★ Cocktail lounge
  ★ Gift Shop
  ★ Marina

WAHWEAP LODGE & MARINA Code: 315	Twin prices per person per night	3rd/4th Adult Price	Children Free*
January–April November–December	£27	£7	
May–October	£40	£9	17

SCOTTSDALE

SCOTTSDALE HILTON RESORT & SPA

Superior First Class
A truly superior first-class hotel with a distinctive Spanish-style, set in 20 acres and built around a landscaped court-yard. Public rooms are spacious and feature high beamed ceilings with large garden and pool area. Guest rooms are of a high standard with colour TV, air conditioning and some with patios.
  ★ Restaurant
  ★ Lounge
  ★ Live entertainment & dancing
  ★ Swimming pool
  ★ 4 lighted tennis courts
  ★ Health spa
  ★ Gift shop
  ★ Beauty salon
  ★ Golf privileges

SCOTTSDALE HILTON RESORT & SPA Code: 324	Twin prices per person per night	3rd/4th Adult Price	Children Free*
January–December	£17	£10	18

PHOENIX

POINTE HILTON AT SQUAW PEAK

Moderate Deluxe
The Pointe Hilton is a deluxe Mediterranean-style mountainside resort. Spacious two-room suites feature air conditioning, a living room, colour TV, phone, refrigerator, wet bar and private balcony. The Pointe Hilton makes a perfect base for a relaxing away-from-it-all stay, yet is within easy access of downtown Phoenix.
  ★ 4 restaurants
  ★ 5 swimming pools
  ★ 8 lighted tennis courts
  ★ Fitness centre with steam room & sauna
  ★ Club for dancing and live entertainment
  ★ Cocktail party nightly
  ★ Racquetball court
  ★ 18-hole championship golf course
  ★ Riding Stables & Hayrides

POINTE HILTON AT SQUAW PEAK Code: 318	Twin prices per person per night	3rd/4th Adult Price	Children Free*
January–December	£18	£3	18

Group discussion
- Each of the four hotels mentioned in this section of the brochure are given a grading: 'Moderate First Class', 'First Class', 'Superior First Class' and 'Moderate Deluxe'. These descriptions derive their meaning in relation to one another. 'First Class', for example, derives meaning in comparison with 'Moderate First Class'. These words are operating within a particular semantic field.

  Compare what is written about the Holiday Inn, Flagstaff and the Wahweap Lodge and Marina at Lake Powell and discuss what might justify one hotel being described as 'Moderate First Class' and the other as 'First Class'. Then compare what is written about the two other hotels and discuss what might make one 'Superior First Class' and the other 'Moderate Deluxe'.
- Discuss why you think the holiday company has used terms such as 'First Class', 'Superior' and 'Deluxe' in this way.
- Imagine there are other hotels available that are not mentioned in this extract. These hotels comprise those at the less expensive and very expensive ends of the scale. How might they be graded in relation to 'Moderate First Class' and 'Moderate Deluxe'?

Writing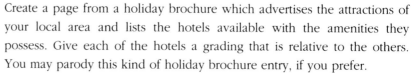
Create a page from a holiday brochure which advertises the attractions of your local area and lists the hotels available with the amenities they possess. Give each of the hotels a grading that is relative to the others. You may parody this kind of holiday brochure entry, if you prefer.

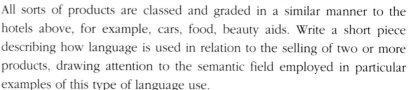
All sorts of products are classed and graded in a similar manner to the hotels above, for example, cars, food, beauty aids. Write a short piece describing how language is used in relation to the selling of two or more products, drawing attention to the semantic field employed in particular examples of this type of language use.

GLOSSARY

Connotation: the emotional or other overtones that words frequently have. Certain words have different connotations for different people, therefore the 'meaning' is not fixed and unvariable.

Semantic field: the framework which enables words to derive a part of their meaning from words of a similar kind. For example, words that might be used by a critic giving a critical guide to films: 'very poor', 'watchable', 'above average', 'not to be missed'.

1.3 The language of persuasion

Everything in a written form, however brief, may be referred to as a *text*. No written text can be fully interpreted or discussed without relating and comparing it to other similar texts.

For example, if we are reading a science fiction or ghost story, we interpret meaning partly in relation to other texts of a similar nature, other science fiction or ghost stories that we have read. The type of language, references, settings and plots used in one text are probably familiar to us from our reading of other texts of the same type. We recognise particular conventions of language use and subject matter through familiarity with particular *text types* or *genres*.

The term ***intertextuality*** may be used to describe how we make texts intelligible through our experience of other similar texts.

We learn to associate certain types of language use with particular kinds of texts. We learn that words have associations and connotations (see the previous section) in particular and differing contexts. The context of the particular use of language is very important in making the text intelligible to us.

To illustrate this, we will examine the use of language in a very short text. Someone has traced these words in the dirt on the back of an unwashed, grimy white car:

ALSO AVAILABLE IN WHITE

To interpret the meaning of this 'text' (we are treating everything 'written' as a text), it helps to be familiar with the kind of language that occurs in the advertising of products in newspapers and department stores. For example, a product of a particular colour may be shown in an magazine advertisement or brochure and the words 'Also available in red' (or other colours) are added.

Consciously or unconsciously, when we appreciate the joke involved in the scrawling of 'Also available in white' on the back of the white car, we are using our familiarity with that particular use of language in a similar context, that is, advertisements of one kind or another. The 'car text' is intelligible in relation to other 'similar' texts.

In this example we can also recognise the use of irony in the language. As the car is (in theory) white, attention is being drawn to how dirty the car is. Irony occurs when the words we hear, read or use ourselves imply a meaning different from the actual words used.

Below are two advertisements for adaptations of two famous novels, one for the stage, the other for the cinema.

Group discussion

- *Jane Eyre* advertisement: discuss in pairs:
    - the different elements that this advertisement consists of, for example, headlines, quotes, names, titles, non-verbal images and any other features.
    - combinations of words that are very familiar from seeing other advertisements of this type.
    - any unusual placing together of words. The term **collocation** is used to describe the placing together of two or more words or phrases. Collocation may mean words in direct sequence (for example, as in 'red roses'), or may refer to words or phrases that are closely related to one another in a text. For example, in these lines:

        The quality of mercy is not strained,

        It droppeth as the gentle rain from heaven

      the words 'quality', 'mercy', 'strained', 'droppeth', 'gentle rain' and 'heaven' are in collocation with one another. Collocation may be entirely predictable and familiar, or unpredictable and unfamiliar.
    - any elements of the typography (the style of print used, bold type, italics, capital letters, etc.) that produce particular meaning.

  Then come together as a group and arrive at a consensus agreement about what the advertisement is made up of.

- *Saturday Night and Sunday Morning* advertisement: discuss in pairs:
    - the meaning produced by the use of the visual images.
    - any meaning created by the way the title of the film and the names of the actors are set out.
    - the 'predictable' and any 'unpredictable' aspects of this advertisement.

  Then, as a group, discuss the elements that go to make up this advertisement.

- Taking into account other advertisements of this kind you have seen and remembering the commercial purpose behind the advertisements themselves (to differentiate one 'product' from another), which of these two do you consider to be the more effective in producing an effective communication with you, the reader?

Writing ☞

Your school or college drama society is to stage a production of an adaptation of one of the books you are studying in your English course. You are asked to design a poster to advertise the production. The poster will be displayed around the building and in the neighbourhood. Create one version that is entirely predictable in its use of language and image. Then create another that is less predictable. You may parody this type of advertising poster, if you prefer.

Intertextuality: we interpret written texts in relation to other similar texts. For example, if we are reading a mystery story, our reading of it may be influenced by our experience of, and familiarity with, other similar texts. It could be claimed that there are no completely original texts, only texts that 'borrow' from one another.

Collocation: the placing of words or phrases together in a text. Unusual collocation may 'surprise' readers and encourage us to re-examine the meaning of words. Predictable collocation may, however, reinforce through familiarity an accepted view of 'reality'.

1.4 Language and discourse

The term 'discourse' was used in the introduction to this section on prose. A *discourse* is an area of language use which embodies a specific way of thinking, speaking or talking. Indeed, all forms of writing (and speaking) involve using language in a way that reflects a particular way of thinking and discussing. We can describe particular areas of language use as employing specific types of discourse.

Different forms of discourse employ different language usage appropriate to the subject and context of the writing or speech, for example, a radio disc jockey will use a particular kind of discourse, which listeners will recognise and interpret according to certain expectations of the kind of discourse that is usually offered by this radio station, whereas an announcer on a classical music station will use a different form of discourse, one that regular listeners will 'tune into' readily. There are 'shared assumptions' between the respective presenters and listeners of these two radio stations about the kind of discourse that will be offered.

It is important to understand that the ideas embodied in a piece of writing or speech are not separate from the words that are used by the writer or speaker. They are inscribed in the words, in the discourse, which is a way of thinking, writing or talking. To illustrate this, here is an extract from *Beyond Power: On Women, Men and Morals* by Marilyn French. This book offers a discourse on power and particularly the power that resides, it is claimed, in the hands of a relatively few men.

> Although many people believe it is women who work harder to maintain gender roles, to teach their daughters to be 'ladies', and their sons to be 'gentlemen', studies have revealed that in late twentieth-century America, men are more concerned than women that their children adopt 'proper' – that is, dictated, traditional – sex-role behaviour. Other studies show that

boys have more difficulty in accepting their appropriate sex role. David Lynn, who has conducted a number of these studies, attributes boys' difficulties to three sources: lack of male models, the rigidity and harshness of masculine roles, and the negative nature of the requirements. Boys especially seem to suffer from the fact that fathers are absent, whether emotionally or physically, and from the lack of other significant males in their young lives. And the male role in patriarchal society consists, as we have seen, largely of sacrifices – men must give up the hope of happiness, the ideal of home, emotional expressiveness and spontaneity, in order to become members of an elite that values power, wandering isolation, individuality, and discipline (order in obedience).

The fact that a male role does not gratify a boy, does not arise from primary desire but from the secondary desire of wanting to be like other boys or wanting to be a man like others he sees (on television, in films, in comic books, in history books), may account for the rigid, almost ritualistic way in which many adult men 'play' their roles. Lynn discovered that boys who lack fathers entirely are more likely to entertain exaggerated and stereotypical images of masculinity than boys who have fathers, no matter how absent or violent.

What Westerners mean when they say they want to make a man out of a boy is that they want a boy to learn that the sacrifices mentioned above are essential, are the characteristics of men. And the schools, or gymnasia, or army training camps to which people send boys to 'make men of them', specialise in brutalisation: rigid discipline, emphasis on physical hardness and strength, and contempt for sensitivity, delicacy and emotion. Fortunately, not all boys are subjected to such treatment, but no boy escapes knowledge of the severities of 'manliness' in our society, and those who feel they have not achieved it live with a lingering self-doubt, self-diminishment. On the other hand, those men who score highest on tests of 'masculinity' refuse to restrain their aggressiveness even when by expressing it they lose the approval of their community.

'Manliness', as defined by patriarchy, means to be or appears to be in control at all times. But remaining in control prevents a person from ever achieving intimacy with another, from ever letting down his guard; it thus precludes easy friendship, fellowship, community. Men may have 'buddies', acquaintances with whom they can engage in ritual competition of banter, sport, or game, but they rarely possess intimate friends. I mentioned before that on tests administered by Carol Gilligan, in which a set of pictures was submitted to male and female subjects, men offered the most violent and threatening narratives as explanations of photographs showing people close to each other, and the least threatening stories to explain photographs of men in isolation. Shut out from the most nourishing parts of life, men seek what they need in the channels they have been told is 'theirs': work, achievement, success. They imagine that success, or the demonstration of 'manliness', will bring them love; instead it often alienates those they love. They feel cheated; and they blame women.

And men have, through patriarchal forms, achieved power-in-the-world. Men own 99 per cent of the world's property and earn 90 per cent of its wages, while producing only 55 per cent of the world's food and performing only one third of the world's work. Men rather exclusively direct the course not just of states and corporations but of culture: religion, arts, education. Despite the assault of various waves of feminism, men have been able to retain their control over the people, creatures, plants, and even some of the elements of this planet. Many men wish to retain those powers.

Group discussion

- Working in pairs, prepare a list of the ideas or points that you consider to be expressed through the language of the extract. Then write a summary of the passage based on this list, using no more than sixty words. Reduce this to forty words by excluding what is not absolutely essential.

  As a class, compare summaries and agree a consensus summary, also of no more than forty words. Then, agree a title for the extract above.

- From the group summary, choose some of the ideas or points that were made in the original passage. Look at how the relevant section of the passage embodies those ideas in language use. Discuss the words used: what kind of discourse is being employed? How formal or informal is the language?

- The *tone* of a piece of writing arises from the language use. Just as the ideas are inscribed in the language, so is the tone. Discuss the tone of this piece: is it scientific, detached, highly subjective, angry, academic, seeking to persuade, dogmatic, balanced?

Writing ☛

You have been asked to write a piece about gender relations for your school or college magazine or newspaper. You are restricted to 400 words. The piece will appear in a regular feature called 'Opinion'. The readers of the piece will be your fellow students and teaching staff. Decide on the subject of the piece, a title and the main points you want to make. What tone will the piece have? What do you think the expectations of your readers will be? Do you want to meet those expectations or not?

GLOSSARY

Discourse: a discourse is an area of language use, a specific way of thinking, speaking or talking.

1.5 The ceremony of language

Language is often used ceremonially and formally with particular codes for specific contexts and purposes. In these formal contexts, the language is distanced from everyday usage in a deliberate attempt to make it 'special' and distinct. For example, clubs and associations of people with particular interests in common often evolve their own manner of communication and vocabulary: freemasons, youth organisations, business organisations, political and pressure groups.

The House of Commons in the United Kingdom is where Members of Parliament meet to debate public issues and enact legislation. Down the centuries, a formal style of address has been established and for an MP to make a contribution to a debate in the House, s/he has to accept this ceremonial way of speaking and obey the accepted rules laid down by the procedures. Below is an extract from *Hansard*, the publication which prints a daily record of the debates held on the floor of the House of Commons.

House of Commons

Thursday 19 May 1994
The House met at half-past Two o'clock

PRAYERS
(Madam Speaker *in the Chair*

PRIVATE BUSINESS
Federation of Street Traders Union (London Local Authorities Act 1990) (Amendment) Bill (By Order.)
Order for Second Reading read.
To be read a Second time on Thursday 16 June.

Oral Answers to Questions

HOME DEPARTMENT
Identity Cards

1. **Mr. Campbell-Savours:** To ask the Secretary of State for the Home Department what further discussions have taken place on the introduction of identity cards.

3. **Mr Gale:** To ask the Secretary of State for the Home Department what further consideration he has given to the introduction of identity cards.

The Secretary of State for the Home Department (Mr. Michael Howard): We keep this issue under constant review. I fully appreciate the widespread support which exists for a national identity card scheme.

Mr. Campbell-Savours: May I suggest that Ministers stop trying to sell a national identity card scheme on the basis that it would be a tool to deal with social security fraud—(Hon. Members: "Why?") Conservative Members should wait. Despite the lobby that wants to insert an element of political correctness into the debate, is not the truth that a national identity card scheme could enhance civil liberties, be a major tool in tracking down crime, particularly tax fraud, and also be of immeasurable benefit to people needing emergency medical treatment?

Mr Howard: The hon. Gentleman has identified a number of advantages that an identity card could have. As he knows, there are considerable practical

---

difficulties and we are trying to find ways to overcome them.

Mr Gale: Given that a properly designed identity card could be used as a travel document throughout the European Union, as a passport for pensions and social benefits and to carry medical and banking information, that people in the Press Gallery, hon. Members, servants of the House and many other people in many walks of life already carry identity cards, that the honest person has nothing to fear from carrying an identity card, and that the introduction of such a scheme has the support of the Association of Chief Police Officers, the Superintendents Association and the Police Federation, will my right hon. and learned Friend bring forward in the next Session of Parliament the measures necessary to introduce such a scheme?

Mr Howard: My hon. Friend makes an even more compelling case than the hon. Member for Workington (Mr. Campbell-Savours). However, the practical difficulties still need to be overcome. My hon. Friend was not, perhaps, entirely accurate in his description of the organisations which support the introduction of an identity card, but I readily accept that there is widespread support for such a scheme.

Mr Spellar: Why does the Home Secretary not come clean and admit that the identity card is a political gimmick with a huge cost? His Department's figures show that a scheme would cost £475 million to set up and £50 million to £100 million per year to run. Will he reflect on the figures produced by his colleagues in the Department of the Environment, which show that council tax registers record a 34 per cent. turnover each year? Would that not result in enormous administrative problems? Those are the real practical difficulties and costs of the scheme.

Mr Howard: I do not conceal from the House that there are practical difficulties. However, the hon. Gentleman would have had a most effective answer to the points that he raised in the early part of his question had he been able to see the number of his hon. Friends shaking their heads as he spoke.

Mr. Batiste: Does my right hon. and learned Friend agree that many organisations are now exploring different technologies for smart ID cards? If the Government act quickly they could co-ordinate that activity and produce a card that would have widespread application in the years ahead.

Mr Howard: Mr hon. Friend makes an extremely important point, which I assure him is not lost on the Government.

Mr Allen: Before the Home Secretary is tempted to snatch at a panacea and cure-all for all the things that are wrong with society, will he heed those who have strong reservations in principle about identity cards, those who feel that they could be discriminatory and those who make the case that professional criminals could easily evade the use of such cards? Before the right hon. and learned Gentleman goes any further, will he conduct some serious Home Office research? If he then intends to bring proposals before the House, will he ensure that it is on the basis of an all-party consensus?

Mr. Howard: Given the difference of views expressed in the past two minutes, it would be difficult to strike a consensus that would satisfy everyone.

Mr. Skinner: It would.

Mr Howard: I am delighted to have the agreement of the hon. Member for Bolsover (Mr Skinner). At the end of the day, we shall have to make a decision on the matter, but I can certainly give an undertaking to the hon. Member for Nottingham, North (Mr. Allen) that we shall listen to all the views that are expressed.

Group discussion

- Read the section between 'House of Commons' and 'Oral Answers to Questions'. Discuss what the language communicates to you. Select any examples of language use that appear to be part of a 'parliamentary discourse' or distinct to the House of Commons.

- Read the first contribution made by the Secretary of State for the Home Department, Mr Howard. Consider the oral statement he makes. How formal is the language used? What examples of language use make it formal?

- Select examples from the *Hansard* report of how MPs refer to one another. What is ceremonial about this? What meaning is produced by the use of this manner of address?

- Read the second contribution made to the debate by Mr Gale. He asks a question of the Secretary of State contained in one sentence, which is very long. The 'question' part of the question comes right at the end of the sentence. What is the effect on the meaning produced of making a series of statements before putting the actual question?

- This is a written record of a debate in the House of Commons, although it is not a *verbatim* (word-for-word) report of the proceedings. Judging by this record, and this one alone, what impression do you receive of the way the House of Commons conducts its debates?

Writing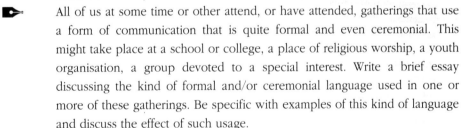

The language used in the debate is formal and polite. Imagine that the MPs in the House were not constrained by the rules of procedure and accepted modes of address. Rewrite part of this *Hansard* report imagining that the MPs used more everyday language and did not address each other so formally.

All of us at some time or other attend, or have attended, gatherings that use a form of communication that is quite formal and even ceremonial. This might take place at a school or college, a place of religious worship, a youth organisation, a group devoted to a special interest. Write a brief essay discussing the kind of formal and/or ceremonial language used in one or more of these gatherings. Be specific with examples of this kind of language and discuss the effect of such usage.

1.6 The language of science

The language that science, of whatever sphere of interest, uses is meant to be neutral and objective. Science, it is claimed, observes, analyses and makes conclusions on the basis of hard evidence. The language that scientists employ is intended to be free of any bias, not charged with emotional undertones and strictly impersonal.

Below is an article from *New Statesman and Society*, a weekly periodical that focuses on social, political, environmental and scientific issues. The article is reporting on what scientists have deduced from information gathered from a space satellite, the COBE.

SCIENCE & ENVIRONMENT

The latest results from the COBE satellite show the oldest and largest structures yet seen and have provided more evidence for the Big Bang, reports John Mather

Ripples in time

The COBE (Cosmic Background Explorer) satellite completed its mission, after four years of successful observations, on 23 December 1993. We now have new and definite confirmation of the ripples in space-time first announced last April, and the COBE observations have led to the most precise measurement of the spectrum of the cosmic microwave background radiation (CMBR) ever obtained.

This radiation is the heat left over from the beginning of time about 15 billion years ago, and fills the universe, although it has now cooled to only 2.726 degrees above absolute zero. The theoretical prediction of the spectrum for the CMBR was confirmed within 0.03 per cent, more than 1,000 times better than was possible before the COBE mission.

The implications of the spectrum measurement are profound: the Hot Big Bang theory is the only one that can explain the precise spectrum, and no others come close. Moreover, at least 99.97 per cent of the energy in the CMBR was released by the end of the first year of expansion. There is little room for exotic effects such as decaying cosmic strings, decaying elementary particles, evaporating or growing black holes, primeval turbulent motions, hot intergalactic gas, or new undiscovered galaxies or quasars.

Very recently we completed the analysis of two years of data showing the cosmic ripples in the CMBR brightness. These primordial lumps and bumps were first reported by the COBE team in April 1992, based on the first year of data, and they made worldwide headlines. Our original results have been confirmed extremely well. The new maps are qualitatively similar to the old, but have been improved in clarity by additional data. The implications are that we have seen the largest and oldest structures that we may ever see, stretching across the cosmos at the dawn of time.

These results are extremely important because despite its brilliant successes, the Big Bang theory harbours great mysteries as well: what caused the universe to begin to expand? Why is the antimatter all gone? Why is the universe so uniform and, conversely, why did gigantic clusters of galaxies develop? What is the dark matter, and why does it seem to be ten to 100 times more abundant than ordinary matter? When and how did galaxies themselves evolve? The COBE CMBR results fit neatly into the cosmological jig-saw puzzle, and strictly limit some of the answers to these questions.

Group discussion

- Working in pairs, read through the first paragraph. Select examples of language use from this paragraph that reflects the enthusiasm of the writer for the advance in scientific knowledge that appears to have happened.

- If discourse means a particular domain of language use, here we are being offered a *scientific discourse*. Make a list of words and phrases used in the article that reflect this type of discourse.

- Discuss whether there are any further examples of language use outside the first paragraph that are more personal and less 'scientific'.

- As a group, discuss whether this article is written from a particular viewpoint and whether any attempt is made to persuade the readers to accept a particular theory.

- This article was written for a particular weekly magazine. Judging by this article, what kind of readership is the magazine aiming at?

Writing 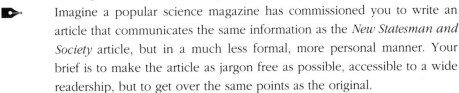 Imagine you have been commissioned by the same magazine to write an article in response to the one above. Your aim is to discredit the scientific findings reported on in the article. You will need to use short quotes from the original in order to make your counter argument.

Imagine a popular science magazine has commissioned you to write an article that communicates the same information as the *New Statesman and Society* article, but in a much less formal, more personal manner. Your brief is to make the article as jargon free as possible, accessible to a wide readership, but to get over the same points as the original.

1.7 Letter writing

Letter writing is a form of written communication that may employ a wide range of language use according to context, purpose and the relationship between the letter writer and the 'receiver' or addressee. Clearly, the level of formality of language will vary according to the context: writing a letter to a department of your local authority will require a different register to a letter to a close friend. The *mode* is the same (written), but the *field* would be different ('official communication' as opposed to personal) and the *tenor* would be quite dissimilar (formal and impersonal in contrast to personal and informal).

On page 24 is an extract from a letter written in the 1940s by Raymond Chandler to his publisher in New York. Raymond Chandler was a famous author of 'tough guy' detective fiction (his most famous creation is private eye Philip Marlowe). He wrote this letter from Hollywood, where he had been working as a scriptwriter for one of the film studios.

Jan. 12, 1946

To: Alfred A. Knopf

. . . I no longer have a secretary because I no longer have a motion picture job. I am what is technically known as suspended. For refusing to perform under a contract which is not a proper expression of my standing in the motion picture business. I requested a cancellation, but was denied that. There is no moral issue involved since the studios have destroyed the moral basis of contracts themselves. They tear them up whenever it suits them. One of the troubles is that it seems quite impossible to convince anyone that a man would turn his back on a whopping salary – whopping by the standards of normal living – for any reason but a tactical manoeuvre through which he hopes to acquire a still more whopping salary. What I want is something quite different: a freedom from datelines and unnatural pressures, and a right to find and work with those few people in Hollywood whose purpose is to make the best pictures possible within the limitations of a popular art, not merely to repeat the old vulgar formulae.

. . . No doubt I have learned a lot from Hollywood. Please do not think I completely despise it, because I don't. The best proof of that may be that every producer I have ever worked for I would work for again, and every one of them, in spite of my tantrums, would be glad to have me. But the overall picture, as the boys say, is of a degraded community whose idealism even is largely fake. The pretentiousness, the bogus enthusiasm, the constant drinking and drabbing, the incessant squabbling over money, the all-pervasive agent, the strutting of the big shots (and their usually utter incompetence to achieve anything they start out to do), the constant fear of losing all this fairy gold and being the nothing they have never ceased to be, the snide tricks, the whole damn mess is out of this world.

It is a great subject for a novel – probably the greatest still untouched. But how to do it with a level mind, that's the thing that baffles me. It is like one of these South American palace revolutions conducted by officers in comic opera uniforms – only when the thing is over the ragged dead men lie in rows against the walls and you suddenly know that this is not funny, this is the Roman circus, and damn near the end of a civilization.

Group discussion

- Working in pairs, read the first paragraph of the letter extract carefully. Then select examples of language use that appears critical of the Hollywood studio that has suspended Chandler. Then select examples of language that produces the meaning of Chandler 'justifying himself'.

- As a group, consider the second paragraph of the letter extract. In what terms does Chandler express his criticisms of Hollywood? Summarise the gist of his complaints.

- There is a use of simile and metaphor in the third paragraph. A **simile** is an object, scene or action that is used to make a comparison between two unlike things for purposes of illustration, explanation or embellishment. Chandler writes 'It is like one of these South American palace revolutions conducted by officers in comic opera uniforms' about Hollywood. What meaning is produced by making this direct comparison? A **metaphor** is a comparison by transferring the qualities of one thing to another thing that is different from it. Chandler writes of Hollywood 'this is the Roman circus', thus he transfers the qualities of a Roman circus to Hollywood. Discuss the force of this metaphor.

- How formal is the language of the letter? Choose examples of formal language and some less formal usage.

- Judging by the manner in which the letter is written, make an assessment about how well Chandler knows the addressee.

Writing ☛

Imagine you are working away from home in a job that you do not particularly care for. You write three letters: one to a close friend in which you express your feelings about the work you are doing; the second to an older relative who has written to you enquiring how you are getting along in your new position; and a third to your employer at head office in which you express your doubts about whether you are really suited to the job and requesting a transfer.

After writing these three letters, write a commentary on the task, commenting on how you felt you had to vary the kind of language and register according to the context.

GLOSSARY

Simile: a direct comparison between two unlike things for the purposes of illustration. For example, he was as jumpy as a cat on a hot tin roof.

Metaphor: an indirect comparison between two unlike things in which the qualities of one thing are given to another. For example, in any struggle for supremacy she was a tiger.

1.8 Language in literature

What is 'literature'? The word means many different things to many different people. However, one way of describing literature would be to say it consists of various examples of language being arranged in particular ways in particular contexts. A novel can be seen as a use of language within a particular context, a 'long' work of prose fiction.

Short stories are examples of how language can be arranged within a particular form, a short piece of fiction. The context of short stories is usually a magazine of some kind, or sometimes a collection of short stories are brought together in a book.

Below is an example of a 'short', short story by Jayne Ann Philips. The story first appeared in a literary periodical, and was printed in a collection of short stories, all by the same author.

Solo dance

She hadn't been home in a long time. Her father had a cancer operation; she went home. She went to the hospital every other day, sitting for hours beside his bed. She could see him flickering. He was very thin and the skin on his legs was soft and pure like fine paper. She remembered him saying 'I give up' when he was angry or exasperated. Sometimes he said it as a joke, 'Jesus Christ, I give up'. She kept hearing his voice in the words now even though he wasn't saying them. She read his get-well cards aloud to him. One was from her mother's relatives. Well, he said, I don't think they had anything to do with it. He was speaking of his divorce two years ago.

She put lather in a hospital cup and he got up to shave in the mirror. He had to lean on the sink. She combed the back of his head with water and her fingers. His hair was long after six weeks in the hospital, a gray-silver full of shadow and smudge. She helped him get slowly into bed and he lay against the pillows breathing heavily. She sat down again. I can't wait till I get some weight on me, he said. So I can knock down that son-of-a-bitch lawyer right in front of the courthouse.

She sat watching her father. His robe was patterned with tiny horses, sorrels in arabesques. When she was very young, she had started ballet lessons. At the first class her teacher raised her leg until her foot was flat against the wall beside her head. He held it there and looked at her. She looked back at him, thinking to herself it didn't hurt and willing her eyes dry.

Her father was twisting his hands. How's your mother? She must be half crazy by now. She wanted to be by herself and brother that's what she got.

Group discussion
- Working in pairs, summarise the story in sixty words. Then reduce the summary to thirty words, including what you consider to be the 'essence' of the story. As a group, compare the summaries and arrive at a consensus summary of thirty words.
- As a group, discuss whether this is an 'unusual' short story. You might consider its length, the narrative, the language and how it ends.
- What words would you use to describe the tone of the story?
- Consider in detail how meaning is produced through the use of language: the vocabulary; the words the **narrative figures** (the 'characters') are given to say; the way the sentences are arranged.
- Discuss any meaning that the story has for you.

Writing ☞

Compared to many short stories, 'Solo dance' ends very abruptly. There is no particular reason why the story should have ended where it does; the author chose this ending, however, and that affects the meaning that is produced. Consider the story as not 'finished'. Continue from the point where it 'ends' above, choosing to develop the story in any way you want, but writing in a similar style to the author, Jayne Anne Philips.

After you have completed the story, write a brief commentary on how you accomplished this, commenting on the problems that this task set you.

GLOSSARY

Narrative figure: this term may be used in place of the more traditional 'character'. The use of the word 'characters' implies that the 'people' in a work of fiction are somehow 'real human beings' rather than descriptions of human beings created through language.

2 The text in context

Any text must be read within its context. *Context* is the total 'real' external situation in which a text is presented. For example, the context of this text is an introduction to a chapter on the subject of 'the text in context', within an 'educational book' for the use of students studying English. When the context of any written text is discussed, its 'surroundings' must be described, the type of publication it appears in, the kind of language and discourse this type of publication habitually employs, the kind of readership it appears to be aimed at and the expectations which that readership has of the publication.

The context of any text affects any meaning that is produced for the reader. For example, if in the midst of a strip cartoon comic full of stories of amazing heroic adventures, there appeared a very philosophical and learned written text, the incongruity of placing such a text in that particular context would affect any meaning the text has. Readers' expectations would be jolted and the 'surroundings' of this text (the comic, the strip cartoon format) would highlight the kind of discourse and language employed by the 'serious' text and would inevitably affect how readers 'read' it. Context, then, is an integral part of a text's meaning.

2.1 Tabloid journalism

Newspapers are often defined as belonging to one of two categories: 'tabloid' or 'quality'. The term 'tabloid' originally referred to a newspaper's size, a smaller format than the broadsheets of the 'qualities' (like a concentrated tablet). However, 'tabloid' has come to mean any newspaper aimed at a mass readership and which is informal, even sensational in style, packed full of headlines, photographs, short news stories and items of gossip.

This section includes the text of a report from a tabloid newspaper about a move towards peace in Ireland. In the next section, we will be looking at how a 'quality' newspaper reported the same event.

ON THE BRINK

by Paul Wilenius
Political Editor

Strife-torn Northern Ireland is on the brink of an historic deal to end 25 years of bloodshed.

As hopes rose yesterday that the IRA would call a permanent halt to the killing that has claimed 3,000 lives, Irish Premier Albert Reynolds said the whole island was "poised for peace". And US President Bill Clinton is ready to pump up to £135 million into the province if there is a ceasefire.

The pledge comes as the IRA were ensured a propaganda coup with the arrival in America later today of veteran Irish republican activist Joe Cahill. However, the hopes of peace were clouded by warnings of civil war from Loyalist terror groups and politicians.

Hardline Unionist leader the Rev Ian Paisley said that the ceasefire smacked of betrayal.

The IRA were only going for peace because they felt they had "won the war", he said. John Major, who heard a detailed outline of the ceasefire from Mr Reynolds on Monday, has been at pains to stress that no concessions have been made to weaken British policy.

Last night senior aides added that the Government would accept nothing less than a "permanent cessation of violence".

The strong words were aimed as much at Tory backbenchers as disgruntled Loyalists.

Tories such as Winston Churchill and Nicholas Budgen said the first whiff of capitulation to the IRA would spark a full-scale rebellion by Tory MPs.

Excessive

"If it was judged that the terms being demanded by the IRA were excessive, then there could be a very great problem in the party," said Mr Churchill.

His remarks follow reports that the Government has agreed to an early release of political prisoners, a sharp reduction in British troops, and the lifting of travel restrictions on leading Republicans.

Number 10 did not deny that informal contacts between the Government and Sinn Fein had taken place in recent weeks.

Group discussion

- Working in pairs, make a summary of the report in not more than sixty words. Then compare your summary with those produced by the rest of the group and agree a consensus summary.
- Consider the use of the headline at the top of the report. Discuss how it affects meaning.
- Working in pairs, analyse the structure of the report in terms of its arrangement into paragraphs: how many sentences are there in each paragraph? how long are the sentences? Then, as a group, share your findings and discuss how this arrangement of language affects meaning.
- Again working in pairs, make a list of words from the report that appear familiar to you as examples of the vocabulary often used in this type of journalism. For example, you should select examples of predictable collocation, the placing of words together that is entirely 'expected' and conventional. Then compare the list you have produced with the rest of the group.
- There are some direct quotes from individuals used in the report as well

as examples of 'reported speech'. Pick out examples of both and discuss how these affect meaning.

- The first paragraph of the report is printed in bold typography. The seventh paragraph is printed in italic print. Discuss how these variations in typography affect meaning.
- The context of this report is a tabloid newspaper. Discuss any general features of the text that reflect this context.

2.2 'Quality' journalism

Below is an extract from a 'quality' newspaper, a report of the same news story that was reported in the tabloid newspaper.

Ireland 'is poised for peace'

David Sharrock in Belfast

THE BRITISH and Irish governments yesterday moved to calm Unionist fears over a "sell-out" to Sinn Fein amid intense speculation that the IRA will announce a permanent cessation of violence today.

In Dublin, the Irish prime minister, Albert Reynolds, said Ireland was "poised for peace . . . In a very short time we will be able to make an entirely new beginning on this island."

Last night, the Sinn Fein leader, Gerry Adams, said it was "time to get away from the past and look forward to a new beginning and to a new future". He told RTE television that it would be unforgivable if John Major failed to take the opportunity before him.

"We are putting 75 years of partition, discrimination, all the inequalities, all the injustices behind us.

Surely the Unionists have within their ranks men and women of courage prepared to take the same risks that we have."

In the event of an IRA ceasefire, Mr Adams said he would demand the immediate recognition of Sinn Fein's electoral mandate. "There must be an immediate end to censorship . . . The bigger issues will take more time and that's why I call for calm.'

The timing of the ceasefire announcement was being linked to the news that Joe Cahill, a founder member of the IRA, had arrived in New York on a visa personally authorised by President Clinton. Mr Cahill is expected to explain the ceasefire decision to Sinn Fein supporters in America.

The White House press secretary, Dee Dee Myers, said yesterday the US was considering an aid package for Northern Ireland in the event of a ceasefire. But a State Department official denied Dublin press reports of $200 million in aid.

A British government spokesman yesterday rejected Unionist and rightwing Tory concerns that its Northern Ireland policy had shifted.

John Major will underline his commitment to the principles enshrined in his Joint Declaration with Mr Reynolds when he meets the Ulster Unionist leader, James Molyneaux, in Downing Street today.

Mr Major reiterated that for Sinn Fein to be involved even in exploratory talks, there would have to be a permanent end to IRA violence. The future status of Northern Ireland could only be changed with the consent of the majority, he said.

Mr Major's position was reinforced in Dublin by the Irish deputy prime minister, Dick Spring, who said the Irish government was only interested in a permanent IRA ceasefire.

Mr Reynolds and his cabinet yesterday received a detailed report on the prospects for peace. He said later: "Nobody should be afraid of peace, since it would open up a whole new vista of opportunity that would economically benefit everyone and create a new prosperity."

Group discussion

- Working in pairs, make a summary of the report in not more than sixty words. Then compare your summary with those of the rest of the group and agree a consensus summary.
- Discuss how the headline is used in the report and compare its use with the headline in the tabloid report.
- Discuss how quotations and reported speech are used in the report. Then compare these aspects of the text with the way quotes are used in the tabloid report.
- Working in pairs, make a list of words and phrases used in the report which you consider would not be used in a tabloid newspaper. Compare your list with those of the rest of the group and discuss what the usage of this vocabulary implies about the readership of the newspaper and reader expectations.
- Compare the tabloid report with the 'quality' report. Discuss similarities and differences. Consider how the respective contexts affect meaning.

Writing ☞ Write two different reports of the same imaginary event, one for a tabloid newspaper and one for a 'quality' newspaper. Use a headline for each report and consider the context in which your report is to appear.

2.3 Journalism: the glossy magazine

The 'glossies', as they are sometimes referred to, are magazines aimed at large groups of potential readers identified by the publishers as likely to be interested in the subject matter and style of particular publications. Publishers may be aiming to attract a readership which shares an interest in such spheres as the private lives of the rich and famous, property or business. Some magazines are aimed at one sex more than the other.

Cosmopolitan is classed as a 'woman's magazine' because its contents are aimed at a female readership. On page 32 is an extract from a feature article entitled 'The New Order: Relax! Get Organised!'

become businesslike

Frontline empowerment, crisis management, business process re-engineering are buzz words that mean little outside the world of management consultancy. But wait – the theories behind them can help you organise your life.

- "Organisations are only groups of individuals with collective goals," says Dr Cheryl Travers, lecturer in organisational behaviour at Loughborough University Business School. "What makes them effective can be applied to individuals, too."

- "Effective is the word," says Debra Allcock, a national project leader on the management team of The Industrial Society. 'You can be efficient – tidying up the files on your computer – when you should be effective, such as preparing yourself for that important meeting.

- "The first thing I'd look for if I were analysing a firm," she adds, "is its mission statement. That's the goal it's working toward. There'd be subsidiary goals but they shouldn't conflict. If they do, it's a question of priorities."

How you apply this: You might add the phrase "aiming for the top" to your own mission statement with lesser goals of completing an extra-mural accountancy course and spending the summer in the States. If you can't manage both the course and the trip, weigh up which one fits more immediately with getting to the top.

- "Next, I'd break the statement into *achievable* chunks," continues Debra. "Then I'd look at who will do what, and to what deadline."

How you apply this: Ask yourself what you need to achieve your mission statement. If it's working abroad, for example, you might need to improve your language skills. Give yourself a schedule.

- "It's at that stage systems go into place," says Debra. "If they're thought through, they smooth out the daily running of a business, though they don't have to be adhered to rigidly."

How you apply this: Think of all the routine but necessary jobs, like shopping. Systematise it with a list of everything you ever buy in one column and stick it on the kitchen wall. Tick the list when you need something, use it as a shopping list, and then stick it back up for next time.

- "Empowering the front line means consulting your staff, and delegating responsibility wherever possible," says Belinda Phipps, a graduate of Ashridge Business school and managing director of a large company.

How you apply this: Don't attempt to do this yourself. "I'm always stunned by how many intelligent women don't 'empower' their partners to do the shopping, and waste time mothering them instead," says Belinda. If you share, ask your flatmates to work out a cleaning rota.

- "Another good tool is problem analysis," says Belinda, "which involves distinguishing between a system problem and a one-off."

How you apply this: Analyse why you didn't have time to prepare for that meeting. Was it a one-off (you had flu?) Or was it a system problem (you have three regular meetings scheduled too close together and should rearrange them better)?

- "One things firms are learning," says Dr Travers, "is that being busy isn't the same as being efficient. Some firms are building in time for reflection, for working out how things can be done better. Effectiveness is doing the right job, properly."

How you apply this: Stop a moment. Is what you're doing simply making you stressed? Did you have to make it a three-course sit-down meal for 10, when your guests would have been happy with salads from M & S?

- Another key phrase, according to Dr Travers, is QA: quality assurance. In business it means not just how much output, but the quality of it.

How you apply this: We're back to making time to examine what you are doing, and how to improve on it.

- Consultants also advise firms on achieving performance. Some employees avoid responsibility, but then end up bored with the monotony of their work. Others overdose on stress.

How you apply this: "When I talk about achieving a balance," says Dr Travers, "I recommend the three Cs: commitment, confidence and control. You get those through having goals, the right training and preparation, and the resources to do the job."

Top 10 points for being more organised in business affairs – with a personal emphasis to follow.

1 Consult your customers and staff. Listen to your inner needs and aims, discuss with family and friends.

2 Identify your mission statement. Set yourself goals in life.

3 Analyse the process. Break down goals into achievable chunks, and work out how they can be achieved.

4 Set deadlines for objectives. When are you going to achieve them?

5 Rationalise – streamline your life. Throw out anything that doesn't fit in with your goals.

6 Empower the front line. Learn to delegate – even the shopping.

7 Be a learning organisation. Build in time for reflection and planning.

8 Open up communication. Really listen to helpful advice, make sure people know you can take it.

9 Avoid short-termism. Don"t necessarily do the easiest thing, especially if it detracts from your main goal.

10 Crisis management. Avoid the worst by imagining it happening. Plan what you'd do and how you'd cope. Then forget about it!

JAY ANDREWS

Group discussion

- 'Frontline empowerment, crisis management, business process re-engineering are buzz words'. Discuss what you interpret 'buzz words' as meaning and then consider what meaning is communicated by the examples of 'buzz words' that are used. Apart from the term 'buzz words', is there any other word or phrase you can think of that might describe this particular type of language use?

- Working in pairs, consider the structure of the extract and how the article is laid out on the page. Make a brief summary of the contents and sections, noting any particular use of print type, subheadings, punctuation and numbering. What effect on the overall meaning is produced by use of these devices?

- Select examples from the extract where business management experts are quoted. Discuss why you think the author of the article has used these statements.

- The type of discourse employed here might be described as 'managerial' as well as educational. Select examples of language used in the article that specifically belong to this type of business management discourse.

- Someone you work for has read this article and decides s/he wants a brief summary of its main points in not more than 80 words. Working in pairs, summarise the main points in not more than 120 words. Then further reduce the summary to a maximum of 80 words by excluding any point you think is not absolutely essential.

- If you had been unaware that this is part of an article which appeared in a 'woman's magazine', what examples of language use might have helped you to make that deduction for yourself?

- Discuss what kind of reader the feature is aimed at, considering the content and the language.

- Write a brief analysis of the advice given in the article and give your own personal response to it.

Writing ☛

Write an article intended for publication in a school or college magazine with the title 'Get Organised!'. The article is meant to offer advice to other students about how to organise their studies and time. Think about how you would set out the article to make it accessible and 'readable'.

If you prefer, you may write a parody of the *Cosmopolitan* type of article.

☛ Write a piece about a magazine that you read regularly. Describe its main subject matter and appeal, and the kind of readership it is aimed at. Give examples of articles or items that you have liked or disliked. Comment in particular on the kind of language use it generally employs.

2.4 The specialist context

The context of a piece of writing affects meaning and the way we produce meaning for ourselves when we read something.

Readers of magazines of a specialist interest, say, a magazine about chess or fashion, have certain expectations of the kind of discourse these magazines will offer. If you are interested in chess and you read an article about the game in a magazine devoted entirely to that subject, then that context will affect meaning and your reading. 'You must see things in their context' is something of a cliché, but it is true about interpreting written texts and how we analyse the way in which meaning is produced.

Here are two reviews of the same film from two different magazines, devoted to writing about the cinema.

TERMINATOR 2: JUDGMENT DAY

DIRECTOR JAMES CAMERON
STARRING ARNOLD
SCHWARZENEGGER
LINDA HAMILTON
ROBERT PATRICK
CERT. 15 USA 136 MINS.
OPENS IN UK ... AUGUST 16

TIPPING THE SCALES AT A REPUTED $100 million dollars, this is allegedly the most expensive movie ever made. Those nice people at Carolco have obviously got their sums right, however, as this sequel has already hauled in more in its first two days of release than the eventual gross of the 1984 original. And it will be difficult for even the fiercest cost-cutter to walk away from this and deny that the moolah is up there on the screen in exploding vehicles, wrecked buildings, monster effects and sheer sweaty action.

It all opens with an intriguing re-run of the original's premise as a gigantic cyborg (Schwarzenegger) and a slimline ordinary Joe (Patrick) are zapped back from the future, this time to seek out ten-year-old John Connor (Edward Furlong), the son of the heroine (Hamilton) of The Terminator, and struggle over his life, with the balance of a future that may or may not be ruined by a cataclysmic war between man and machines up for grabs in the titanic struggle. The twist, however, is that Patrick, a fresh-faced type who impersonates a cop, is the deadly mechanical baddy, while Arnie, in biker leathers and mean shades, has been reprogrammed to protect the brat and his mom and, in between the extensive carnage, gets to reveal that biomechanical killing machines from the future can have their sensitive sides.

While the rewiring of Arnie's persona smacks of a sop to the Kindergarten Cop audience, this strategy really pays off when it comes to Patrick's villain, a fearsome creature constructed from a liquid metal and capable of shaping itself into anything it so desires. A high-tech version of The Blob, utilising some of the most astonishing and surreal effects ever filmed, Patrick's T-1000 stands as one of the great monsters of the cinema.

As with all James Cameron movies, this shuffles its character stuff out of the way in the first two-thirds, then delivers a succession of apparently untoppable climaxes that are routinely outawesomed by the next set-piece. Because it's a sequel, it's less satisfying than the more idea-driven original, but this is still top-flight kick-ass entertainment, and, when Arnie does his shotgun twirl, fire power fans everywhere will reside in hog heaven. ★★★★

KIM NEWMAN

James Cameron's sense of his own mission seems to be growing as fast as his production budgets. *Terminator 2* is less a sequel to *The Terminator* than a benign revision of the earlier film, a parable in which Arnold Schwarzenegger's matchless T-800 is transformed from an unstoppable killing machine into man's best friend and an ideal father figure. This transformation is, of course, in line with the shift in Arnie's image from macho action star to potential Republican candidate and family favourite, but it has been clear since The Abyss that Cameron is a writer-director who takes his messages very seriously. Here he gives Sarah Connor an occasional voice-over narration that points up the moral of the story as preachily as anything in a 30s social-problem picture: "If a machine can learn the value of human life," she gasps, "then maybe we can too."

If the original film flirted with the idea of a secular alternative to New Testament myth, *Terminator 2* goes the whole hog by subtitling itself "Judgment Day" and introducing a redeemer-to-be with the initials J. C. The film sentimentally rhymes the T-800's 'personal growth' with the boy John Connor's discovery of his social conscience as he moves from skateboarding, video-game-playing and petty crime to filial piety. Like much else in the movie, this is accomplished with economy and a fair measure of wit. When the T-800 starts trashing an innocently obstructive bystander, the boy intervenes: "Jeez, you were gonna kill that guy". "Of course", intones Arnie, "I'm a Terminator". From this point on, the T-800 goes out of its way to avoid terminating anything except its implacable foe, the T-1000.

This caring sensibility extends even to the embittered Sarah, who vengefully clobbers her way out of captivity in the asylum but then cannot bring herself to kill the black scientist Miles Dyson when she discovers him at home in the bosom of his Cosby Show family. Sarah's incarceration, incidentally, is one of several non-sequiturs from the original film (she is locked up for babbling on about Terminators and impending nuclear devastation, as if no one else had seen the old T-800). But she is none the less a clear descendant of the heroine of *Aliens* – another in Cameron's gallery of strong and resourcefully maternal women. The price she has to pay for her independence, inevitably, is exclusion from the tremulous male bonding between her son and the T-800: it's hard to project her role beyond the final fade-out.

The element that enables Cameron to reconcile his conviction that human life is sacred with the more profane demands of the genre is the appearance of the T-1000, without doubt the most sophisticated monster so far in screen history. The T-1000 marks the point where computer-generated imagery equals and overtakes the protean effects achieved with lower-tech resources by the Rob Bottin crew for John Carpenter's *The Thing*. The T-1000 is essentially a puddle of liquid metal capable of taking on human and mechanical forms instantaneously, resulting in both a series of ingenious physical transformations and numerous shots in which the actor Robert Patrick appears part-human, part-metal.

There's no disputing that its quaint morality earns *Terminator 2* the label "A James Cameron Film", but there is equally no doubt that it represents another triumph for corporate film-making. What price the auteur in the days of five-minute credit-title sequences? Maybe the Academy should introduce a new Oscar for the Camerons, Burtons, Verhoevens and McTiernans of the New Hollywood: Best Ringmaster?

Tony Rayns

Group discussion

- From the first review, make a list of words and phrases that are relatively informal, even colloquial. Discuss how this affects meaning.
- From the second review, pick out examples of more formal and perhaps more 'difficult' language than has been used in the first review. What does the use of such language suggest about how the magazine views its readership?
- Make a list of things that the two reviews have in common.
- Which of the articles gives the more favourable review of the film? Back up your opinion with evidence from both reviews.

- Suppose you were in charge of the advertising campaign for this film. You want to choose quotes of no more than six words from both reviews to feature in the poster used to advertise the film. Choose at least three such quotes from each review. Then imagine you have been given the task of highlighting the deficiencies of the movie. Choose at least three short quotes from each review.
- Having read these reviews out of context, discuss what kind of magazines you think each appeared in. You could mention the type of readership the magazine appears to be aimed at and the general approach to the subject of cinema which each magazine appears to take.

Writing ✏

Write two reviews of a film you have seen recently, one for a tabloid newspaper and one for the arts pages of a 'quality' newspaper.

Then write a brief commentary on how the context of the two pieces influenced the way you wrote, particularly the language you used.

2.5 Humorous writing

Some magazines (such as *Private Eye* or *Mad*) specialise in satirical or 'oddball' humorous writing. Regular readers of these magazines become accustomed to their style and approach. The main intention of the magazines and their writers is to make readers laugh. Readers themselves bring their expectations to the reading of these humorous texts. Indeed, ***reader expectation*** is a term that can be useful in discussing any particular example of written text in particular contexts.

Quite often, humorous pieces appear first in newspapers and magazines and then the writings of a particular author are collected and published in book form. Garrison Keillor is an American humorist who started out broadcasting features on radio, which were then 'translated' into printed form, in collections of his writing. Below is a complete piece from one of these collections. It is about a fictional place called Lake Wobegon in Minnesota, and its inhabitants.

Life is good

It has been a quiet week in Lake Wobegon. Lightning struck the Tollerud farm Tuesday, about six o'clock in the evening. Daryl and his dad were walking the corn rows, talking, and the clouds were dark and strange but it wasn't storming yet, and Daryl said, "If I were you, I'd take Mother out to Seattle tomorrow and enjoy the trip and not worry about this." Right then it hit, up by the house: a burst of light and a slam and a sizzle like bacon. They ran for the house to find her in the kitchen, sitting on the floor. She was okay but it was close. It hit a crab apple tree thirty feet from the kitchen window.

Some people in town were reminded of Benny Barnes, who was hit by lightning six times. After three, he was nervous when a storm approached, and got in his car and drove fast, but it got him the fourth time, and the fifth time it was sunny with just one little cloud in the sky and, bam, lightning again. He had burn scars down his legs and his ears had been ringing for years. After the fifth, he quit running. The sixth one got him sitting in the yard on an aluminium lawn chair. After that he more or less gave up. When the next thunderstorm came through, he took a long steel pipe and stood out on the hill, holding it straight up. He had lost the will to live. But just the same it took him fifteen more years to die. It wasn't from lightning: he caught cold from the rain and died of pneumonia.

Daryl wished the bolt had come closer to his dad. His dad has a character flaw that drives Daryl crazy: he hates plans. The trip to Seattle was planned before Thanksgiving, letters were written to relatives, calls were made; June 30th was the date set to go, but the old man gets uneasy when plans are made and feels trapped and cornered, even if the plans are his own, so one night after chores he said, "Well, I don't know about that trip to Seattle, I might be too busy, we'll have to see about that," which made everybody else want to shoot him.

Daryl jumped up. "How can you say that? Are you crazy?" No, just nervous about plans. Always was. To agree to do something and have people expect you to do it: it bothers him. When his kids were little, he'd tell them, "Now, I'm not promising anything, but maybe next week sometime I could take you swimming, up to your uncle Carl's, but don't count on it, it all depends." As next week came around, he'd say, "I don't know about that swimming, we're going to have to see about that. Maybe Thursday.' Thursday the kids would get their bathing suits out and he'd say, "We'll see how it goes this morning, if I get my work done we'll go." Right up to when they got in the car, he was saying, "I don't know. I really ought to get to work on that drain pipe," and even when he stuck the key in the ignition, he'd hesitate. "Gosh, I'm not sure, maybe it'd be better if we went tomorrow." He couldn't bring himself to say, "Thursday we swim," and stick to it. Daryl and his brothers and sisters learned not to look forward to things because Dad might change his mind.

The old man is the same with his grandkids. He says, "Well, we'll see. Maybe. If I can." But the Seattle trip beats all. Ruby got the train tickets and had the suitcase packed three weeks ago, then he said, "I don't know how I can leave with the corn like it is." Ruby put her head in her hands. He said, "You know, the Grand Canyon is a place I always wanted to see, maybe we should go there." She sighed, and he said, "You know, I never agreed to this Seattle trip, this was your idea from day one." And then Ruby went to Daryl's to talk to Daryl and Marilyn. They sat drinking coffee and getting madder and Ruby said, "Oh well, you have to understand Dad." Marilyn stood up and said, "I do not have to understand him. He's crazy. he doesn't just have a screw loose, the whole top has come off."

She is reading a book, *Get Down and Garden*, about getting tough with plants. She has yanked a bunch of slow movers out of her flower garden, the dullards and the dim bulbs, and it's improved her confidence. Now she often begins sentences with "Look," as in "Look. It's obvious." She used to begin with "Well" as in "Well, I don't know," but now she says, "Look. This is not that hard to understand."

She said to Ruby, "Look. It's obvious what he's doing. He wants to be the Grand Exalted Ruler and come down in the morning and hear his subjects say, 'What is your pleasure, sire?' and he'll say, 'Seattle,' so they head for the luggage and then he says, 'No, we'll stay home,' so they sit down, and then 'Grand Canyon' and they all jump up. As long as you keep jumping, he'll keep holding the hoop up there."

Not only does Old Man Tollerud hate to commit himself to trips, he also likes to stay loose in regard to drawing up a will or some other legal paper that gives Daryl and Marilyn some right to the farm that they've worked on for fifteen years. When Daryl mentions it, his dad says, "Well, we'll have to see. We'll talk about it in a few months." Daryl is forty-two years old and he's got no more ownership of this farm that if he'd gone off and been a drunk like his brother Gunnar. Sometimes he gets so mad at the old man, he screams at him. But always when he's on the tractor in the middle of the field with the motor running. Once he left a rake in the yard with the tines up, hoping his dad would step on it and brain himself.

Last April he saw a skunk waddling toward the barn and got a can of catfood and lured the skunk into the tractor shed, hoping his dad would start up the John Deere the next morning and get a snootful. He fed the skunk day after day, waiting for it to do the job for him. Sweet justice. Blast the old bastard with skunk sauce at close range so nobody would care to see him for about a year. Then the skunk started following Daryl, who fed him such rich food, so Daryl quit and the skunk disappeared.

Daryl got some satisfaction at the Syttende Mai dinner at the Lutheran church in May, Norwegian Independence Day, where his dad went through the buffet and loaded up and was heading for a table when his paper plate started to collapse on him. He balanced his coffee cup on his wrist to get his other hand under the plate, and it was *hot*—the meatballs had sat in a chafing dish over a candle. The old man winced and looked for a place to dump the load; then the hot gravy burned right through the paper plate and he did a little tango and everything sloshed down the front of his pants. Daryl watched this with warm satisfaction.

But that was months ago, the satisfaction has worn off. The day after the lightning strike, Daryl drove up to the house to have it out once and for all. He practised his speech in the pickup. "You don't treat me like I'm your son at all, you've never treated me like a son." He got to the house and found a note on the door: "Gone to Saint Cloud for windowshades. Back soon. Clean the haybarn."

Clean the haybarn! He ripped the note off and wadded it up and drop-kicked it into the peonies. He stalked to the end of the porch and back and stood and yelled at the door. "You don't treat me like I was your son, you bastard, you treat me like I was a—" And then the terrible truth dawned on him. His mother had said, "If anything happens to us in Seattle, I left you a letter in my dresser drawer. I've been meaning to give it to you for years." So he wasn't their son. He was adopted. That's why his dad wouldn't make out the will.

Daryl had wondered about this before, if he was his father's son. He thought, "I'm forty-two, it's time to find out." He walked in and climbed the stairs, step by deep purple step, and turned and entered his parents' bedroom, the forbidden chamber, and walked to the dresser and heard something move on the bed. He turned—it was their old tabby cat, Lulu, on the bed—his hand, hit a bottle and it crashed on the floor. She didn't jump at the crash, she sat up and gave him a long look that said: "You're not supposed to be in here and you know it. You ought to be ashamed of yourself. You're no good and you know it. Shame on you." He clapped his hands—*Ha! Git!*—and she climbed down and walked away, stopped, looked over her shoulder, and said: You'll suffer for this, you just wait.

He picked up the shards of perfume bottle and opened both dormer windows to air out the room. Unbelievable that his mother would ever smell like this, it smelled like old fruit salads. He dug down into the dresser drawer where he'd seen her stick old pictures, under her stockings and underwear. There was a book, *Sexual Aspects of Christian Marriage: A Meditation* by Reverend E. M. Mintner, that he'd read when he was twelve, and he dug beneath it to a packet of envelopes tied with a thick rubber binder, tight. He slipped if off: they were his dad's pay slips from the Co-op; each envelope held a year's worth; there were more than thirty envelopes.

He sat on the bed, feeling weak. Of all his parents' secrets, this was the darkest: how much money did they make? They would no more talk about that than discuss sexual aspects of marriage. One Sunday little Daryl piped up at dinner and asked, "Dad, how much money do you make?"

His dad has several different voices, a regular one ("So how come you went down there then when I told you I needed you? I don't get it") and a prayer voice ("Our Father, we do come before Thee with hearts filled with thanksgiving, remembering Thy many blessings to us, and we do ask Thee now. . ."). When he discussed money he used the second voice and he said, "I don't care to discuss that and I don't want to discuss it with anyone else. Is that clear?"

Oh yes. We don't talk about money, that is very clear. Except to say, "I got this window fan for four dollars; it's brand-new except for this scratch, and you know those things run ten, twelve dollars." Bargains yes, but salaries no.

So here was the secret. He opened the first envelope, 1956. Forty-five dollars. That was for a whole week. Not much for a good mechanic. Forty-five dollars and five kids: it explained all that scrimping, his mother darning socks and canning tomatoes. When the old man forked over their allowance, he counted the two quarters twice to make sure he wasn't overpaying. It explained why he was such a pack rat, saving tinfoil, string, paper, rags— once Daryl looked around for string and found a box full of corks, another of bits of wire, and one box with hundreds of odd jigsaw-puzzle pieces, labelled "Puzzle: Misc."

It dawned on him that he wasn't adopted, he was their boy all right. He'd inherited their frugality and stoicism. If his paper plate fell apart, he'd try to save it, even if his hand was burning. Same as his dad. They raised him to bear up under hardship and sadness and disappointment and disaster, but what if you're brought up to be stoic and your life turns out lucky—you're in love with your wife, you're lucky in your children, and life is lovely to you—what then? You're ready to endure trouble and pain, and instead God sends you love—what do you do? He'd been worried about inheriting the farm, meanwhile God had given him six beautiful children. What happens if you expect the worst and you get the best? *Thank you, Lord*, he thought. Thank you for sending me up here to the bedroom. It was wrong to come, but thank you for sending me.

He heard Lulu tiptoe in, and when she brushed against his leg he was sorry for chasing her out. He scratched her head. It didn't feel catlike. He looked down and saw the white stripes down its back.

The skunk sniffed his hand, wondering where the catfood was. Then it raised its head and sniffed the spilled perfume. It raised its tail, sensing an adversary. It walked toward the window. It seemed edgy.

"Easy, easy," he said. If he opened the window wider, it might go out on the roof and find a route down the oak tree to the ground. He was opening the window wider when he heard the feet padding up the stairs. He hollered, "No, Shep, no!" and raised his leg to climb out of the window as the dog burst into the room, barking. The skunk turned and attacked. Daryl went out the window, but not quite fast enough. He tore off all his clothes and threw them down to the ground, and climbed back in. The bedroom smelled so strong he couldn't bear it. The skunk was under the bed. He ran down and got the shotgun and loaded it. Daryl was almost dying of the smell, but he crept into the bedroom. He heard the skunk grunt, trying to squeeze out more juice. Daryl aimed and fired. Feathers exploded and the skunk dropped down dead.

He carried it out on a shovel and buried it, but that didn't help very much: the deceased was still very much a part of the Tollerud house when his parents arrived home a little while later. Daryl sat on the porch steps, bare naked except for a newspaper. he smelled so bad, he didn't care about modesty. Ruby said, "Oh dear. Are you all right?" She stopped, twenty feet away. She thought he looked naked, but he smelled so bad she didn't care to come closer.

His dad said, "You know, Daryl, I think you were right about Seattle."

And they left. They didn't take clothes with them. They went straight out the driveway.

That was Tuesday. Daryl has been living at his parents' house all week. But life is good. I'm sure he still believes this. Life is good, friends. It's even better if you stay away from Daryl, but basically life is good.

Group discussion

- 'Life is good' was originally a radio 'talk' before it was printed as part of a book. (It is part of a BBC cassette tape called *Leaving Home* by Garrison Keillor). If you can, listen to the author reading his own story. Discuss what aspects of the language reflect the origins of this piece: that it was intended to be read aloud on the radio rather than to appear in print.
- Listening to someone reading aloud is a different experience from reading the same material yourself. If you do manage to listen to the original recording, discuss whether the piece makes more of an impact on you as a listener than as a reader. Try to assess what the differences are.
- We all have different expectations of what makes for genuinely humorous writing. In pairs, discuss what kinds of humorous writing you appreciate and then share your thoughts as a whole group.
- Perhaps Garrison Keillor's humour could fairly be described as 'gentle' satire. He genuinely seems to like the 'people' and 'communities' he satirises. Would you say this is a fair description of the kind of humorous writing he offers?
- If any meaning the story has is produced through the language used, how are the 'humorous effects' of the piece achieved? Select examples of language use that are intended to produce a humorous response.
- Trace the structure of the piece by summarising in sequence the events described. Decide whether it has a very definite, linear structure or whether it meanders somewhat. Either way, how does this affect meaning?

Writing Garrison Keillor starts almost all his stories about the fictional community he writes about with this sentence: 'It has been a quiet week in Lake Wobegon.' Decide on a real or fictional community you want to write a piece about and start it with the words 'It has been a quiet week in ...'. You are writing this piece to be read aloud on radio, then later printed in an anthology of humorous writing. Its aim should be to present a humorous portrait of the people and community you have chosen.

After you have written this piece, write a brief commentary on how you approached the task, mentioning any problems you had to overcome in the process (for example, thinking about writing for radio).

Write a short comic piece on any subject for inclusion in a humorous publication that you read, or have read, such as *Mad, Private Eye, Punch*, a fanzine of some kind, or any other periodical. Take into account 'reader expectations' when you write this piece: think about the kind of readers the publication sells to, and their expectations of the kind of humorous writing the publication specialises in.

GLOSSARY

Reader expectation: the expectation that readers have about particular examples of writing in terms of the way language is used. For example, readers of horror fiction might well have definite expectations about storylines, settings, vocabulary, incidents, narrative figures. These expectations are built up through familiarity with types of writing and can in part affect how readers respond to the view of reality represented.

2.6 The autobiographical text

An autobiographical piece of writing is generally understood to mean an individual writing about his or her own life. However, the difference between fiction and autobiography is not always easy to define. This is not just a matter of writers deliberately making up things to include in the story of their lives, that is, of 'fictionalising' the things that have happened to them, but more a blurring of the division between what we mean by 'a true story' and what we mean by 'fiction'. For example, the description 'based on a true story' is sometimes used to sell a film (*Schindler's List, What's Love Got To Do With It*). However, when does the 'based on a true story' edge over into fiction? What is 'a true story'? Can any individual give a wholly truthful account of his or her own life, can the story of anyone's life be anything more than just a 'representation' of that person's life, or are biography and autobiography necessarily always going to be highly subjective and selective and, therefore, a ***representation of reality*** rather than 'reality' itself?

Below is an extract from Maya Angelou's autobiography, *I Know why the Caged Bird Sings*. She is an African-American who grew up in one of the most rigorously racially segregated states in the American South. In the extract below, she describes growing up in Georgia during the Depression (the worldwide economic slump of the thirties).

Stamps, Arkansas, was Chitlin' Switch, Georgia; Hang 'Em High, Alabama; Don't Let the Sun Set on You Here, Nigger, Mississippi; or any other name just as descriptive. People in Stamps used to say that the whites in our town were so prejudiced that a Negro couldn't buy vanilla ice cream. Except on July Fourth. Other days he had to be satisfied with chocolate.

A light shade had been pulled down between the Black community and all things white, but one could see through it enough to develop a fear, admiration, contempt for the white 'things' white folks' cars and white glistening houses and their children and their women. But, above all, their wealth that allowed them to waste was the most enviable. They had so many clothes that they were able to give perfectly good dresses, worn just under the arms, to the sewing class at our school for the larger girls to practise on.

Although there was always generosity in the Negro neighbourhood, it was indulged on pain of sacrifice. Whatever was given by Black people to other Blacks was most probably needed as desperately by the donor as by the receiver. A fact which made the giving and receiving a rich exchange.

I couldn't understand whites and where they got the right to spend money so lavishly. Of course, I knew God was white too, but no one could have made me believe he was prejudiced. My grandmother had more money than all the powhitetrash. We owned land and houses, but each day Bailey, and I were cautioned, 'Waste not, want not.'

Momma bought two bolts of cloth each year for winter and summer clothes. She made my school dresses, underslips, bloomers, handkerchiefs, Bailey's shirts, shorts, her aprons, house dresses and waists from the rolls shipped to Stamps by Sears and Roebuck. Uncle Willie was the only person in the family who wore readytowear clothes all the time. Each day, he wore fresh white shirts and flowered suspenders, and his special shoes cost twenty dollars. I thought Uncle Willie sinfully vain, especially when I had to iron seven stiff starched shirts and not leave a cat's face anywhere.

During the summer we went barefoot, except on Sunday, and we learned to resole our shoes when they 'gave out', as ready-to-wear used to say. The Depression must have hit the white section of Stamps with cyclonic impact, but it seeped into the Black area slowly, like a thief with misgivings. The country had been in the throes of the Depression for two years before the Negroes in Stamps knew it, I think that everyone thought that the Depression, like everything else, was for the whitefolks, so it had nothing to do with them. Our people had lived off the land and counted on cotton-picking and hoeing and chopping seasons to bring in the cash needed to buy shoes, clothes, books and light farm equipment. It was when the owners of cotton fields dropped the payment of ten cents for a pound of cotton to eight, seven and finally five that the Negro community realised that the Depression, at least, did not discriminate.

Welfare agencies gave food to the poor families. Black and white. Gallons of lard, flour, salt, powdered eggs and powdered milk. People stopped trying to raise hogs because it was too difficult to get slop rich enough to feed them, and no one had the money to buy mash or fish meal.

Mamma spent many nights figuring on our tablets, slowly. She was trying to find a way to keep her business going, although her customers had no money.

Group discussion
- In any piece of writing, whether it be labelled 'fiction' or 'non-fiction', readers are offered a representation of reality. Language serves to communicate a writer's experience of the 'real' world. The reality that is presented to the reader is constructed through language, but it is not reality itself, however 'true-to-life' it may seem. It is a highly subjective view of the world. Discuss how language is used in the extract to create a picture of day-to-day reality through a subjective point of view.
- Pick out examples of language that is used to communicate the differences between the lives of white and black people in Georgia at that time.
- You have already learnt that discourse is a particular area of language use that embodies a way of thinking, speaking or writing. This extract offers an autobiographical discourse. However, suppose the introduction to the extract had described the piece of writing as fiction rather than autobiography. Is there anything in the way the extract is written that would have led you to question that it was fiction?

Writing
A community writing project in your area has decided to publish a collection of short autobiographical pieces by local people. You decide to write a piece as a contribution to this collection. The maximum length for a contribution is 500 words.

Then write a commentary on the writing process, discussing in particular whether you thought there was much difference between writing this autobiographical piece and writing a piece of fiction.

GLOSSARY

Representation of reality: how language can create a view of reality or the illusion of reality. Language in speech or written modes can create this representation of reality, but it is only a representation of it, not reality itself.

2.7 More autobiographical writing

Below is an extract from *Wild Swans* by Jung Chang, an autobiography which tells the story of the author's life in China under communist rule. This extract deals with a period in the 1960s when a 'cultural revolution' was being encouraged by China's rulers, particularly Mao Tse Tung, Chairman of the Communist Party. Mao and his supporters encouraged the Red Guards, mainly youthful followers of Mao, to root out all examples of 'bourgeois' culture and to force people to be true revolutionaries.

After 1964, following Mao's calls for an austere life-style, more suited to the atmosphere of class struggle, I put patches on my trousers to try to look 'proletarian' and wore my hair in the uniform style of two plaits with no colours, but long hair had not been condemned as yet. My grandmother cut it for me, muttering all the while. Her hair survived, because she never went out at that time.

The famous teahouses in Chengdu also came under attack as 'decadent.' I did not understand why, but did not ask. In the summer of 1966 I learned

to suppress my sense of reason. Most Chinese had been doing that for a long time.

A Sichuan teahouse is a unique place. It usually sits in the embrace of a bamboo grove or under the canopy of a large tree. Around the low, square wooden tables are bamboo armchairs which give out a faint aroma even after years of use. To prepare the tea a pinch of tea leaves is dropped into a cup and boiling water is poured on top. Then a lid is sunk loosely onto the cup, allowing the steam to seep through the gap, bringing out the fragrance of the jasmine or other blossoms. Sichuan has many kinds of tea. Jasmine alone has five grades.

Teahouses are as important to the Sichuanese as pubs are to the British. Older men, in particular, spend a lot of time there, puffing their long-stemmed pipes over a cup of tea and a plateful of nuts and melon seeds. The waiter shuttles between the seats with a kettle of hot water which he pours from a couple of feet away with pinpoint accuracy. A skilful waiter makes the water level higher than the edge of the cup without it spilling over. As a child I was always mesmerized watching the water fall from the spout. I was rarely taken to a teahouse, though. It had an air of indulgence of which my parents disapproved.

Like European cafés, a Sichuan teahouse provides newspapers on bamboo frames. Some customers go there to read, but it is primarily a place to meet and chat, exchanging news and gossip. There is often entertainment – storytelling punctuated with wooden clappers.

Perhaps because they had an aura of leisure, and if people were sitting in one they were not out making revolution, teahouses had to be closed. I went with a couple of dozen pupils between thirteen and sixteen years old, most of whom were Red Guards, to a small one on the bank of the Silk River. Chairs and tables were spread outside under a Chinese scholar tree. The summer evening breeze from the river fanned out a heavy scent from the clusters of white blossoms. The customers, mostly men, raised their heads from their chessboards as we approached along the uneven cobble-stones that paved the bank. We stopped under the tree. A few voices from our group started to shout: 'Pack up! Pack up! Don't linger in this bourgeois place!' A boy from my form snatched a corner of the paper chessboard on the nearest table and jerked it away. The wooden pieces scattered on the ground.

The men who had been playing were quite young. One of them lunged forward, his fists clenched, but his friend quickly pulled the corner of his jacket. Silently they began to pick up the chess pieces. The boy who had jerked away their board shouted: 'No more chess playing! Don't you know it is a bourgeois habit?' He stooped to sweep up a handful of pieces and threw them toward the river.

I had been brought up to be courteous and respectful to anyone older than me, but now to be revolutionary meant being aggressive and militant. Gentleness was considered 'bourgeois.' I was repeatedly criticized for it, and it was one reason given for not allowing me into the Red Guards. Over the years of the Cultural Revolution, I was to witness people being attacked for saying 'thank you' too often, which was branded as 'bourgeois hypocrisy'; courtesy was on the brink of extinction.

But now, outside the teahouse, I could see that most of us, including the Red Guards, were uneasy about the new style of speaking and lording it over others. Not many of us opened our mouths. Quietly, a few started to paste rectangular slogans onto the walls of the teahouse and the trunk of the scholar tree.

The customers silently began to walk away along the bank. Watching their disappearing figures, a feeling of loss overwhelmed me. A couple of months before, these adults probably would have told us to get lost. But now they knew that Mao's backing had given the Red Guards power. Thinking back, I can see the thrill some children must have felt at demonstrating their power over adults. A popular Red Guard slogan went: 'We can soar to heaven, and pierce the earth, because our Great leader Chairman Mao is our supreme commander!' As this declaration reveals, the Red Guards were not enjoying genuine freedom of self-expression. From the start they were nothing but the tool of a tyrant.

Standing on the riverbank in August 1966, though, I was just confused. I went into the teahouse with my fellow pupils. Some asked the manager to close down. Others started pasting slogans on the walls. Many customers were getting up to go, but in a far corner one old man was still sitting at his table, calmly sipping his tea. I stood beside him, feeling embarrassed that I was supposed to assume the voice of authority. He looked at me, and resumed his noisy sipping. He had a deeply lined face that was almost stereotypical 'working class' as shown in propaganda pictures. His hands reminded me of one of my textbook stories which described the hands of an old peasant: they could bundle thorny firewood without feeling any pain.

Perhaps this old man was very sure of his unquestionable background, or his advanced age, which had hitherto been the object of respect, or perhaps he simply did not think I was very impressive. Anyway, he remained in his seat taking no notice of me. I summoned up my courage and pleaded in a low voice, 'Please, could you leave?' Without looking at me, he said, 'Where to?' 'Home, of course,' I replied. He turned to face me. There was emotion in his voice, though he spoke quietly. 'Home? What home? I share a tiny room with my two grandsons. I have a corner surrounded by a bamboo curtain. Just for the bed. That's all. When the kids are home I come here for some peace and quiet. Why do you have to take this away from me?'

His words filled me with shock and shame. This was the first time I had heard a first-hand account of such miserable living conditions. I turned and walked away.

This teahouse, like all the others in Sichuan, was shut for fifteen years – until 1981, when Deng Xiaoping's reforms decreed it could be reopened. In 1985 I went back there with a British friend. We sat under the scholar tree. An old waitress came to fill our cups with a kettle from two feet away. Around us, people were playing chess. It was one of the happiest moments of that trip back.

Group discussion

- In the first two paragraphs of the extract, two words have single inverted commas round them. How does this use of punctuation affect meaning?
- Consider how language is used to describe the teahouses. Select examples of words that acquire special significance because of their associations and connotations. How is the reader's view of teahouses possibly influenced by this use of language?
- Discuss the contrast between the way the customers of the teahouses and the Red Guard are described. How are the sympathies of the reader guided one way or another?
- This extract is from an autobiographical book. Discuss whether this extract could have been 'mistaken' for fiction and what features, if any, identify it as being autobiographical rather than a fictional story.
- Compare this extract with the Maya Angelou extract in the previous section. Discuss features they have in common, and ways in which they are different.

Writing ☞

Choose an autobiographical work of some kind, preferably a book, but a 'biopic' (a film about the life of someone famous) will suffice. Describe what the book or film tells us about the life of the person portrayed, what impression of the person is produced and whether you think the work can be accepted as an accurate account of the person's life, or merely a 'version' of the life.

☞ Write a brief piece of autobiography yourself, concentrating on one important incident in your life. Then rewrite the section as though a biographer (rather than yourself) were writing the 'story'.

Write a commentary on the way you completed the task, dealing in particular with the problem of how to convey on paper the 'truth' about your own life.

3   Will the author please stand up?

When we read a novel, a short story, a poem or most written texts, we can usually identify one individual as the author. Even when a piece of written text does not have a named author (a leaflet providing information, a report in a newspaper), we assume that one individual has been responsible for the authorship of it.

In literature especially, individual works are traditionally in part defined by their authorship: *David Copperfield* by Charles Dickens or George Eliot's *Middlemarch*. The traditional view of the literary text is that it is the expression of an individual author who is responsible for any 'meaning' the text has. It is assumed that the author has a vision of reality that s/he communicates through the medium of the novel, short story, poem or other form that s/he has used. The reader of the text then has to decipher the author's intentions and 'meaning'. This view of the relationship between author/text/reader leads to the concept that the text has a fixed meaning which stems from the author and which the reader has to discover.

However, recent development in literary theory has challenged this traditional view of the text, and the relationship of the author and the reader to it. One result of this challenge is to 'unseat' the author. The author is no longer seen as the source of all meaning in the text. The 'meaning' of the text becomes a matter of interpretation for the reader without any 'interference' from the author. The author's intentions become far less important, even irrelevant, and the idea that the text has one fixed meaning is discarded. Indeed, texts are perceived as having a plurality of meanings, which will vary from reading to reading and from individual reader to individual reader. Some theorists have gone so far as to claim that 'the author is dead', meaning the tyranny of the individual author over the text has been broken. The text belongs to the reader to do with as s/he wishes.

In this unit, we will be looking at questions of authorship and alternative ways of discussing the issue of who writes the text, and the meaning of texts.

3.1 The omniscient author

When we are reading a work of fiction, say, a novel, an ***illusion of reality*** is usually created for us, the readers. We are invited to accept this reality, suspend our disbelief and consider the events of the narrative and the characters in it as 'real'. The narrative figures are represented as actual human beings. Traditional literary criticism, and many a question in literature examinations, has analysed these characters as though they were living human beings instead of the product of a particular way of using language to create the illusion of real persons.

It is worthwhile considering the role of the author in creating this illusion of reality and these 'characters'. The author of a work of fiction is usually seen as 'omniscient' and ubiquitous: s/he knows all and is everywhere. In other words, the author is put in the position of a god who looks down on the events and people s/he has created with an all-seeing eye. What we have to consider, if this traditional view of the ***omniscient author*** is to be questioned, is how this is worked out in the language of the text.

Below is an extract from a nineteenth-century novel, *Wives and Daughters* by Elizabeth Gaskell. Mrs Gaskell is usually discussed as a 'realist', a novelist who attempted to create an authentic picture of English life in the middle of the nineteenth century. In this extract, Molly Gibson is anxiously awaiting the return of her newly-remarried father, Mr Gibson, a doctor, to the family home in a Midland town.

> On Tuesday afternoon Molly returned home – to the home which was already strange, and what Warwickshire people would call 'unked', to her. New paint, new paper, new colours; grim servants dressed in their best, and objecting to every change – from their master's marriage to the new oilcloth in the hall, 'which tripped 'em up, and threw 'em down, and was cold to the feet, and smelt just abominable'. All these complaints Molly had to listen to, and it was not a cheerful preparation for the reception which she already felt to be so formidable.
>
> The sound of their carriage-wheels was heard at last, and Molly went to the front door to meet them. Her father got out first, and took her hand and held it while he helped his bride to alight. Then he kissed her fondly, and passed her on to his wife; but her veil was so securely (and becomingly) fastened down, that it was some time before Mrs Gibson could get her lips clear to greet her new daughter. Then there was luggage to be seen about; and both the travellers were occupied in this, while Molly stood by trembling with excitement, unable to help, and only conscious of Betty's rather cross looks, as heavy box after heavy box jammed up the passage.
>
> 'Molly, my dear, show – your mamma to her room!'

Mr Gibson had hesitated, because the question of the name by which Molly was to call her new relation had never occurred to him before. The colour flashed into Molly's face. Was she to call her 'mamma'? – the name long appropriated in her mind to some one else – to her own dead mother. The rebellious heart rose against it, but she said nothing. She led the way upstairs, Mrs Gibson turning round, from time to time, with some fresh direction as to which bag or trunk she needed most. She hardly spoke to Molly till they were both in the newly-furnished bedroom, where a small fire had been lighted by Molly's orders.

'Now, my love, we can embrace each other in peace. O dear, how tired I am!' – (after the embrace had been accomplished). 'My spirits are so easily affected with fatigue; but your dear papa has been kindness itself. Dear! what an old-fashioned bed! And what a – But it doesn't signify. By-and-by we'll renovate the house – won't we, my dear? And you'll be my little maid tonight, and help me to arrange a few things, for I'm just worn out with the day's journey.'

'I've ordered a sort of tea-dinner to be ready for you,' said Molly. 'Shall I go and tell them to send it in?'

'I'm not sure if I can go down again tonight. It would be very comfortable to have a little table brought in here, and sit in my dressing-gown by this cheerful fire. But, to be sure, there's your dear papa. I really don't think he would eat anything if I were not there. One must not think about oneself, you know. Yes, I'll come down in a quarter of an hour.'

But Mr Gibson had found a note awaiting him, with an immediate summons to an old patient, dangerously ill; and, snatching a mouthful of food while his horse was being saddled, he had to resume at once his old habits of attention to his profession above everything.

As soon as Mrs Gibson found that he was not likely to miss her presence – he had eaten a very tolerable lunch of bread and cold meat in solitude, so her fears about his appetite in her absence were not well founded – she desired to have her meal upstairs in her own room; and poor Molly, not daring to tell the servants of this whim, had to carry up first a table, which, however small, was too heavy for her; and afterwards all the choice portions of the meal, which she had taken great pains to arrange on the table, as she had seen such things done at Hamley, intermixed with fruit and flowers that had that morning been sent in from various great houses where Mr Gibson was respected and valued. How pretty Molly had thought her handiwork an hour or two before! How dreary it seemed as, at last released from Mrs Gibson's conversation, she sat down in solitude to cold tea and the drum-sticks of the chicken! No one to look at her preparations, and admire her deft-handedness and taste! She had thought that her father would be grati-fied by it, and then he had never seen it. She had meant her cares as an offering of good-will to her stepmother, who even now was ringing her bell to have the tray taken away, and Miss Gibson summoned to her bedroom.

Molly hastily finished her meal, and went upstairs again.

'I feel so lonely, darling, in this strange house; do come and be with me, and help me to unpack. I think your dear papa might have put off his visit to Mr Craven Smith for just this one evening.'

'Mr Craven Smith couldn't put off his dying,' said Molly bluntly.

'You droll girl!' said Mrs Gibson, with a faint laugh. 'But if this Mr Smith is dying, as you say, what's the use of your father's going off to him in such a hurry? Does he expect any legacy, or anything of that kind?'

Molly bit her lips to prevent herself from saying something disagreeable. She only answered:

'I don't know that he is dying. The man said so; and papa can sometimes do something to make the last struggle easier. At any rate, it's always a comfort to the family to have him.'

'What dreary knowledge of death you have learned for a girl of your age! Really, if I had heard all these details of your father's profession, I doubt if I could have brought myself to have him!'

'He doesn't make the illness or the death; he does his best against them. I call it a very fine thing to think of what he does or tries to do. And you will think so, when you see how he is watched for, and how people welcome him!'

'Well, don't let us talk any more of such gloomy things, tonight! I think I shall go to bed at once, I am so tired, if you will only sit by me till I get sleepy, darling. If you will talk to me, the sound of your voice will soon send me off.'

Molly got a book, and read her stepmother to sleep, preferring that to the harder task of keeping up a continual murmur of speech.

Group discussion
- Working in pairs, discuss what is represented as happening in the narrative and the nature of the relationships between the narrative figures. Then as a group, come to a consensus agreement about the content of the extract.
- Some of the extract consists of narrative, where the unseen author tells the reader about events that are supposed to have already happened. In terms of narrative, this is an example of the author *telling* the reader what has supposedly happened within the fiction. Most of the extract, however, consists of 'dramatisation' of incident involving the *showing* of incidents as though the author had been present when the fictional incidents took place. The 'showing' of these incidents in detail, with the utterances of the narrative figures included, helps to create the illusion that these incidents have taken place in the 'real' world and that these narrative figures

are 'real' people. The arrival of Mr and Mrs Gibson and the section in which Molly goes to her 'mother's' bedroom are dramatised in this way.

Divide the extract into sections consisting of narrative ('telling') and the dramatisation of incident ('showing').

- We, the readers, see the events of the narrative through the eyes of Molly. It is from her perspective that we see Mr Gibson and his new bride. This perspective has been chosen by the author deliberately. How does this 'imposed' viewpoint affect meaning? Are we meant to feel sympathy for Molly rather than for Mrs Gibson? If so, how is this reflected in the language used by the author?

- The creation of 'character' is a matter of a particular use of language in a specific context. 'Mrs Gibson' as a character is the result of language use by the author which builds a picture of 'her' in our minds. Analyse how Mrs Gaskell does this by her use of language, selecting examples of language that is intended to produce particular meaning.

- If Mrs Gaskell is the all-knowing, all-seeing author of this extract from the novel and the creator of the 'characters', does she in any way 'judge' them? Does it appear that she has an 'agenda' in this passage, say, to show Molly's aggrieved feelings and Mrs Gibson's selfishness? If so, is it important that we recognise and accept those intentions as being the 'meaning' of the extract, or, can we afford to ignore the author's intentions and make our own interpretation as an independent reader?

Writing   Summarise the subject matter of the extract in no more than eighty words.

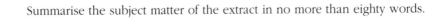   Analyse how the author uses language to build up an illusion of reality (detail, description, dialogue).

GLOSSARY

Illusion of reality: the representation of the 'world' through language, which the reader is implicitly invited to accept as 'real', involving 'real' incidents and 'real' people. Most television soap operas, for example, create this illusion of reality so that viewers begin to think of the events and characters depicted as being 'real'.

The omniscient author: the author as the God-like figure who knows everything about the story and the characters in it.

3.2 The author as personality

More and more in contemporary publishing, authors of books are sold to us as 'products'. Writers have to play their part in publicising their books so that they sell as many copies as possible. Television and radio interviews, chat shows, book signings and literary festivals are some of the ways in which the author as a personality is promoted, as well as the more traditional methods of advertising and book reviews in newspapers and magazines.

The cult of the 'personality author' is not a new phenomenon; Victorian novelists such as Charles Dickens and William Thackeray became famous not only for their novels, but also as celebrities. However, it seems that the cult of the celebrity author has today reached a new pitch of intensity.

One way in which interest in the personality of an author is generated is through literary biography. These biographies raise the issue of how much we need to know about an author's life to read his or her work. Does a biography of a writer help us to understand a writer's intentions in writing novels or poetry, for example?

This, in turn, raises the issue of the ***intentional fallacy***. This term is often used to discredit the idea that we need pay any attention to a writer's intentions when s/he wrote something, or that we can possibly analyse those intentions in the first place. What we should be concentrating on, according to this argument, is what the text says and how meaning is produced, and not what we *think* an author intended to say.

Literary biography, the study of the life of a writer, would appear to run counter to this viewpoint. Most literary biographers would argue that exploring the life of the author helps us to understand her/his creative works that much better. The counter argument might be that many literary biographies are no more than rather superior gossip or intrusions into private lives, which are of little relevance or interest to people who read the author's works.

Below is an extract from a literary biography of the author, Bruce Chatwin, who died in 1989 at the age of 48. This is followed by an extract from Chatwin's most famous book, *On the Black Hill.*

With his third book, Bruce Chatwin sprang a surprise. Established as a chronicler of extraordinary events in extraordinary places he published, in 1982, a book about two Welsh hill farmers whose lives could only be seen as mundane in comparison with the characters he had drawn in Patagonia or Dahomey. He explained himself in an interview with Michael Ignatieff:

It always irritated me to be called a travel writer. So I decided to write something about people who never went out. That's how *On the Black Hill* came into being. (Granta, p.27)

There is perhaps more to the genesis of the book than this. Chatwin's involvement with the Welsh border country dated back, as has been discussed earlier, to a childhood trip with his father. His next visit was from Marlborough as part of a youth club summer camp that had the aim of mixing the social classes through activities such as walling and roofing. Later, he stayed at Llanthony Abbey, once owned by Walter Savage Landor and now a hotel but, at the time Chatwin stayed, occupied by an Italian contessa who set up her table in the cloister like a nineteenth century landlord to receive rents from her tenants. He told the poet Hugo Williams: 'Hardly anything has changed around here since my grandparents came on bicycling tours as teenagers. Even the clothes are the same. You can still get the double-fronted striped shirts in Hay-on-Wye.' In an interview given to Melvyn Bragg on London Weekend Television's *South Bank Show*, Chatwin said that he had often thought of the landscape of the Welsh borders, of the Black Mountains and the Radnor Forest, 'as if it were my home in many ways'. He had come there as a child 'and it's my home base, a sort of metaphorical home base if you like and it's the place I love.'

Chatwin had friends in the area: he stayed regularly with Penelope Chetwode (Lady Betjeman) another adventurous traveller who lived above Hay, and with Diana Melly at her thirteenth century Norman watchtower near Brecon where much of the book was eventually written. He stayed, too, with an old friend, Martin Wilkinson, near Clun, where the book was begun. It was at Lady Betjeman's table that he was introduced to some of the more prominent members of Hay society like the bookseller Richard Booth, the self-styled 'King of Hay'. Booth found the writer too much of an intellectual for his taste, and accuses him now of taking a romantic view of the people of the Black Mountains. 'I felt very strongly that he was taking an intellectual view of it,' he says, 'without realising how the local economy works, how it did still continue.' Booth is unimpressed by the fact that most local people loved the book and found it a fair reflection of the Radnorshire reality. 'These people are too inclined to go down well locally,' he observes tartly.

Ros Fry, who worked at the Blue Board in Hay, recalls that Chatwin frequently came in for lunch: 'He was always watching people, how they spoke, and their mannerisms.' He was also able to efface himself in the interests of observation and recording ('No-one really knew him') but when he wished to he could shine: 'He had quite a theatrical way about him if he wanted to. He had a face that you really wanted to look at. His eyes really glittered. If he had been born in the twelfth century he would have been a wizard.' Chatwin insisted that Rhulen in the book could have been any one of the border towns (he mentions specifically Kington or Knighton) but it would be unwise to suggest that to the citizens of Hay. Certainly, an identification of the topography of the novel with the Llanthony valley seems reasonable enough, although Chatwin was drawing on explorations and researches up and down the border, even as far north as Clun.

A typical local reader of *On the Black Hill* was Mrs Nancy Powell who lives at a hill farm near Hay and who read the book with great eagerness, recognising many of the stories in it. The shooting at Lower Brechfa, for example, was based on a real incident, thought to have happened in 1926. Certainly the *Hereford Times* for that year records two very similar incidents. In May 1926 a man called Godfrey Thomas, who lived with his aged mother at Henllys Farm, Tregare, near Raglan in Monmouthshire, attempted to shoot Alice Powell of Ty Pwll Farm, Tregare, following a lovers' quarrel and then shot himself dead with the same shotgun. In September, also near Raglan, Albert Rudge, a farm-worker, shot dead 19-year old Doris Moody at her home, Pentre Cottage, Llandenny. In spite of shooting himself and then trying to drown in the village pond, Albert was brought before Monmouth magistrates with his arm in a sling, looking, understandable, 'ill and haggard'. At the assizes his love letter to the girl, which was also a suicide note, was read out. She had apparently returned his engagement ring by post. Rudge was found guilty but detained as criminally insane 'until His Majesty's pleasure be known'. The inquest jury at Monmouth Assizes was so moved by the girl's mother's plight that they handed her their fees.

Mrs Powell also recalls many cases of twins who would not marry for fear of losing part of the farm to the other's widow. And she remembers a well-known case of a vicar's daughter, like Mary Jones, who ran off with a carpenter and had two bachelor sons who farmed together until the 1960s when a divorcee 'managed to prise them apart' by marrying one of them. For Mrs Powell the book was 'very convincing, very good on farm life'. She adds: 'He painted a wonderful picture of my mother's day and age.' Pressed on whether there was any element of condescension in the book, a frequent charge levelled at those who write from outside a community, she replies simply: 'He had no bones to pick with the people.'

Group discussion
- What explanation is given for Chatwin's decision to write *On the Black Hill*? Discuss whether his biographer, Nicholas Murray, communicates that he thinks there were more complex reasons for Chatwin's decision than the explanation given.
- What evidence is provided in the first paragraph of the extract that Chatwin was a well-known writer and a 'public person'?
- List the details about Chatwin's life that his biographer includes in the first two paragraphs of the extract.

- We are given two contrasting views of Chatwin and his attitude to the area and the people who lived there. One is fairly negative, the other fairly positive. How are these negative and positive impressions created through the speakers' use of language?
- What evidence is provided that Chatwin based some of the incidents in his book on real events?
- Pressed on whether there was any element of condescension in the book, a frequent charge levelled at those who write from outside a community, she replies simply: 'He had no bones to pick with the people.'

What does the phrase 'any element of condescension' communicate to you? What do you understand from the woman's response to the question? How would you describe the contrast in the kind of language used in the question put to the woman and the language used by the interviewer, the writer of the biography?

* * *

Below is an an extract from the first chapter of Bruce Chatwin's novel *On the Black Hill.*

> For forty-two years, Lewis and Benjamin Jones slept side by side, in their parents' bed, at their farm which was known as 'The Vision'.
>
> The bedstead, an oak four-poster, came from their mother's home at Bryn-Draenog when she married in 1899. Its faded cretonne hangings, printed with a design of larkspur and roses, shut out the mosquitoes of summer, and the draughts in winter. Calloused heels had worn holes in the linen sheets, and parts of the patchwork quilt had frayed. Under the goose-feather mattress, there was a second mattress, of horsehair, and this had sunk into two troughs, leaving a ridge between the sleepers.
>
> The room was always dark and smelled of lavender and mothballs.
>
> The smell of mothballs came from a pyramid of hatboxes piled up beside the washstand. On the bed-table lay a pincushion still stuck with Mrs Jones's hatpins; and on the end wall hung an engraving of Holman Hunt's 'Light of the World', enclosed in an ebonized frame.
>
> One of the windows looked out over the green fields of England: the other looked back into Wales, past a clump of larches, at the Black Hill.
>
> Both the brothers' hair was even whiter than the pillowcases.
>
> Every morning their alarm went off at six. They listened to the farmers' broadcast as they shaved and dressed. Downstairs, they tapped the barometer, lit the fire and boiled a kettle for tea. Then they did the milking, and foddering before coming back for breakfast.

A still from the 1987 film version of On the Black Hill

The house had roughcast walls and a roof of mossy stone tiles and stood at the far end of the farmyard in the shade of an old Scots pine. Below the cowshed there was an orchard of wind-stunted apple trees, and then the fields slanted down to the dingle, and there were birches and alders along the stream.

Long ago, the place had been called Ty-Cradoc – and Caractacus is still a name in these parts – but in 1737 an ailing girl called Alice Morgan saw the Virgin hovering over a patch of rhubarb, and ran back to the kitchen, cured. To celebrate the miracle, her father renamed his farm 'The Vision' and carved the initials A.M. with the date and a cross on the lintel above the porch. The border of Radnor and Hereford was said to run right through the middle of the staircase.

The brothers were identical twins.

As boys, only their mother could tell them apart: now age and accidents had weathered them in different ways.

Lewis was tall and stringy, with shoulders set square and a steady long-limbed stride. Even at eighty he could walk over the hills all day, or wield an axe all day, and not get tired.

He gave off a strong smell. His eyes – grey, dreamy and astygmatic – were set well back into the skull, and capped with thick round lenses in white metal frames. He bore the scar of a cycling accident on his nose and, ever since, its tip had curved downwards and turned purple in cold weather.

His head would wobble as he spoke: unless he was fumbling with his watch-chain, he had no idea what to do with his hands. In company he always wore a puzzled look; and if anyone made a statement of fact, he'd say, 'Thank you!' or 'Very kind of you!' Everyone agreed he had a wonderful way with sheepdogs.

Benjamin was shorter, pinker, neater and sharper-tongued. His chin fell into his neck, but he still possessed the full stretch of his nose, which he would use in conversation as a weapon. He had less hair.

He did all the cooking, the darning and the ironing; and he kept the accounts. No one could be fiercer in a haggle over stock-prices and he would go on, arguing for hours, until the dealer threw up his hands and said, 'Come off, you old skinflint!' and he'd smile and say, 'What can you mean by that?'

For miles around the twins had the reputation of being incredibly stingy – but this was not always so.

They refused, for example, to make a penny out of hay. Hay, they said, was God's gift to the farmer; and providing The Vision had hay to spare, their poorer neighbours were welcome to what they needed. Even in the foul days of January, old Miss Fifield the Tump had only to send a message with the postman, and Lewis would drive the tractor over with a load of bales.

Benjamin's favourite occupation was delivering lambs. All the long winter, he waited for the end of March, when the curlews started calling and the lambing began. It was he, not Lewis, who stayed awake to watch the ewes. It was he who would pull a lamb at a difficult birth. Sometimes, he had to thrust his forearm into the womb to disentangle a pair of twins; and afterwards, he would sit by the fireside, unwashed and contented, and let the cat lick the afterbirth off his hands.

In winter and summer, the brothers went to work in striped flannel shirts with copper studs to fasten them at the neck. Their jackets and waistcoats were made of brown whipcord, and their trousers were of darker corduroy. They wore their moleskin hats with the brims turned down; but since Lewis had the habit of lifting his to every stranger, his fingers had rubbed the nap off the peak.

From time to time, with a show of mock solemnity, they consulted their silver watches – not to tell the hour but to see whose watch was beating faster. On Saturday nights they took turns to have a hip-bath in front of the fire; and they lived for the memory of their mother.

Because they knew each other's thoughts, they even quarrelled without speaking. And sometimes – perhaps after one of these silent quarrels, when they needed their mother to unite them – they would stand over her patchwork quilt and peer at the black velvet stars and the hexagons of printed calico that had once been her dresses. And without saying a word they could see her again – in pink, walking through the oatfield with a jug of draught cider for the reapers. or in green, at a sheep-shearers' lunch. Or in a blue-striped apron bending over the fire. But the black stars brought back a memory of their father's coffin, laid out on the kitchen table, and the chalk-faced women, crying.

Group discussion
- Consider the varied length of the paragraphs in this extract from the novel. Some paragraphs consist of one short sentence. Working in pairs, analyse the paragraph structure of the extract in terms of the number of sentences and how long the sentences are. Then as a group, discuss what effect this variation in the length of paragraphs has on the meaning produced and whether the one short sentence paragraphs have particular significance.
- Consider the second paragraph of the extract. How does the author use language to represent a detailed picture of the four-poster bed?
- Consider the sequence of the paragraphs. Does one paragraph necessarily follow on from the previous one, or does the order seem more haphazard than most narratives?
- How does the writer use physical description and illustrations of how the twins characteristically behaved to create a picture of the two men?

- Read the extract from the biography of Bruce Chatwin again. Consider whether any information contained in that extract is helpful in understanding more deeply the extract you have read from the novel.

Writing ☛ Write a piece about whether you think we need to know about a writer's life to understand fully her/his work. Try to use illustrations involving writers whose work you like. Address the issue of whether a writer's intentions are relevant to our reading of a work.

GLOSSARY

Intentional fallacy: this term refers to the idea that the 'meaning' of a text somehow resides in the intentions of the author. This 'meaning', according to the fallacy, may only be discovered if we understand fully what those intentions are. The intentional fallacy explodes that theory: it states that the author's intentions are irrelevant. The text itself is the only 'site' of meaning.

3.3 The ironic voice

Irony involves us being able to attribute to a statement or utterance a meaning that appears to be contrary to the surface meaning. For example, the phrase 'Great weather!' spoken by someone on a rainy day can be classed as irony because the apparent meaning of the words is undermined by the tone of voice and the fact that we can see the weather is not 'great'. The statement then appears to mean the opposite of what is actually said. In written texts, however, the use of irony is often more subtle.

Another use of irony is when the reader knows something that a narrative figure in the text is not aware of. In plays, this is called **_dramatic irony_**.

Jane Austen published her novels in the first twenty years of the nineteenth century. She is often alluded to as a writer with a command of irony. In her novels she sometimes makes ironic statements herself, as the 'absent' story-teller; often, she uses a narrative figure to make ironic statements for her.

On page 63 is an extract from *Pride and Prejudice*, one of Austen's most famous novels. Mr Bingley, a rich, aristocratic young man, has moved into the area, arousing the interest of Mrs Bennet, the mother of five unmarried daughters, who is anxious to find rich husbands for them. Mrs Bennet has been trying to persuade her husband to pay a visit to Mr Bingley, so that the daughters may have an opportunity to get to know him.

A still from the 1940 film version of Pride and Prejudice

Mr Bennet was among the earliest of those who waited on Mr Bingley. He had always intended to visit him, though to the last always assuring his wife that he should not go; and till the evening after the visit was paid, she had no knowledge of it. It was then disclosed in the following manner. Observing his second daughter employed in trimming a hat, he suddenly addressed her with, 'I hope Mr Bingley will like it, Lizzy.'

'We are not in a way to know *what* Mr Bingley likes,' said her mother resentfully, 'since we are not to visit.'

'But you forget, Mama,' said Elizabeth, 'that we shall meet him at the assemblies, and that Mrs Long has promised to introduce him.'

'I do not believe Mrs Long will do any such thing. She has two nieces of her own. She is a selfish, hypocritical woman, and I have no opinion of her.'

'No more have I,' said Mr Bennet: 'and I am glad to find that you do not depend on her serving you.'

Mrs Bennet deigned not to make any reply; but unable to contain herself, began scolding one of her daughters.

'Don't keep coughing so, Kitty, for heaven's sake! Have a little compassion on my nerves. You tear them to pieces.'

'Kitty has no discretion in her coughs,' said her father; 'she times them ill.'

'I do not cough for my own amusement,' replied Kitty fretfully.

'When is your next ball to be, Lizzy?'

'Tomorrow fortnight.'

'Aye, so it is,' cried her mother, 'and Mrs Long does not come back till the day before: so, it will be impossible for her to introduce him, for she will not know him herself.'

'Then, my dear, you may have the advantage of your friend, and introduce Mr Bingley to *her*.'

'Impossible, Mr Bennet, impossible, when I am not acquainted with him myself; how can you be so teasing?'

'I honour your circumspection. A fortnight's acquaintance is certainly very little. One cannot know what a man really is by the end of a fortnight. But if *we* do not venture, somebody else will; and after all, Mrs Long and her nieces must stand their chance; and therefore, as she will think it an act of kindness, if you decline the office, I will take it on myself.'

The girls stared at their father. Mrs Bennet said only, 'Nonsense, nonsense!'

'What can be the meaning of that emphatic exclamation?' cried he. 'Do you consider the forms of introduction, and the stress that is laid on them, as nonsense? I cannot quite agree with you *there*. What say you, Mary? for you are a young lady of deep reflection, I know, and read great books, and make extracts.'

Mary wished to say something very sensible, but knew not how.

'While Mary is adjusting her ideas,' he continued, 'let us return to Mr Bingley.'

'I am sick of Mr Bingley,' cried his wife.

'I am sorry to hear *that*; but why did not you tell me so before? If I had known as much this morning, I certainly would not have called on him. It is very unlucky; but as I have actually paid the visit, we cannot escape the acquaintance now.'

The astonishment of the ladies was just what he wished—that of Mrs Bennet perhaps surpassing the rest—though when the first tumult of joy was over, she began to declare that it was what she had expected all the while.

'How good it was in you, my dear Mr Bennet! But I knew I should persuade you at last. I was sure you loved your girls too well to neglect such an acquaintance. Well, how pleased I am! and it is such a good joke, too, that you should have gone this morning, and never said a word about it till now.'

'Now, Kitty, you may cough as much as you choose,' said Mr Bennet; and, as he spoke, he left the room, fatigued with the raptures of his wife.

'What an excellent father you have girls,' said she, when the door was shut. 'I do not know how you will ever make him amends for his kindness; or me either, for that matter. At our time of life it is not so pleasant, I can tell you, to be making new acquaintance everyday; but for your sakes, we would do anything. Lydia, my love, though you are the youngest, I dare say Mr Bingley will dance with you at the next ball.'

'Oh!' said Lydia stoutly, 'I am not afraid; for though I *am* the youngest, I'm the tallest.'

The rest of the evening was spent in conjecturing how soon he would return Mr Bennet's visit, and determining when they should ask him to dinner.

Group discussion
- We have already made a distinction between 'telling' and 'showing' in narrative writing. In the first paragraph down to 'no knowledge of it', the author tells the reader what has happened. She then signals her intention to 'show' or to dramatise a scene by the use of the words 'It was then disclosed in the following manner.'

  Discuss Austen's use of language here and where that places her in relation to the events and 'characters' of the narrative.
- Working in pairs, consider each utterance that the author has Mr Bennet say in the extract. To how many of these utterances can the reader attribute an ironic intention?
- Show how the narrative figure, Mrs Bennet, is contrasted with the figure

of her husband, and how what she is given to say makes him look intelligent and she rather foolish.

- *Pride and Prejudice* was first published in 1813. Select examples of language use that you think would not appear in a twentieth-century novel.
- Discuss whether you think Jane Austen deliberately uses the narrative figure of Mr Bennet to communicate her own view of the other narrative figures and the events represented. If so, how does she do this?

Writing You have been asked to write a short story for the school or college magazine. You decide to write a story consisting mainly of a conversation between two narrative figures, one of whom makes only ironic statements.

Write a piece about the use of irony in everyday speech, illustrating your text with as many examples of ironic usage as you can think of.

GLOSSARY

Dramatic irony: a term used to describe how an audience in a theatre seems to be in possession of information or an understanding of a character that the characters in the play are not aware of.

3.4   The 'traditional' short story

The forerunners of the short story form are fairy stories, fables, essays, myths and legends. However, the short story as such is a genre of literature that emerged during the nineteenth century because of the requirement of magazines and other periodicals to supply fiction for their readership that could be read over a brief period of time (anything from a few minutes to a couple of hours). Early practitioners of the short story included Sir Walter Scott, Edgar Allen Poe and Gogol.

The 'traditional' short story focuses on one incident or 'character' and tells an uncomplicated narrative that often ends with some kind of 'twist'. Editors commissioning short stories of writers would probably stress the need for conciseness, a clear narrative and a neat, rounded conclusion, if not a surprise ending. Below is an example of this kind of 'well-made' short story by Graham Greene.

Alas, poor Maling

Poor inoffensive ineffectual Maling! I don't want you to smile at Maling and his borborygmi, as the doctors always smiled when he consulted them, as they must have smiled even after the sad climax of September 3rd, 1940, when his borborygmi held up for twenty-four fatal hours the amalgamation of the Simcox and Hythe Newsprint Companies. Simcox's interests had always been dearer to Maling than life: hard-driven, conscientious, happy in his work, he wanted no position higher than their secretary, and those twenty-four hours happened for reasons it is unwise to go into here, for they involve intricacies in British income-tax law – to be fatal to the company's existence. After that day he dropped altogether out of sight, and I shall always believe he crept away to die of a broken heart in some provincial printing works. Alas, poor Maling!

It was the doctors who called his complaint borborygmi: in England we usually call it just 'tummy rumbles'. I believe it's quite a harmless kind of indigestion, but in Maling's case it took a rather odd form. His stomach, he used to complain, blinking sadly downwards through his semi-circular reading glasses, had 'an ear'. It used to pick up notes in an extraordinary way and give them out again after meals. I shall never forget one embarrassing tea at the Piccadilly Hotel in honour of a party of provincial printers: it was the year before the war, and Maling had been attending the Symphony Concerts at Queen's Hall (he never went again). In the distance a dance orchestra had been playing 'The Lambeth Walk' (how tired one got of that tune in 1938 with its waggery and false bonhomie and its 'ois'). Suddenly in the happy silence between dances, as the printers sat back from a ruin of toasted tea-cakes, there emerged – faint as though from a distant part of the hotel, sad and plangent – the opening bars of a Brahms Concerto. A Scottish printer, who had an ear for good music, exclaimed with dour relish, 'My goodness, how that mon can play.' Then the music stopped abruptly, and an odd suspicion made me look at Maling. He was red as beetroot. Nobody noticed because the dance orchestra began again to the Scotsman's disgust with 'Boomps-a-Daisy', and I think I was the only one who detected a curious faint undertone of 'The Lambeth Walk' coming from the chair where Maling sat.

It was after ten, when the printers had piled into taxis and driven away to Euston, that Maling told me about his stomach. 'It's quite unaccountable,' he said, 'like a parrot. It seems to pick up things at random.' He added with tears in his voice, 'I can't enjoy food any more. I never know what's going to happen afterwards. This afternoon wasn't the worst. Sometimes it's quite loud.' He brooded forlornly. 'When I was a boy I liked listening to German bands . . .'

'Haven't you seen a doctor?'

'They don't understand. They say it's just indigestion and nothing to worry about. Nothing to worry about! But then when I've been seeing a doctor it's always lain quiet.' I noticed that he spoke of his stomach as if it were a detested animal. He gazed bleakly at his knuckles and said, 'Now I've become afraid of any new noise. I never know. It doesn't take any notice of some, but others seem . . . well, to fascinate it. At a first hearing. Last year when they took up Piccadilly it was the road drills. I used to get them all over again after dinner.'

I said rather stupidly, 'I suppose you've tried the usual salts,' and I remember – it was my last sight of him – his expression of despair as though he had ceased to expect comprehension from any living soul.

It was my last sight of him because the war pitched me out of the printing trade into all sorts of odd occupations, and it was only at second-hand that I heard the account of the strange board meeting which broke poor Maling's heart.

What the papers called the blitz-and-pieces krieg against Britain had been going on for about a week: in London we were just settling down to air-raid alarms at the rate of five or six a day, but the 3rd of September, the anniversary of the war, had so far been relatively peaceful. There was a general feeling, however, that Hitler might celebrate the anniversary with a big attack. It was therefore in an atmosphere of some tension that Simcox and Hythe had their joint meeting.

It took place in the traditional grubby little room above the Simcox offices in Fetter Lane: the round table dating from the original Joshua Simcox, the steel engraving of a printing works dated 1875, and an irrelevant copy of a Bible which had always been the only book in the big glass bookcase except for a volume of type faces. Old Sir Joshua Simcox was in the chair: you can picture his snow-white hair and the pale pork-like Nonconformist features. Wesby Hythe was there, and half a dozen other directors with narrow faces and neat black coats: they all looked a little strained. If the new income-tax regulations were to be evaded, they had to work quickly. As for Maling he crouched over his pad, nervously ready to advise anybody on anything.

There was one interruption during the reading of the minutes. Wesby Hythe, who was an invalid, complained that a typewriter in the next room was getting on his nerves. Maling blushed and went out: I think he must have swallowed a tablet because the typewriter stopped. Hythe was impatient. 'Hurry up,' he said, 'hurry up. We haven't all night.' But that was exactly what they had.

After the minutes had been read Sir Joshua began explaining elaborately in a Yorkshire accent that their motives were entirely patriotic: they hadn't any intention of evading tax: they just wanted to contribute to the war effort, drive, economy . . . he said, 'The proof of the pudden' . . .' and at that moment the air-raid sirens started. As I have said a mass attack was expected: it wasn't the time for delay: a dead man couldn't evade income tax. The directors gathered up their papers and bolted for the basement.

All except Maling. You see, he knew the truth. I think it had been the reference to pudding which had roused the sleeping animal. Of course he should have confessed, but think for a moment: would you have had the courage, after watching those elderly men with white slips to their waist-coats pelt with a horrifying lack of dignity to safety? I know I should have done exactly what Maling did, have followed Sir Joshua down to the base-ment in the desperate hope that for once the stomach would do the right thing and make amends. But it didn't. The joint boards of Simcox and Hythe stayed in the basement for twelve hours, and Maling stayed with them, saying nothing. You see, for some unaccountable reason of taste, poor Maling's stomach had picked up the note of the Warning only too effec-tively, but it had somehow never taken to the All Clear.

Group discussion

- Working in pairs, make a summary of the narrative in no more than eighty words. Then reduce your summary further to a maximum of fifty words. As a group, compare the summaries you have produced and agree a consensus summary of fifty words.
- Consider the first paragraph. How does the writer attempt to draw the reader into the story?
- The story is written in first-person narrative. The 'I' of the narrative is unnamed, but we may think it is the author himself. Read through the story and note which incidents he dramatises when the narrator was present. How does he get round the difficulty of telling about an event at which the narrator was not present?
- Discuss whether you think the author, in the guise of the first-person narrator, 'intrudes' into the story and comments directly on the narrative and the narrative figures. How is this 'intrusion' expressed in language?
- Re-read the introduction to this section and discuss whether 'Alas, poor Maling' fits into the category of a 'traditional' short story.
- Discuss what kind of magazine this short story might have been first published in, and the kind of readership it might have been aimed at.
- On the surface, it is the story of a man who suffered from a rather unusual complaint. Does it produce any other meaning for you as a reader, or is it merely a narrative without much significance?

Writing ☛

You have been asked to contribute a story to a monthly periodical that publishes at least one short story per issue. The editor has stipulated that it should be about a person with an unusual power of some kind. It must have an uncomplicated narrative, dramatise a few incidents and have a definite conclusion, preferably some kind of 'twist' ending. Because of the need to conserve space in the magazine, the editor limits the story to 500 words.

After you have written the story write a brief commentary on the writing process: how you decided to construct the narrative; how you kept the story uncomplicated; any difficulties you had in delivering the kind of story the editor wanted.

3.5 The 'no tricks' short story

The short story in the previous section could be described as using conventional 'tricks' of the genre, especially in terms of the neat, rounded-off ending. Raymond Carver (1938-1988) was an American writer who employed what has been described as a 'no tricks' manner of short story writing. Below is a Carver short story, 'Intimacy'.

Intimacy

I have some business out west anyway, so I stop off in this little town where my former wife lives. We haven't seen each other in four years. But from time to time, when something of mine appeared, or was written about me in the magazines or papers – a profile or an interview – I sent her these things. I don't know what I had in mind except I thought she might be interested. In any case, she never responded.

It is nine in the morning, I haven't called, and it's true I don't know what I am going to find.

But she lets me in. She doesn't seem surprised. We don't shake hands, much less kiss each other. She takes me into the living room. As soon as I sit down she brings me some coffee. Then she comes out with what's on her mind. She says I've caused her anguish, made her feel exposed and humiliated.

Make no mistake, I feel I'm home.

She says, But then you were into betrayal early. You always felt comfortable with betrayal. No, she says, that's not true. Not in the beginning, at any rate. You were different then. But I guess I was different too. Everything was different, she says. No, it was after you turned thirty-five, or thirty-six, whenever it was, around in there anyway, your mid-thirties somewhere, then you started in. You really started in. You turned on me. You did it up pretty then. You must be proud of yourself.

She says, Sometimes I could scream.

She says she wishes I'd forget about the hard times, the bad times, when I talk about back then. Spend some time on the good times, she says. Weren't there some good times? She wishes I'd get off that other subject. She's bored with it. Sick of hearing about it. Your private hobbyhorse, she says.

What's done is done and water under the bridge, she says. A tragedy, yes. God knows it was a tragedy and then some. But why keep it going? Don't you ever get tired of dredging up that old business?

She says, Let go of the past, for Christ's sake. Those old hurts. You must have some other arrows in your quiver, she says.

She says, You know something? I think you're sick. I think you're crazy as a bedbug. Hey, you don't believe the things they're saying about you, do you? Don't believe them for a minute she says. Listen, I could tell them a thing or two. Let them talk to me about it, if they want to hear a story.

She says, Are you listening to me?

I'm listening, I say. I'm all ears, I say.

She says, I've had a bellyful of it buster! Who asked you here today anyway? I sure as hell didn't. You just show up and walk in. What the hell do you want from me? Blood? You want more blood? I thought you had your fill by now.

She says, Think of me as dead. I want to be left in peace now. That's all I want any more is to be left in peace and forgotten about. Hey, I'm forty-five years old, she says. Forty-five going on fifty-five, or sixty-five. Lay off, will you.

She says, Why don't you wipe the blackboard clean and see what you have left after that? Why don't you start with a clean slate? See how far that gets you, she says.

She has to laugh at this. I laugh too, but it's nerves.

She says, You know something? I had my chance once, but I let it go. I just let it go. I don't guess I ever told you. But now look at me. Look! Take a good look while you're at it. You threw me away, you son of a bitch.

She says, I was younger then and a better person. Maybe you were too, she says. A better person, I mean. You had to be. You were better then or I wouldn't have had anything to do with you.

She says, I loved you so much once. I loved you to the point of distraction. I did. More than anything in the whole wide world. Imagine that. What a laugh that is now. Can you imagine it? We were so *intimate* once upon a time I can't believe it now. I think that's the strangest thing of all now. The memory of being that intimate with somebody. We were so intimate I could puke. I can't imagine ever being that intimate with somebody else. I haven't been.

She says, Frankly, and I mean this, I want to be kept out of it from here on out. Who do you think you are anyway? You think you're God or somebody? You're not fit to lick God's boots, or anybody else's for that matter. Mister, you've been hanging out with the wrong people. But what do I know? I don't even know what I know any longer. I know I don't like what you've been dishing out. I know that much. You know what I'm talking about, don't you? Am I right? Right, I say. Right as rain.

She says, You'll agree to anything, won't you? You give in too easy. You always did. You don't have any principles, not one. Anything to avoid a fuss. But that's neither here nor there.

She says, You remember that time I pulled the knife on you?

She says this as if in passing, as if it's not important.

Vaguely, I say, I must have deserved it, but I don't remember much about it. Go ahead, why don't you, and tell me about it.

She says, I'm beginning to understand something now. I think I know why you're here. Yes. I know why you're here, even if you don't. But you're a slyboots. You know why you're here. You're on a fishing expedition. You're hunting for *material*. Am I getting warm? Am I right?

Tell me about the knife, I say.

She says, If you want to know, I'm really sorry I didn't use that knife. I am. I really and truly am. I've thought and thought about it, and I'm sorry I didn't use it. I had the chance. But I hesitated and was lost, as somebody or other said. But I should have used it, the hell with everything and everybody. I should have nicked your arm with it at least. At least that.

Well, you didn't, I say. I thought you were going to cut me with it, but you didn't. I took it away from you.

She says, You were always lucky. You took it away and then you slapped me. Still, I regret I didn't use that knife just a little bit. Even a little would have been something to remember me by.

I remember a lot, I say. I say that, then wish I hadn't.

She says, Amen, brother. That's the bone of contention here, if you hadn't noticed. That's the whole problem. But like I said, in my opinion you remember the wrong things. You remember the low, shameful things. That's why you got interested when I brought up the knife.

She says, I wonder if you ever have any regret. For whatever that's worth on the market these days. Not much, I guess. But you ought to be a specialist in it by now.

Regret, I say. It doesn't interest me much, to tell the truth. Regret is not a word I use very often. I guess I mainly don't have it. I admit I hold to the dark view of things. Sometimes, anyway. But regret? I don't think so.

She says, You're a real son of a bitch, did you know that? A ruthless, cold-hearted son of a bitch. Did anybody ever tell you that?

You did, I say. Plenty of times.

She says, I always speak the truth. Even when it hurts. You'll never catch me in a lie.

She says, My eyes were opened a long time ago, but by then it was too late. I had my chance but I let it slide through my fingers. I even thought for a while you'd come back. Why'd I think that anyway? I must have been out of my mind. I could cry my eyes out now, but I wouldn't give you that satisfaction.

She says, You know what? I think if you were on fire right now, if you suddenly burst into flame this minute, I wouldn't throw a bucket of water on you.

She laughs at this. Then her face closes down again.

She says, Why in hell *are* you here? You want to hear some more? I could go on for days. I think I know why you turned up, but I want to hear it from you.

When I don't answer, when I just keep sitting there, she goes on.

She says, After that time, when you went away, nothing much mattered after that. Not the kids, not God, not anything. It was like I didn't know what hit me. It was like I had *stopped living*. My life had been going along, going along, and then it just stopped. It didn't just come to a stop, it screeched to a stop. I thought, If I'm not worth anything to him, well, I'm not worth anything to myself or anybody else either. That was the worst thing I felt. I thought my heart would break. What am I saying? It did break. Of course it broke. It broke, just like that. It's still broke, if you want to know. And so there you have it in a nutshell. My eggs in one basket, she says. A tisket, a tasket. All my rotten eggs in one basket.

She says, You found somebody else for yourself, didn't you? It didn't take long. And you're happy now. That's what they say about you anyway: 'He's happy now.' Hey, I read everything you send! You think I don't? Listen, I know your heart, mister. I always did. I knew it back then, and I know it now. I know your heart inside and out, and don't you ever forget it. Your heart is a jungle, a dark forest, it's a garbage pail, if you want to know. Let them talk to me if they want to ask somebody something. I know how you operate. Just let them come around here, and I'll give them an earful. I was there. I served, buddy boy. Then you held me up for display and ridicule in your so-called work. For any Tom or Harry to pity or pass judgement on. Ask me if I cared. Ask me if it embarrassed me. Go ahead, ask.

No I say, I won't ask that. I don't want to get into that, I say.

Damn straight you don't! she says. And you know *why*, too!

She says, Honey, no offence, but sometimes I think I could shoot you and watch you kick.

She says, You can't look me in the eyes, can you?

She says, and this is exactly what she says, You can't even, look me in the eyes when I'm talking to you.

So, OK, I look her in the eyes.

She says, Right. OK, she says. Now we're getting someplace, maybe. That's better. You can tell a lot about the person you're talking to from his eyes. Everybody knows that. But you know something else? There's nobody in this whole world who would tell you this, but I can tell you. I have the right. I *earned* that right, sonny. You have yourself confused with somebody else. And that's the pure truth of it. But what do I know? they'll say in a hundred years. They'll say, Who was she anyway?

She says, In any case, you sure as hell have me confused with somebody else. I don't even have the same name any more! Not the name I was born with, not the name I lived with you with, not even the name I had two years ago.

What is this? What is this in hell all about anyway? Let me say something. I want to be left alone now. Please. That's not a crime.

She says, Don't you have someplace else you should be? Some plane to catch? Shouldn't you be somewhere far from here at this very minute?

No, I say. I say it again: No. No place, I say. I don't have any place I have to be.

And then I do something. I reach over and take the sleeve of her blouse between my thumb and forefinger. That's all. I just touch it that way, and then I just bring my hand back. She doesn't draw away. She doesn't move.

Then here's the thing I do next. I get down on my knees, a big guy like me, and I take the hem of her dress. What am I doing on the floor? I wish I could say. But I know it's where I ought to be, and I'm there on my knees holding on to the hem of her dress.

She is still for a minute. But in a minute she says, Hey, it's all right, stupid. You're so dumb, sometimes. Get up now. I'm telling you to get up. Listen, it's OK. I'm over it now. It took me a while to get over it. What do you think? Did you think it wouldn't? Then you walk in here and suddenly the whole cruddy business is back. I felt a need to ventilate. But you know, and I know, it's over and done with now.

She says, For the longest while, honey, I was inconsolable. *Inconsolable*, she says. Put that word in your little notebook. I can tell you from experience that's the saddest word in the English language. Anyway, I got over it finally. Time is a gentleman, a wise man said. Or else maybe a worn-out old woman, one or the other anyway.

She says, I have a life now. It's a different kind of life than yours, but I guess we don't need to compare. It's my life, and that's the important thing I have to realize as I get older. Don't feel *too* bad, anyway, she says. I mean, it's all right to feel a *little* bad, maybe. That won't hurt you, that's only to be expected after all. Even if you can't move yourself to regret.

She says, Now you have to get up and get out of here. My husband will be along pretty soon for his lunch. How would I explain this kind of thing?

It's crazy, but I'm still on my knees holding the hem of her dress. I won't let it go. I'm like a terrier, and it's like I'm stuck to the floor. It's like I can't move.

She says, Get up now. What is it? You still want something from me. What do you want? Want me to forgive you? Is that why you're doing this? That's it, isn't it? That's the reason you came all this way. The knife thing kind of perked you up, too. I think you'd forgotten about that. But you needed me to remind you. OK, I'll say something if you'll just go.

She says, I forgive you.

She says, Are you satisfied now? Is that better? Are you happy? He's happy now, she says.

But I'm still there, knees on the floor.

She says, Did you hear what I said? You have to go now. Hey, stupid, Honey, I said I forgive you. And I even reminded you about the knife thing. I can't think what else I can do now. You got it made in the shade baby. Come *on* now, you have to get out of here. Get up. That's right. You're still a big guy, aren't you. Here's your hat, don't forget your hat. You never used to wear a hat. I never in my life saw you in a hat before.

She says, Listen to me now. Look at me. Listen carefully to what I'm going to tell you.

She moves closer. She's about three inches from my face. We haven't been this close in a long time. I take these little breaths that she can't hear, and I wait. I think my heart slows way down, I think.

She says, You just tell it like you have to, I guess, and forget the rest. Like always. You been doing that for so long now anyway it shouldn't be hard for you.

She says, There, I've done it. You're free, aren't you? At least you think you are anyway. Free at last. That's a joke, but don't laugh. Anyway, you feel better, don't you?

She walks with me down the hall.

She says, I can't imagine how I'd explain this if my husband was to walk in this very minute. But who really cares any more, right? In the final analysis, nobody gives a damn any more. Besides which, I think everything that can happen that way has already happened. His name is Fred, by the way. He's a decent guy and works hard for his living. He cares for me.

So she walks me to the front door, which has been standing open all this while. The door that was letting in light and fresh air this morning, and sounds off the street, all of which we had ignored. I look outside and, Jesus, there's this white moon hanging in the morning sky. I can't think when I've ever seen anything so remarkable. But I'm afraid to comment on it. I am. I don't know what might happen. I might break into tears even. I might not understand a word I'd say.

She says, Maybe you'll be back sometime, and maybe you won't. This'll wear off, you know. Pretty soon you'll start feeling bad again. Maybe it'll make a good story, she says. But I don't want to know about it if it does.

I say goodbye. She doesn't say anything more. She looks at her hands, and then she puts them into the pockets of her dress. She shakes her head. She goes back inside, and this time she closes the door.

I move off down the sidewalk. Some kids are tossing a football at the end of the street. But they aren't my kids, and they aren't her kids either. There are these leaves everywhere, even in the gutters. Piles of leaves wherever I look. They're falling off the limbs as I walk. I can't take a step without putting my shoe into leaves. Somebody ought to make an effort here. Somebody ought to get a rake and take care of this.

Group discussion

- The story is written in the ***historic present*** tense. This means that the events described have supposedly taken place in the past, but the writer chooses to write about them as though they are happening 'now'. Working in pairs, discuss the use of tense in the story and then rewrite the opening paragraph in the past tense. Discuss whether this alters the meaning in any way.

- Another 'unconventional' aspect of the story is the absence of speech marks around the ***utterances***, the words the narrative figures in the story say. There is a great deal of repetition of 'she says' and 'I say'. Discuss how this affects meaning.

- Pick out any examples of language use that in your judgement would not be used in ordinary everyday speech, bearing in mind the setting of the story (the American west in the very recent past).

- Discuss the connotations of any language use in the story that particularly strikes you, and how these connotations affect tone and meaning.

Writing

Write a short story on a theme of your choice, but written in the manner adopted by Raymond Carver. Then write a commentary on the writing process.

Write an analysis of 'Intimacy', commenting particularly on whether the term 'no tricks' is appropriate to this style of writing short stories.

GLOSSARY

The historic present: the use of the present tense in a narrative to describe events that have taken place in the past.

Utterances: a term used to describe the words that narrative figures in a piece of writing are given to say.

3.6　Who is telling the story?

Sometimes in fiction the author, the usually invisible story-teller, has a narrative figure who tells a 'story-within-a-story'. Below is a story by the South African writer, Bessie Head, in which this occurs.

Heaven is not closed

All her life Galethebege earnestly believed that her whole heart ought to be devoted to God, yet one catastrophe after another occurred to swerve her from this path.

It was only in the last five years of her life, after her husband Ralokae had died, that she was able to devote her whole mind to her calling. Then, all her pent-up and suppressed love for God burst forth and she talked only of Him day and night – so her grandchildren, solemnly and with deep awe, informed the mourners at her funeral. And all the mourners present at her hour of passing were utterly convinced that they had watched a profound and holy event.

They talked about it for days afterwards.

Galethebege was well over ninety when she died and not at all afflicted by crippling ailments like most of the aged. In fact, only two days before her death she had complained to her grandchildren of a sudden fever and a lameness in her legs and she had remained in bed.

A quiet and thoughtful mood fell upon her. On the morning of the second day she had abruptly demanded that all the relatives be summoned.

'My hour has come,' she said, with lofty dignity.

No one quite believed it, because that whole morning she sat bolt upright in bed and talked to all who had gathered about God, whom she loved with her whole heart.

Then, exactly at noon, she announced once more that her hour had indeed come and lay down peacefully like one about to take a short nap. Her last words were:

'I shall rest now because I believe in God.'

Then, a terrible silence filled the hut and seemed to paralyze the mourners because they all remained immobile for some time; each person present cried quietly, as not one of them had witnessed such a magnificent death before.

They only stirred when the old man, Modise, suddenly observed, with great practicality, that Galethebege was not in the correct position for death. She lay on her side with her right arm thrust out above her head.

She ought to be turned over on her back, with her hands crossed over her chest, he said. A smile flickered over the old man's face as he said this, as though it was just like Galethebege to make a miscalculation.

Why, she knew the hour of her death and everything, then forgot at the last minute the correct sleeping posture for the coffin. And later that evening, as he sat with his children near the out-door fire for the evening meal, a smile again flickered over his face.

'I am of a mind to think that Galethebege was praying for forgiveness for her sins this morning,' he said slowly. 'It must have been a sin for her to marry Ralokae. He was an unbeliever to the day of his death . . .'

A gust of astonished laughter shook his family out of the solemn mood of mourning that had fallen upon them and they all turned eagerly towards their grandfather, sensing that he had a story to tell.

'As you know,' the old man said, wisely, 'Ralokae was my brother. But none of you present knows the story of Galethebege's life, as I know it . . .'

And as the flickering firelight lit up their faces, he told the following story: 'I was never like Ralokae, an unbeliever. But that man, my brother, draws out my heart. He liked to say that we as a tribe would fall into great difficulties if we forgot our own customs and laws. Today, his words seem true. There is thieving and adultery going on such as was not possible under Setswana law.'

In those days when they were young, said the old man, Modise, it had become the fashion for all Black people to embrace the Gospel. For some it was the mark of whether they were 'civilized' or not. For some, like Galethebege, it was their whole life.

Anyone with eyes to see would have known that Galethebege had been born good and under any custom, whether Setswana or Christian, she would still have been good. It was this natural goodness of heart that made her so eagerly pursue the word of the Gospel. There was a look on her face, absent, abstracted, as though she needed to share the final secret of life with God, who would understand all things. So she was always on her way to church, and in hours of leisure in life would have gone on in this quiet and worshipful way, had not a sudden catastrophe occurred in the yard of Ralokae.

Ralokae had been married for nearly a year when his young wife died in childbirth. She died when the crops of the season were being harvested, and for a year Ralokae imposed on himself the traditional restraints and disciplines of *boswagadi* or mourning for the deceased.

A year later, again at the harvest time, he underwent the cleansing ceremony demanded by custom and could once more resume the normal life of a man. It was the unexpectedness of the tragic event and the discipline it imposed on him that made Ralokae take note of the life of Galethebege.

She lived just three yards away from his own yard and formerly he had barely taken note of her existence; it was too quiet and orderly. But during that year of mourning it delighted him to hear that gentle and earnest voice of Galethebege inform him that such tragedies 'were the will of God'.

As soon as he could, he began courting her. He was young and impatient to be married again and no one could bring back the dead. So a few days after the cleansing ceremony, he made his intentions very clear to her.

'Let us two get together,' he said. 'I am pleased by all your ways.'

Galethebege was all at the same time startled, pleased and hesitant. She was hesitant because it was well known that Ralokae was an unbeliever; he had not once set foot in church. So she looked at him, begging an apology, and mentioned the matter which was foremost in her mind.

'Ralokae,' she said, uncertainly, 'I have set God always before me,' implying by that statement that perhaps he was seeking a Christian life too, like her own. But he only looked at her in a strange way and said nothing. This matter was to stand like a fearful sword between them but he had set his mind on winning Galethebege as his wife. That was all he was certain of. He would turn up in her yard day after day.

'Hello, girl friend,' he'd greet her, enchantingly.

He always wore a black beret perched at a jaunty angle on his head, and his walk and manner were gay and jaunty too. He was so exciting as a man that he threw her whole life into a turmoil. It was the first time love had come her way and it made the blood pound fiercely through her whole body till she could feel its very throbbing at the tips of her fingers. It turned her thoughts from God a bit to this new magic life was offering her. The day she agreed to be his wife, that sword quivered like a fearful thing between them. Ralokae said quietly and finally: 'I took my first wife according to the old customs. I am going to take my second wife according to the old customs too.'

He could see the protest on her face. She wanted to be married in church according to the Christian custom, but he also had his own protest to make. The God might be all right, he explained. But there was something wrong with the people who had brought the word of the Gospel to the land. Their love was enslaving Black people and he could not stand it.

That was why he was without belief. It was the people he did not trust. They were full of tricks. They were a people who, at the sight of a Black man, pointed a finger in the air, looked away into the distance and said, impatiently: 'Boy! Will you carry this! Boy! Will you fetch this!'

They had brought a new order of things into the land and they made the people cry for love. One never had to cry for love in the customary way of life. Respect was just there for the people all the time. That was why he rejected all things foreign.

What did a woman do with a man like that who knew his own mind? She either loved him or she was mad. From that day on Galethebege knew what she would do. She would do all that Ralokae commanded, as a good wife should.

But her former life was like a drug. Her footsteps were too accustomed to wearing down the foot-path to the church, so they carried her to the home of the missionary which stood just under its shadow.

The missionary was a short, anonymous-looking man who wore glasses. He had been the resident missionary for some time and, like all his fellows, he did not particularly like the people. He always complained to his kind that they were terrible beggars and rather stupid. So when he opened the door and saw Galethebege there his expression with its raised eyebrows clearly said: 'Well what do you want now?'

'I am to be married, sir,' Galethebege said, politely, after the exchange of greetings.

The missionary smiled: 'Well come in, my dear. Let us talk about the arrangements.'

He stared at her with polite, professional interest. She was a complete nonentity, a part of the vague black blur which was his congregation – oh, they noticed chiefs and people like that, but not the silent mass of the humble and lowly who had an almost weird capacity to creep quietly through life. Her next words brought her sharply into focus.

'The man I am to marry, sir, does not wish to be married in the Christian way. He will only marry under Setswana custom,' she said softly.

They always knew the superficial stories about 'heathen customs'; an expression of disgust crept into his face – sexual malpractices had been associated with the traditional ceremony and (shudder!) they draped the stinking intestinal bag of the ox around the necks.

'That we cannot allow!' he said sharply. 'Tell him to come and marry in the Christian way.'

Galethebege started trembling all over. She looked at the missionary in alarm. Ralokae would never agree to this. Her intention in approaching the missionary was to acquire his blessing for the marriage, as though a compromise of tenderness could be made between two traditions opposed to each other.

She trembled because it was beyond her station in life to be involved in controversy and protest. The missionary noted the trembling and alarm and his tone softened a bit, but his next words were devastating.

'My dear,' he said, persuasively, 'Heaven is closed to the unbeliever . . .'

Galethebege stumbled home on faint legs. It never occurred to her to question such a miserable religion which terrified people with the fate of eternal damnation in hell-fire if they were 'heathens' or sinners. Only Ralokae seemed quite unperturbed by the fate that awaited him. He smiled when Galethebege relayed the words of the missionary to him.

'Girl friend,' he said, carelessly, 'You can choose what you like, Setswana custom or Christian custom. I have chosen to live my life by Setswana custom.'

Never once in her life had Galethebege's integrity been called into question. She wanted to make the point clear.

'What you mean, Ralokae,' she said firmly, 'is that I must choose you over my life with the church. I have a great love in my heart for you so I choose you. I shall tell the priest about this matter because his command is that I marry in church.'

Even Galethebege was astounded by the harshness of the missionary's attitude. The catastrophe she never anticipated was that he abruptly excommunicated her from the church. She could no longer enter the church if she married under Setswana custom.

It was beyond her to reason that the missionary was the representative of both God and something evil, the mark of 'civilization'. It was unthinkable that an illiterate and ignorant man could display such contempt for the missionary's civilization. His rage and hatred were directed at Ralokae, but the only way in which he could inflict punishment was to banish Galethebege from the church. If it hurt anyone at all, it was only Galethebege.

The austere rituals of the church, the mass, the sermons, the intimate communication in prayer with God – all this had thrilled her heart deeply. But Ralokae was also representative of an ancient stream of holiness that people had lived with before any white man had set foot on the land, and it only needed a small protest to stir up loyalty for the old customs.

The old man, Modise, paused at this point in the telling of his tale, but his young listeners remained breathless and silent, eager for the conclusion.

'Today,' he continued, 'it is not a matter of debate because the young care neither way about religion. But in that day, the expulsion of Galethebege from the church was a matter of debate. It made the people of our village ward think.

'There was great indignation because both Galethebege and Ralokae were much respected in the community. People then wanted to know how it was that Ralokae, who was an unbeliever, could have heaven closed to him.

'A number of people, all the relatives who officiated at the wedding ceremony, then decided that if heaven was closed to Galethebege and Ralokae, it might as well be closed to them too, so they all no longer attended church.

'On the day of the wedding, we had all our own things. Everyone knows the extent to which the cow was a part of the people's life and customs.

'We took our clothes from the cow and our food from the cow and it was the symbol of our wealth. So the cow was a holy thing in our lives. The elders then cut the intestinal bag of the cow in two, and one portion was placed around the neck of Galethebege and one portion around the neck of Ralokae to indicate the wealth and good luck they would find together in married life.

'Then the porridge and meat were dished up in our *mogopo* bowls which we had used from old times. There was much capering and ululating that day because Ralokae had honoured the old customs . . .'

A tender smile once more flickered over the old man's face.

'Galethebege could never forsake the custom in which she had been brought up. All through her married life she would find a corner in which to pray. Sometimes Ralokae would find her so and ask: 'What are you doing, Mother?' And she would reply: 'I am praying to the Christian God.''

The old man leaned forward and stirred the dying fire with a partially burnt-out log of wood. His listeners sighed, the way people do when they have heard a particularly good story. As they stared at the fire they found themselves debating the matter in their minds, as their elders had done forty or fifty years ago. Was heaven really closed to the unbeliever, Ralokae?

Or had Christian custom been so intolerant of Setswana custom that it could not bear the holiness of Setswana custom? Wasn't there a place in heaven too for Setswana custom? Then that gust of astonished laughter shook them again. Galethebege had been very well known in the village ward over the past five years for the supreme authority with which she talked about God. Perhaps her simple and good heart had been terrified that the doors of heaven were indeed closed on Ralokae and she had been trying to open them.

Group discussion

- Working in pairs, summarise the story in not more than sixty words.
- Working in pairs, analyse how the telling of the story is shared between the 'unseen' author and the narrative figure of Modise. Then as a group discuss how this sharing of the narrative affects meaning.
- In the previous two sections, we have looked at one 'traditional' short story and one 'no tricks' story. Discuss whether 'Heaven is not closed' belongs in either category. Consider the structure of the story and the events the narrative describes and the manner in which the story ends.
- The story deals with aspects of a culture that will be unfamiliar to most of you: African customs and rituals; a rural community in Southern Africa; a country that has been colonised by foreigners. Discuss whether this causes any difficulty of interpretation for you.

Writing ▶

Write an appreciation of 'Heaven is not closed', making clear what meaning the story has for you.

▶ Write a short story in which you, the author, use a narrative figure to tell a story-within-the-story.

3.7 Narrative sequence

The traditional narrative or story is constructed on a 'beginning, middle and end' structure. Children's stories, for example, often start with the words 'Once upon a time...' whereby the teller sets the scene and introduces the narrative figures. Then the story is developed and brought to a neat resolution – often of the 'they lived happily ever after' kind. This kind of ***closure*** implies permanence, a certain view of reality that is complete, unchangeable and permanent.

However, as we saw from our reading of 'Solo dance' (section 1.8), not all fiction need end like that. If a writer chooses a definite closure, then that affects meaning. Equally, the lack of a definite ending or closure produces a different kind of meaning.

How a ***narrative sequence*** is put together and what decision is made about the openings and closings of stories is clearly crucial to the meaning that is produced. Below is printed 'Over', a complete short story by Rose Tremain. However, the narrative sequence of the original has been all 'jumbled up' and divided into sections that are 'out of order'. The writer, when she wrote the story, had to make definite decisions about how to order the narrative sequence: what followed on from what, how to start the narrative and how to end it. This is the task you are being asked to do now.

The original short story has been divided into fifteen sections, which have been printed in random order. Read each section and then piece together the narrative by ordering the sections in the sequence you think most effective. Work in pairs and agree a finished version of the story.

Come together as a group and compare the versions and titles that have been produced. Discuss why you decided on a particular narrative sequence, the variations that have been produced and agree on a consensus version of the story. After this stage, consult Appendix 1 and compare the group's version with the original version of the story as published. Discuss any variations and how these might affect meaning.

1   It was then that the old man began his hatred of time. He couldn't bear to see anything endure. What he longed for was for things to be over. He did the *Times* crossword only to fill up the waiting spaces. He read the newspaper only to finish it and fold it and place it in the waste-paper basket. He snipped off from the rose bushes not only the dead heads but blooms that were still living. At mealtimes, he cleared the cutlery from the table before the meal was finished. He drove out with his wife to visit friends to find that he longed, upon arrival, for the moment of departure. When he made his bed in the morning, he would put on the bedcover then turn it down again, ready for the night.

2   His curtains are drawn back and light floods into the room. To him, light is time. Until nightfall, it lies on his skin, seeping just a little into the pores yet never penetrating inside him, neither into his brain nor his heart nor any crevice or crease of him. Light and time, time and light lie on him as weightless as the sheet. He is somewhere else. He is in the place where the jokes come from, where the dreams of stoats lie. He refuses ever to leave it except upon one condition.

3   The boy, still dizzy with sleep, opened his mouth and opened wide his blue eyes. He knew he must not move so he did not even look round when his father left his side and went back into the house. He shivered a little in the dewy air. He wanted to creep forward so that he could be in the sun. He tiptoed out across the gravel that hurt his feet onto the soft wet lawn. The stoat saw him and whipped its body to a halt, head up, tail flat, regarding the boy. The boy could see its eyes. He thought how sleek and slippery it looked and how he would like to stroke its head with his finger.

4   That condition is so seldom satisfied, yet every morning, after his teeth are in, he asks the nurse: 'Is my son coming today?'

    'Not that I know of, Sir,' she replies.

    So then he takes no notice of the things he does. He eats his boiled egg. He pisses into a jar. He puts a kiss as thin as air on his wife's cheek. He tells the nurse the joke about the Talking Dog. He folds his arms across his chest. He dreams of being asleep.

    But once in a while – once a fortnight perhaps, or once a month? – the nurse will say as she lifts him up onto his pillows: 'Your son's arrived, Sir.'

    Then he'll reach up and try to neaten the silk scarf he wears at his throat. He will ask for his window to be opened wider. He will sniff the room and wonder whether it doesn't smell peculiarly of water-weed.

5   Waking is the hardest thing they ask of him.

6   The son is a big man, balding, with kind eyes. Always and without fail he arrives in the room with a bottle of champagne and two glasses held upside down between his first and second finger.

    'How are you?' he asks.

    'That's a stupid question,' says the father.

    The son sits by the bed and the father looks and looks for him with faded eyes and they sip the drink. Neither the nurse nor the wife disturbs them.

    'Stay a bit,' says the father, 'won't you?'

'I can't stay long,' says the son.

Sometimes the father weeps without knowing it. All he knows is that with his son here, time is no longer a thing that covers him, but an element in which he floats and which fills his head and his heart until he is both brimming with it and buoyant on the current of it.

When the champagne has all been drunk, the son and the nurse carry the father downstairs and put him into the son's Jaguar and cover his knees with a rug. The father and the son drive off down the Hampshire lanes. Light falls in dapples on the old man's temples and on his folded hands.

7   His wife watched and suffered. She felt he was robbing her of life. She was his second wife, less beautiful and less loved than the first (the mother of his son) who had been a dancer and who had liked to spring into his arms from a sequence of three cartwheels. He sometimes dismayed the second wife by telling her about the day when the first wife did a cartwheel in the revolving doors of the Ritz. 'I've heard that story, darling,' she'd say politely, ashamed for him that he could tell it so proudly. And to her bridge friends she'd confide: 'It's as if he believes that by rushing through the *now* he'll get back to the *then*.'

8   The father took aim with his shotgun and fired. He hit the stoat right in the head and its body flew up into the air before it fell without a sound. The man laughed with joy at the cleanness and beauty of the shot. He laughed a loud, happy laugh and then he looked down at his son to get his approval. But the boy was not there. The boy had walked back inside the house, leaving his father alone in the bright morning.

9   When the war ended he was still married to the dancer. His son was five years old. They lived in a manor house with an ancient tennis court and an east-facing croquet lawn. Though his head was still full of the war, he had a touching faith in the future and he usually knew, as each night descended, that he was looking forward to the day.

Very often, in the summer of 1946, he would wake when the sun came up and, leaving the dancer sleeping, would go out onto the croquet lawn wearing his dressing gown and his slippers from Simpson's of Piccadilly and stare at the dew on the grass, at the shine on the croquet hoops and at the sky, turning. He had the feeling that he and the world made a handsome pair.

10   The father returned. 'Don't move!' he whispered to his son, so the boy did not turn.

11   One morning, he saw a stoat on the lawn. The stoat was running round the croquet hoops and then in and out of them in a strange repeated pattern, as if it were taking part in a stoat gymkhana. The man did not move, but stood and watched. Then he backed off into the house and ran up the stairs to the room where his son was sleeping.

'Wake up!' he said to the little boy. 'I've got something to show you!'

He took his son's hand and led him barefoot down the stairs and out into the garden. The stoat was still running round and through the croquet hoops and now, as the man and the boy stood watching, it decided to leap over the hoops, jumping twice its height into the air and rolling over in a somersault as it landed, then flicking its tail as it turned and ran in for another leap.

12   There was a period of years that arrived as the father was beginning to get old when the son went to work in the Middle East and came home only once or twice a year, bringing presents made in Japan which the father did not trust.

13   The nurse always wakes him with the word 'morning', and the word 'morning' brings a hurting into his head which he cannot control or ameliorate or do anything about. Very often, the word 'morning' interrupts his dreams. In these dreams there was a stoat somewhere. This is all he can say about them.

14   The nurse opens his mouth, which tastes of seed and fills it with teeth. 'These teeth have got too big for me,' he sometimes remarks, but neither the nurse nor his wife replies to this just as neither the nurse nor his wife laughs when from some part of his ancient self he brings out a joke he did not know he could still remember. He isn't even certain they smile at his jokes because he can't see faces any longer unless they are no more and no less than two feet from his eyes. 'Aren't you even smiling?' he sometimes shouts.

'I'm smiling, Sir,' says the nurse.

'Naturally, I'm smiling,' says his wife.

15   He began a practice of adding things up. He would try to put a finite number on the oysters he had eaten since the war. He counted the cigarettes his wife smoked in a day and the number of times she mislaid her lighter. He tried to make a sum of the remembered cartwheels. Then when he had done these additions, he would draw a neat line through them, like the line a captive draws through each recorded clutch of days, and fold the paper in half and then in quarters and so on until it could

not be folded any smaller and then place it carefully in the waste-paper basket next to the finished *Times*.

'Now we know,' his wife once heard him mutter. 'Now we know all about it.'

Writing 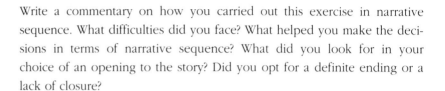 Write a commentary on how you carried out this exercise in narrative sequence. What difficulties did you face? What helped you make the decisions in terms of narrative sequence? What did you look for in your choice of an opening to the story? Did you opt for a definite ending or a lack of closure?

GLOSSARY

Closure: how a piece of writing ends. Usually, texts are 'rounded-off' with definite and recognisable endings; some contemporary fiction, however, avoids such 'closed' endings.

Narrative sequence: the order in which narrative incident is arranged.

3.8 Genre: science fiction

Science fiction can be described as a particular 'genre' of narrative fiction. Genre is a conventional text type, a common arrangement of language in a recognised form with its own conventions of language and areas of subject matter.

As a group, discuss the following questions:

• When you think of science fiction, what characteristics of this genre come to mind?

• Are there any specific kinds of discourse that characterise science fiction?

• What kind of 'implied reader' is inscribed in most science fiction?

Having discussed these questions, read the short story below, which is by Isaac Asimov.

Margie even wrote about it that night in her diary. On the page headed May 17, 2157, she wrote, 'Today Tommy found a real book!'

It was a very old book. Margie's grandfather once said that when he was a little boy *his* grandfather told him that there was a time when all stories were printed on paper.

They turned the pages, which were yellow and crinkly, and it was awfully funny to read words that stood still instead of moving the way they were supposed to – on a screen, you know. And then, when they turned back to the page before, it had the same words on it that it had had when they read it the first time.

'Gee,' said Tommy, 'what a waste. When you're through with the book, you just throw it away, I guess. Our television screen must have had a million books on it and it's good for plenty more. I wouldn't throw *it* away.'

'Same with mine,' said Margie. She was eleven and hadn't seen as many textbooks as Tommy had. He was thirteen.

She said, 'Where did you find it?'

'In my house.' He pointed without looking, because he was busy reading. 'In the attic.'

'What's it about?'

'School.'

Margie was scornful. 'School? What's there to write about school? I hate school.'

Margie always hated school, but now she hated it more than ever. The mechanical teacher had been giving her test after test in geography and she had been doing worse and worse until her mother had shaken her head sorrowfully and sent for the County Inspector.

He was a round little man with a red face and a whole box of tools with dials and wires. He smiled at Margie and gave her an apple, then took the teacher apart. Margie had hoped he wouldn't know how to put it together again, but he knew how all right, and, after an hour or so, there it was again, large and black and ugly, with a big screen on which all the lessons were shown and the questions were asked. That wasn't so bad. The part Margie hated most was the slot where she had to put homework and test papers. She always had to write them out in a punch code they made her learn when she was six years old, and the mechanical teacher calculated the mark in no time.

The inspector had smiled after he was finished and patted Margie's head. He said to her mother, 'It's not the little girl's fault, Mrs Jones. I think the geography sector was geared a little too quick. Those things happen some-times. I've slowed it up to an average ten-year level. Actually, the over-all pattern of her progress is quite satisfactory.' And he patted Margie's head again.

Margie was disappointed. She had been hoping they would take the teacher away altogether. They had once taken Tommy's teacher away for nearly a month because the history sector had blanked out completely.

So she said to Tommy, 'Why would anyone write about school?'

Tommy looked at her with very superior eyes. 'Because it's not our kind of school, stupid. This is the old kind of school that they had hundreds and hundreds of years ago.' He added loftily, pronouncing the word carefully, '*Centuries* ago.'

Margie was hurt. 'Well, I don't know what kind of school they had all that time ago.' She read the book over his shoulder for a while, then said, 'Anyway, they had a teacher.'

'Sure they had a teacher, but it wasn't a *regular* teacher. It was a man.'

'A man? How could a man be a teacher?'

'Well, he just told the boys and girls things and gave them homework and asked them questions.'

'A man isn't smart enough.'

'Sure he is. My father knows as much as my teacher.'

'He can't. A man can't know as much as a teacher.'

'He knows almost as much, I betcha.'

Margie wasn't prepared to dispute that. She said, 'I wouldn't want a strange man in my house to teach me.'

Tommy screamed with laughter. 'You don't know much, Margie. The teachers didn't live in the house. They had a special building and all the kids went there.'

'And all the kids learned the same thing?'

'Sure, if they were the same age.'

'But my mother says a teacher has to be adjusted to fit the mind of each boy and girl it teaches and that each kid has to be taught differently.'

'Just the same they didn't do it that way then. If you don't like it, you don't have to read the book.'

'I didn't say I didn't like it,' Margie said quickly. She wanted to read about those funny schools.

They weren't even half-finished when Margie's mother called, 'Margie! School!'

Margie looked up. 'Not yet, Mamma.'

'Now!' said Mrs Jones. 'And it's probably time for Tommy, too.'

Margie said to Tommy, 'Can I read the book some more with you after school?'

'Maybe,' he said nonchalantly. He walked away whistling, the dusty old book tucked beneath his arm.

Margie went into the schoolroom. It was right next to her bedroom, and the mechanical teacher was on waiting for her. It was always on at the same time every day except Saturday and Sunday, because her mother said little girls learned better if they learned at regular hours.

The screen was lit up, and it said: 'Today's arithmetic lesson is on the addition of proper fractions. Please insert yesterday's homework in the proper slot.'

Margie did so with a sigh. She was thinking about the old schools they had when her grandfather was a little boy. All the kids from the whole neighbourhood came, laughing and shouting in the schoolyard, sitting together in the schoolroom, going home together at the end of the day. They learned the same things, so they could help one another on the homework and talk about it.

And the teachers were people . . .

The mechanical teacher was flashing on the screen 'When we add the fractions $1/2$ and $1/4$—'

Margie was thinking about how the kids must have loved it in the old days. She was thinking about the fun they had.

Group discussion

- Summarise in eighty words the content of the short story. Then reduce the eighty-word summary to one of only fifty. As a group compare the individual summaries you have produced and agree on a consensus summary.
- From the extract, make a list of language use that you consider to be characteristic of science fiction, giving your reasons for the selection you have made. Compare your list with those of others in the group.
- Working in pairs, decide on a title for the story. Then as a group compare titles before checking the published title as listed in Appendix 2.
- As described by the language of the extract, what is 'ordinary' and 'everyday' as compared to the 'extraordinary' and 'science fiction' elements?

Writing

You have been asked to contribute a feature article to a local newspaper with the title 'Why I read science fiction'. Write this article, making sure that in the process you refer to specific characteristics of the genre.

Write a science fiction story set in the distant future in which the narrative figures look back on some aspect of life in the 1990s and regret that things are different now.

3.9 Genre: detective fiction

Detective fiction is generally perceived as being a particular genre of fiction. Some readers and critics of detective fiction would differentiate between this genre and the genre of 'crime fiction'. Detective or 'private eye' fiction has a central narrative figure whose task it is to unravel a mystery of some kind involving a crime, usually murder. Crime fiction generally deals with the world of criminality, involving police and criminals.

Another distinction within these genres can be drawn between the tradition of American crime and detective fiction, and the British tradition. The

American tradition of crime fiction has been described as 'hard-boiled'; its main characteristics are wisecracking, ironic dialogue, complex plots, violent incident and the central figure of a world-weary detective or private eye who tries to maintain some kind of ethical standards in a corrupt world.

The British tradition is less urban and hard-edged. Below is an extract from *An Unsuitable Job for a Woman* by P.D. James, an example of the detective fiction genre.

Cordelia had no premonition of tragedy as she pushed open the street door which was kept perpetually on the latch for the convenience of the secretive and mysterious tenants and their equally mysterious visitors. The new bronze plaque to the left of the door gleamed brightly in the sun in incongruous contrast to the faded and dirt-encrusted paint. Cordelia gave it a short glance of approval.

Pryde's Detective Agency
(*Props:* Bernard G. Pryde   Cordelia Gray)

It had taken Cordelia some weeks of patient and tactful persuasion to convince Bernie that it would be inappropriate to append the words 'ex-C.I.D. Metropolitan Police' to his name or prefix 'Miss' to hers. There had been no other problem over the plaque since Cordelia had brought no qualifications or relevant past experience to the partnership and indeed no capital, except her slight but tough twenty-two-year-old body, a considerable intelligence which Bernie, she suspected, had occasionally found more disconcerting than admirable, and a half exasperated, half pitying affection for Bernie himself. It was obvious very early to Cordelia that in some undramatic but positive way life had turned against him. She recognized the signs. Bernie never got the enviable front left hand seat in the bus; he couldn't admire the view from the train window without another train promptly obscuring it; the bread he dropped invariably fell buttered side downwards; the Mini, reliable enough when she drove it, stalled for Bernie at the busiest and most inconvenient intersections. She sometimes wondered whether, in accepting his offer of a partnership in a fit of depression or of perverse masochism, she was voluntarily embracing his ill-luck. She certainly never saw herself as powerful enough to change it.

The staircase smelt as always of stale sweat, furniture polish and disinfectant. The walls were dark green and were invariably damp whatever the season as if they secreted a miasma of desperate respectability and defeat. The stairs with their ornate wrought-iron balustrade, were covered with split and stained linoleum patched by the landlord in various and contrasting colours only when a tenant complained. The Agency was on the third floor. There was no clatter of typewriter keys as Cordelia entered and she saw that

Miss Sparshott was engaged in cleaning her machine, an ancient Imperial which was a constant cause of justified complaint. She looked up, her face blotched with resentment, her back as rigid as the space bar.

'I've been wondering when you would turn up, Miss Gray. I'm concerned about Mr Pryde. I think he must be in the inner office but he's quiet, very quiet, and the door's locked.'

Cordelia, chill at heart, wrenched at the door handle: 'Why didn't you do something?'

'Do what, Miss Gray? I knocked at the door and called out to him. It wasn't my place to do that. I'm only the temporary typist. I've no authority here. I should have been placed in a very embarrassing position if he had answered. After all, he's entitled to use his own office I suppose. Besides, I'm not even sure if he's there.'

'He must be. The door's locked and his hat is here.'

Bernie's trilby, the stained brim turned up all round, a comedian's hat, was hanging on the convoluted hatstand, a symbol of forlorn decrepitude. Cordelia was fumbling in her shoulder bag for her own key. As usual, the object most required had fallen to the bottom of the bag. Miss Sparshott began to clatter on the keys as if to disassociate herself from impending trauma. Above the noise she said defensively:

'There's a note on your desk.'

Cordelia tore it open. It was short and explicit. Bernie had always been able to express himself succinctly when he had something to say:

'I'm sorry, partner, they've told me it's cancer and I'm taking the easy way out. I've seen what the treatment does to people and I'm not having any. I've made my will and it's with my solicitor. You'll find his name in the desk. I've left the business to you. Everything, including *all* the equipment. Good luck and thank you.' Underneath with the inconsiderateness of the doomed he had scribbled a final unfair plea:

'If you find me alive, for God's sake wait before calling help. I rely on you for this, partner. Bernie.'

She unlocked the door of the inner office and went inside, closing the door carefully behind her.

It was a relief to see that there was no need to wait. Bernie was dead. He lay slumped over the desk as if in an extremity of exhaustion. His right hand was half-clenched and an open cut-throat razor had slithered over the desk top leaving a thin trail of blood like a snail's track and had come to rest precariously poised on the extreme edge of the desk. His left wrist, scored with two parallel cuts, lay palm upwards in the enamel bowl which Cordelia used for the washing-up. Bernie had filled it with water but it was now brimful with a pale pinky liquid smelling sickly sweet, through which the fingers, curved as if in supplication and looking as white and delicate as those of a child, gleamed as smooth as wax. The blood and water had overflowed on to the desk and floor soaking the oblong of garish rug which Bernie had recently bought in the hope of impressing visitors with his status but which Cordelia privately thought had only drawn attention to the shabbiness of the rest of the office. One of the cuts was tentative and superficial but the other had gone deep as the bone and the severed edges of the wound, drained of blood, gaped cleanly like an illustration in an anatomy text book.

Group discussion
- Make a list of words and phrases from the extract that belong to a 'literary' language rather than the language of everyday use. Then share your list with the group and discuss what effect this usage has on meaning.
- Discuss how the author uses language to create a picture of Bernie as a 'failure'.
- Consider how language is used to create a picture of the physical surroundings of the detective agency.
- What impression of the narrative figure of Cordelia is created by selective use of detail through language.
- Why do you think the author has gone into so much detail about the details of Bernie's suicide?

Writing

In the above extract, we, the readers, are provided with an impression of Cordelia Gray, private detective. This impression is created through the language of the passage. Imagine you have been asked to write a series of stories for a magazine centred round the narrative figure of a private detective. Write the opening section to the first of these stories in which, through your use of language, you create an impression of this narrative figure.

Write a critical appreciation of any example of crime fiction you have read, discussing how much it depended on familiar elements of the genre and what kind of language use predominated.

3.10 Realism

We have discussed how fiction, and most other uses of prose, creates a view of reality through its use of language. Traditional criticism has encouraged readers to accept this view of reality created by the individual author as 'real' and the narrative figures as 'real people'. We are invited to sink ourselves into the fiction, suspend our disbelief and view the reality represented as how the world really is.

Much of contemporary criticism challenges this traditional view, encouraging readers not to be seduced into accepting this representation of reality as somehow real. 'Realism', however, is still very prevalent in literary works as a means of creating this illusion of reality. Realism involves the painting of a seemingly accurate picture of the world through detailed description and the use of recognisable settings. The 'people' portrayed in these narratives are often 'ordinary' and the events described the kind that normally happen in most people's lives.

However, realism does not actually create a reality, but a **representation** of reality. The 'reality' is constructed through language and we may accept it as accurate or not, according to our reading of the text. Most realistic works of fiction lead to a definite closure in which the social status quo is restored. Thus, the reader's preconceived view of the world is reinforced.

Below is an extract from a 'realist' novel by the nineteenth-century French writer, Gustave Flaubert. It is from *Madame Bovary*, which tells the story of its main narrative figure, Emma Bovary, a farmer's daughter, who dreams of romance and riches, though she finds herself trapped in an unhappy marriage to a poor country doctor. At the point of the narrative from which the translated extract below is chosen, Emma and her husband, Charles, have been invited to the nearby chateau to a ball given by the local aristocrat.

The quadrilles had begun. Guests were arriving. People pushed against one another. She sat down near the door on a bench.

When the dance was over, the floor was left free for groups of men who stood about, talking, and for liveried servants carrying large trays. Along the line of seated women, painted fans fluttered, bouquets half concealed smiles upon faces and gold-stoppered vials were toyed with by hands whose white gloves outlined the form of the fingernails and squeezed the flesh at the wrist. Ornaments and lace, diamond brooches, medallion bracelets, gleamed on bosoms, whispered on bare arms. Hair was dressed flat across foreheads, twisted into a knot in back, and was crowned with garlands of forget-me-nots, jasmine, pomegranate blossoms, feathery grasses or bluets, in clusters or in sprays. Peaceful in their places, mothers with intent faces wore red turbans.

Emma's heart beat a little faster when, her partner holding her finger tips, she went to take her place in line and waited for the stroke of the bow to start the dance. But soon emotion vanished; and, swaying to the rhythm of the orchestra, she moved forward with delicate motions of the head. A smile rose to her lips at certain graceful passages from the violin, which sometimes played alone while the other instruments were silent; the clear sound of gold coins could be heard as they were flung down on baize tables at one side; then all would take up the melody again, the cornet giving forth a sonorous note. Feet stepped in the measure, skirts billowed and rustled, hands joined and parted; the same eyes, lowering before you, returned to gaze into yours.

A few of the men, perhaps fifteen, ranging from twenty-five to forty years of age, scattered among the dancers or standing talking at doorways, were distinguished from the rest by a family look, whatever the differences in their ages, dress or features.

Their suits, better made, seemed to be of a richer material, and their hair, drawn back in curls at the temples, given luster by finer pomades. They had the complexion of wealth, that white complexion which enhances the translucency of porcelains, the sheen of satin, the finish of beautiful furniture, and which keeps up its health by means of a discreet diet of exquisite foods. Their necks turned in comfort above low cravats; their long side-whiskers fell to their turned-back collars; they wiped their lips with handkerchiefs embroidered with large monograms, from which drifted a pleasant fragrance. Those who were beginning to age had a youthful air, while there was an element of maturity upon the faces of the younger ones. In their indifferent glances was the serenity of passions daily gratified; and through their agreeable manners penetrated that particular brutality communicated by domination in fairly unexacting matters where force is employed and in which vanity takes pleasure: the handling of blooded horses and the society of abandoned women.

The air in the ballroom was heavy; the lamps were growing dim. The throng flowed into the billiard room. A servant climbed upon a chair and broke two windows; at the sound of glass splintering, Emma turned her head and saw in the garden, against the panes, the faces of peasants who were watching. Then the memory of Les Bertaux returned to her. She saw again the farm, the marshy pond, her father in shirt sleeves beneath the apple tree, and she saw herself, as she had once been, skimming the cream from the earthen pans of milk in the dairy with her finger. But in the vivid brilliance of the present hour her past life, so clear until that time, faded away altogether, and she almost doubted having experienced it. She was here; then, surrounding the ball, there was only shadow, spread out over all the rest. At that moment she was eating a maraschino ice in a silver-gilt cup which she held in her left hand, and half closed her eyes, the spoon between her teeth.

A lady near her dropped her fan. A dancer passed.

'Would you be so kind, Monsieur,' the lady said, 'as to pick up my fan? It's behind this couch.'

The gentleman bent and, as he was stretching out his arm, Emma saw the young lady's hand throw something white, folded into a triangle, into his hat. The gentleman, recovering the fan, offered it respectfully to the lady; she thanked him with a nod and began to sniff at her bouquet.

After supper, at which were served many Spanish wines and Rhine wines, bisque soups and soups made with milk of almonds, Trafalgar puddings and all sorts of cold meats in aspic which quivered on the platters, the carriages began to leave, one after another. Pulling aside a corner of the muslin curtain, one saw the light of their lanterns slipping through the dark. The benches were deserted; a few card players still remained; the musicians cooled their fingers with the tips of their tongues; Charles was half asleep, his back propped against a door.

Group discussion
- Working in pairs, make a list of the detail created by language use that the writer has packed into the second paragraph to create a representation of reality.
- Discuss from whose perspective we view the ball and how this affects the meaning produced for us.
- Read through the fifth paragraph again. How is language used to create a picture of the men at the ball?
- Discuss how Emma's present situation is contrasted with her past.
- Discuss how the writer uses language to create a picture of opulence and waste.
- As a group, discuss the extract as a representation of reality. How effective is it in creating this 'reality'? As readers of fiction, do you think we should accept the representation of reality presented in a text or 'stand back' from it, reminding ourselves that it is only an illusion of reality? If we remain objective and detached as readers, do we risk losing some enjoyment through identification with the narrative figures?

Writing ▶
Write a piece about the extract, analysing the use of language that helps create such a detailed picture of 'reality' and making a judgement about how effective it is as a piece of writing.

3.11 Magic realism

Magic realism is a term used to describe stories and novels which mix a representation of a 'realistic' world with elements of fairy tales or mythology, and in the narrative of which unexpected and inexplicable events take place, often of a symbolic nature. Most magic realist writers, such as Angela Carter, Salman Rushdie and Lisa St. Aubin, strive to create a believably real world and then introduce bizarre events that seem to escape rational explanation.

Isabel Allende is a contemporary writer who was born in Peru. Her novel

Of Love and Shadows is set in a country in South America where the military has seized power and imposed a dictatorship that uses arbitrary arrests and executions to maintain power. Evangelina is a young girl who suffers from mysterious fits.

Evangelina had not gone to school since the first signs of her disturbance appeared. Her mother remembered the precise moment their misfortune began. It was the day of the convention of frogs, although she was sure that that episode was not related to her daughter's sickness.

They had been discovered very early one morning, two fat and majestic frogs observing the landscape near the railroad crossing. Soon many more arrived, coming from every direction, little pond frogs, larger well frogs, white ones from irrigation ditches, gray ones from the river. Someone sounded the alarm and everyone came to see them. Meanwhile the amphibians had formed compact rows and begun an orderly march. Along the road others joined in, and soon there was a green multitude advancing toward the highway. The word spread, and the curious came on foot, on horseback, and in buses, commenting on this never-before-seen marvel. The enormous living mosaic occupied the asphalt of the principal road to Los Riscos, halting any vehicles travelling at that hour. One imprudent truck attempted to drive forward, but skidded on squashed corpses and overturned amid the enthusiasm of the children, who avidly appropriated the merchandise scattered in the underbush. The police flew over the area in a helicopter, ascertaining that two hundred and seventy meters of road were covered with frogs so closely packed that they resembled a glistening carpet of moss. The news was broadcast by radio, and in a short time newspapermen arrived from the capital, accompanied by a Chinese expert from the United Nations who reported that he had witnessed a similar phenomenon during his childhood in Peking. This stranger descended from a dark automobile with official licence plates, bowed to the right and to the left, and the crowd applauded, very naturally confusing him with the director of the Choral Society. After observing that gelatinous mass for a few moments, the Oriental concluded that there was no cause for alarm, this was merely a convention of frogs. That was what the press called it, and as it occurred during a time of poverty and shortages, they joked about it, saying that instead of manna, God was raining down frogs from the sky so that the chosen people could cook them with garlic and coriander.

When Evangelina had her attack, the participants in the convention had dispersed and the television crews were removing their equipment from the trees. It was twelve o'clock noon; the air sparkled, washed by the rain. Evangelina was alone inside the house, and in the patio Digna and her grandson Jacinto were slopping the pigs with the kitchen garbage. After going to take a look at the spectacle, they had realized that there was nothing to be seen but a revolting mass of slimy creatures, and had returned to their chores. A sharp cry and the sound of breaking crockery alerted them that something was happening inside the house. They found Evangelina on her back on the floor, weight on her heels and neck, arched backward like a bow, frothing at the mouth and surrounded by broken cups and plates.

The terrified mother resorted to the first remedy that came to her mind; she emptied a bucket of cold water over the girl, but far from calming her, the alarming signs grew worse. The froth turned into a rosy slobber when the girl bit her tongue; her eyes rolled backward in her head, lost in infinity; she shook in shuddering convulsions, and the room was impregnated with anguish and the smell of excrement. The tension was so high that the thick adobe walls seemed to vibrate as if a secret trembling were coursing through their entrails. Digna Ranquileo hugged Jacinto close, covering his eyes to spare him that dreadful sight.

The attack lasted several minutes and left Evangelina drained, the mother and the brother terrorized, and the house turned upside down. When Hipólito and the other children returned from watching the convention of frogs, it was all over; the girl was resting in her chair and the mother was picking up the broken pottery.

'She was stung by a black widow spider' was the father's diagnosis when they told him about it.

Group discussion
- Read the second paragraph of the extract. Discuss how language is used to represent a bizarre event and the subsequent reactions of the onlookers, the 'expert' and the newspapermen. What meaning is produced for you by the representation of this incident?
- Read the third paragraph of the extract. Select details used by the writer to represent everyday reality and discuss language use that represents the attitude of Digna and Jacinto to the appearance of the frogs.
- You have read this extract out of its context: a novel. However, consider how the novel is described in the introduction to this section. In that context, discuss what the description of the frogs might symbolise.
- Compare this extract with the previous extract. Discuss any similarities and any differences between them.

Writing
You have been asked to submit a short story to a magazine that specialises in tales of the unexpected. You decide to write a story set against a 'realistic' background, but to mix bizarre events with 'normality'.

Once you have written the story, write a commentary on the writing process, discussing in particular how you managed to mix the 'real' with the 'uncanny'.

4   You, the reader

Any kind of discourse, in whatever area of language use, assumes there is a 'speaker' and a 'hearer', a writer and a reader. You, the reader of any written text, are addressed either directly or indirectly. In a sense, the reader is 'inscribed' into the text. Many written texts assume a certain kind of reader; for example, many comics 'assume' a young readership with an interest in strip cartoon adventures, jokes and regular features. We can use the term 'the implied reader' to describe this relationship between the text and the kind of reader the text appears to assume.

However, you as the reader can reject this position within the text as the implied reader. For example, you may choose to resist the blandishments of the text and not 'sink yourself' into the view of reality that the text offers. You may decide to 'keep your distance' from the text and analyse it as objectively as you can. You may remain 'sceptical' of the text and its 'transparent' meaning.

Let us use an illustration from prose fiction to clarify this. Most realist fiction that aims to represent a view of 'everyday reality' centres on the subjective responses of a few main characters, or even a single individual, through whose perspective we, the reader, see the events of the narrative. Implicitly, the reader is invited to identify with these narrative figures and share the view of reality that they have. In empathising with the narrative figures the reader is more likely to accept the values embodied in the text.

Thus, the reader is already 'positioned' in the text by being invited to identify with the 'voice' of the narrative, whether it be the invisible story-teller (the omniscient author) or the narrative figures. The reader shares the 'all-knowingness' of the author and is perhaps flattered by it.

Are readers, then, helpless in their relationship to the text? Do they have to accept that they are the implied readers the text seems to assume? Hardly surprisingly, the answer is no. Readers, for example, can reject this ready-made relationship to the text and decide to read with more detachment. Readers can put themselves in control of the text and produce *their* own meaning from their reading of it, no longer trying to winkle out the 'meaning' which the writer may have tried to impose upon the text. Instead of there being one single meaning to the text, and that deriving from the author, there can be a plurality of meanings, which may vary from reading to reading and from reader to reader. The reader may also resist identification with the narrative figures. S/he may identify with the 'people' and yet remember that what is being served up is an illusion of reality, not reality itself.

Think of the many differences that exist between people: differences of gender, age, nationality, race, culture, social class, experience, beliefs and many others. These 'differences' will undoubtedly affect how we approach any given text. Each of us is likely to have different interpretations of the same text.

In a sense, we may read into any text whatever meaning it produces for us. If that is so, then it is no longer acceptable to put forward the idea that a text has one single, closed meaning.

4.1   The implied reader

Romantic fiction is a best-selling genre. Romantic novels sell in their millions and the star authors of such works make huge royalties from sales of their books. Romantic fiction also appears in the form of short stories or serials in mass circulation magazines.

What kind of reader is 'implied' by these types of fictional texts? As individuals, answer the following questions, then pool your answers and arrive at a consensus about the kind of reader most romantic fiction implies.

QUESTIONNAIRE

1   Do you ever read romantic fiction?

Yes/No

2   Do you think romantic fiction is aimed at one sex more than the other?

Yes/No

3   If so, which sex is it?   Male/female

4   Which age range do you think romantic fiction is mostly read by?

12-18 ☐   19-30 ☐   31-45 ☐   46-65 ☐

the elderly ☐   all age ranges ☐

5   Which of these statements do you think best describes the appeal of romantic fiction to readers?

a) It provides harmless romantic escapism. ☐

b) It makes up for a lack in their own lives. ☐

c) It provides a model for their own lives. ☐

d) It represents the world as it is. ☐

e) It is usually just a good, entertaining read. ☐

f) It reinforces gender roles. ☐

The genre of romantic fiction is not that easy to define. Often 'romantic fiction' is a pejorative term used to describe 'love stories' that appear in women's magazines or crowd the fiction shelves of public libraries. However, if the subject matter of romantic fiction is courtship, love affairs and romantic entanglements in general, then many a so-called serious novel could fairly be included in this category as well (for example, consider the extract from *Pride and Prejudice* by Jane Austen in section 3.3).

These 'serious' novels that deal mainly with the subject matter of love and marriage inevitably share generic characteristics with the kind of 'formula' romantic fiction of mass circulation magazines and pulp fiction.

Below is an extract from a novel, *Hotel du Lac* by Anita Brookner. At the beginning of the extract from the novel, the narrative has reached that familiar juncture in romantic fiction where the principal male narrative figure, Mr Neville, proposes marriage to the heroine, Edith Hope, who is herself supposed to be a writer of romantic novels. The setting is a restaurant on the shores of Lake Geneva in Switzerland.

'I think you should marry me, Edith,' he said. She stared at him, her eyes widening in disbelief.

'Let me explain,' he said, rather hurriedly, taking a firm grip on his composure. 'I am not a romantic youth. I am in fact extremely discriminating. I have a small estate and a very fine house, Regency Gothic, a really beautiful example. And I have a rather well-known collection of *famille rose* dishes. I am sure you love beautiful things.'

'You are wrong,' she said, her voice cold. 'I do not love *things* at all.'

'I have a lot of business overseas,' he went on, ignoring her. 'And I like to entertain. I am away a certain amount of the time. But I dislike having to come back to a house only occupied by the couple who live in it when I am not there. You would fit perfectly into that setting.'

A terrible silence installed itself between them. Edith concentrated her attention on the bill, fluttering unnoticed under an ashtray. When she spoke her voice was unsteady.

'You make it sound like a job specification,' she said. 'And I have not applied for the job.'

'Edith, what else will you do? Will you too go back to an empty house?'

She shook her head, wordless.

'You see,' he went on, 'I cannot afford another scandal. My wife's adventure made me look a laughing stock. I thought I could sit it out with dignity, but dignity doesn't help. Rather the opposite. People seem to want you to break down. However, that's all in the past. I need a wife, and I need a wife whom I can trust. It has not been easy for me.'

'And you are not making it easy for me,' she said.

'I am making it easier for you. I have watched you, trying to talk to these women. You are desolate. And without the sort of self-love which I have been urging on you, you are never going to learn the rules, or you are going to learn them too late and become bitter. And when you think you are alone, your expression is full of sorrow. You face a life of exile of one sort or another.'

'But why should you think me such a hopeless case?'

'You are a lady, Edith. They are rather out of fashion these days, as you may have noticed. As my wife, you will do very well. Unmarried, I'm afraid you will soon look a bit of a fool.'

She studied him sadly. 'And what will I do in your fine house, when you are away?' she asked. And when you are not away, she thought, but kept the thought to herself.

'Whatever you do now, only better. You may write, if you want to. In fact, you may begin to write rather better than you ever thought you could. Edith Neville is a fine name for an author. You will have a social position, which you need. You will gain confidence, sophistication. And you will have the satisfaction of knowing that you are doing me credit. You are not the sort of woman of whom men are afraid, hysterics who behave as though they are the constant object of scandal or desire, who boast of their conquests and their performance, and who think they can do anything so long as they entertain their friends and keep a minimal bargain with their husbands.'

'Women too are afraid of that sort of woman,' murmured Edith.

'No,' he said. 'Most women *are* that sort of woman.'

She looked up at him. 'But I thought that men preferred that kind of woman. I thought that they despised the sort of conjugal peace that you prescribe for me.'

'In a sense, yes,' he replied. 'Men do like that kind of woman. They feel they are missing out if they get anything that is less than tricky and fantastic; they like the danger of that sort of attachment. They like the feeling that they have had to fight other men for possession. That is what it is all about, really. Knocking other men down. It is only when those other men get up and start fighting for possession all over again that they realize how fragile, how *tiring*, that particular kind of partnership is. One gets no work done.'

'Again you are paying me the tremendous compliment of assuming that no one else will want me, ever.'

'I am paying you the compliment of assuming that you know the difference between flirtation and fidelity. I am paying you the compliment of assuming that you will never indulge in the sort of gossipy indiscretions that so discredit a man. I am paying you the compliment of believing that you will not shame me, will not ridicule me, *will not hurt my feelings*. Do you realise how hard it is for a man to own up to being hurt in that way? I simply cannot afford to let it happen again.'

'And yet the other day you were preaching a doctrine of selfishness. Centrality was your word. How is that to be shared?'

'Much more easily than you think. I am not asking you to lose all for love. I am asking you to recognize your own true self-interest. I am simply telling you what you may already have begun to suspect: that modesty and merit are very poor cards to hold. I am proposing a partnership of the most enlightened kind. A partnership based on esteem, if you like. Also out of fashion, by the way. If you wish to take a lover, that is your concern, so long as you arrange it in a civilized manner.'

'And if you . . .'

'The same applies, of course. For me, now, that would always be a trivial matter. You would not hear of it nor need you care about it. The union between us would be one of shared interests, of truthful discourse. Of companionship. To me, these are the important things. And for you they should be important. Think, Edith. Have you not, at some time in your well-behaved life, desired vindication? Are you not tired of being polite to rude people?'

Edith bowed her head.

'You will be able to entertain your friends, of course. And you will find that they treat you quite differently. This comes back to what I was saying before. You will find that you can behave as badly as you like. As badly as everybody else likes, too. That is the way of the world. And you will be respected for it. People will at last feel comfortable with you. You are lonely, Edith.'

After a long pause she looked up and said, 'It's getting cold. Shall we go back?'

Group discussion
- Working in pairs, discuss how the author represents the narrative figure of Mr Neville in this extract. Consider the utterances he is given and the responses from the narrative figure of Edith. From your reading of the text, what image of Mr Neville do you form? Then share your analysis of Mr Neville with the rest of the group.
- Again working in pairs, discuss how the narrative figure of Edith Hope is represented in the extract. Consider what she is given to say and any other details about the character the language provides us with. Then share your analysis with the rest of the group.
- Summarise in not more than eighty words the essence of what Mr Neville says to Edith. Then summarise what Edith says. As a group compare summaries and agree a consensus summary for each set of utterances.
- On a measuring gradient ranging from one extreme of 'very informal' to the other extreme of 'very formal', discuss how you would measure the degree of formality in the language of the extract.

- Think of the 'stock' heroes and heroines of popular romantic fiction. Judging by this extract, how does the representation of Mr Neville and Edith differ from the stereotypical representation of romantic heroes and heroines?

Writing ☛ The above extract comes very close to the end of the novel from which it was taken. Continue the story from the point at which the extract ends. The two narrative figures leave the restaurant and take a boat across the lake to the hotel at which they are both staying. In your writing, imitate the style of language of the original.

☛ Compare this extract with the extract from *Pride and Prejudice* (section 3.3). Discuss any similarities and differences of subject-matter and language use.

4.2 The 'tough guy' tradition

'Tough guy' writing is usually associated with American fiction. The characteristics of the 'tough guy' tradition are a clipped, terse use of language and descriptions of men facing danger of one kind or another consisting of narrative incidents that are meant to represent a test of their 'masculinity'. Ernest Hemingway and Norman Mailer are two American novelists who have been described as writing within this tradition. Crime writers such as Chandler and Hammett also use this 'tough guy' persona in their writing of crime fiction. A contemporary crime writer is Elmore Leonard. Below is the opening of one of his novels set in the city of Detroit, *Unknown Man No. 89*.

A friend of Ryan's said to him one time, 'Yeah, but at least you don't take any shit from anybody.'

Ryan said to his friend, 'I don't know, the way things've been going, maybe it's about time I started taking some.'

This had been a few years ago. Ryan remembered it as finally waking up, deciding to get off his ass and make some kind of run.

His sister drove him down to the Detroit police car auction, where he bought a 1970 maroon and white Cougar for $250. His sister didn't like the Cougar because it had four bullet holes in the door on the driver's side. Ryan said he didn't mind the holes. Didn't *mind*; he loved them.

The friend of Ryan's who told him about the car auctions was a police officer with long hair and jeans and a big Mag under his leather jacket who worked out of the Criminal Investigation Division at 1300 Beaubien. His name was Dick Speed. He showed Ryan around the Frank Murphy Hall of

Justice and what went on behind the courtrooms and told him about serving papers and how a guy could do pretty well if he didn't mind driving around in his car all day. The way Dick Speed explained it, it didn't look too hard.

Ryan met a few process servers. He studied them to see if there was a process server 'look'. There didn't seem to be one. They could have been working on the line or delivering dry cleaning. Only one of them stood out, a short and sort of fat Jewish guy who wore leisure suits and seemed to know everybody in the Frank Murphy Hall of Justice. His name was Jay Walt. Ryan couldn't figure out what made the guy so sure of himself.

Ryan was thirty-six by then and starting to worry that maybe he was a misfit, a little out of touch with reality, that all the people strapped to their boring nine-to-fives were right and he was wrong.

He had sold insurance one time, for three weeks. He had sold new cars for several different Detroit dealerships; but, each place, the sales manager or the owner turned out to be a pain in the ass. He'd worked construction and driven a truck. He'd been with Local 299 of the Teamsters as a business agent for a while and got into a couple of fistfights that were interesting. He's worked on the line at Chevrolet truck assembly in Flint, quit before he went out of his mind, and got a job at Abercrombie's store in Troy, but only lasted two weeks. One day during the Christmas rush he told a lady if she didn't like the service why didn't she go someplace else. He'd said to her, 'Why should a nice person like you stand around taking a lot of shit?' Ryan was always polite. He had also been into a little breaking and entering when he was much younger and working for a carpet-cleaning company; but it was more for fun than profit: see if he could get away with it. He had been arrested only once, for felonious assault – belting a migrant crew chief the summer he picked cucumbers up in the Thumb – but the charge was dismissed. He had never served time.

What he got into serving was legal papers and it surprised him he liked it and was good at it. It surprised him that he was patient and had a knack for finding people. He wasn't afraid to walk up and hand someone a writ or a summons. As long as he didn't know anything about them personally it was all right. What they did, whatever trouble they were in, was their business, not his. He was polite, soft-spoken. He never hassled anybody. He would identify the individual and hand over the paper and say thank you, best of luck, and that was it. He couldn't remember many of the faces and he liked it that way.

Group discussion
- Working in pairs, make a list of words and phrases from the extract that could be described as examples of 'American English'.
- There are a couple of examples of what could be described as 'bad language' in the extract. As a group, discuss whether this use is acceptable in a context such as this. If it is, why is it? If it is not, why not?
- Consider the type of sentence that predominates in the extract. What sentence structure is used more than others and how does this repetitive sentence structure affect meaning?
- The narrative makes references to numerous interests and jobs. Is there anything particularly 'male' about these references?
- There are also references to bullet holes, violence and crime in the extract. Discuss how this may or may not be associated with the 'tough guy' tradition mentioned in the introduction.
- Is there an attempt through use of language to invite the reader to identify with the narrative figure of Ryan?
- Judging by this opening to the novel, is there an 'implied reader' for this kind of writing? Is it likely to appeal more to one gender than the other?

Writing Write an appreciation of any story or novel that you consider to be an example of 'tough guy' writing. Give examples of language use that could be described as in the 'tough guy' tradition.

Write a short parody of 'tough guy' writing, perhaps placing a narrative figure in your local area and having him or her use 'tough guy' dialogue.

4.3 Writing within the community

We have often referred to the 'context' of a piece of writing and the importance of reading and interpreting any written text within that context. An important part of 'context' is the immediate community from which the writing emerges.

Below is a complete short story by Maura Treacy, a writer living in Northern Ireland. The narrative is told from the perspective of a group of Irish women encountering a British army truck. The context includes the situation of the recent 'troubles' in contemporary Northern Ireland.

The Army truck had passed them earlier on the road. The driver had kept close to the edge, forcing them to pull the prams onto the grass verge, to press back against the hedge until the briars pricked their shoulders. The covered truck passed so close to them, looming above them, that the children cried with fright. Then it was gone. Shaken, they stepped out into the road again. From the back of the truck the soldiers grinned.

Captain barked as he raced along on the other side of the hedge. He had broken away from them earlier and now rushed back to the sound of the motor, scrambling through a gap to shake himself and bark at the truck. But it was too far off by then and when Sara shouted to him, he gave up and went back to her. He squatted in front of her, still panting, his pink tongue rippling between the white rows of spiky teeth, his bushy tail swishing clouds of dust off the road. He blocked her way until she patted him and talked to him, and then he fell in behind and followed tamely for another while.

They had walked too far in the heat and now on the way home Sara lagged behind the others. Her mother and Mrs Martin walked on in front, pushing their prams. Mrs Flynn stooped to lift up her child. He had stumbled again and dropped his bottle of milky tea and she would have to carry him the rest of the way. She was going to have another baby soon. Her leg was bandaged. Her hair kept on falling in around her face and when she was out of earshot Mrs Martin would whisper about her until she caught up with them again. When their own baby awoke, Sara's mother sat him up and lifted Mrs Flynn's child onto the end of the pram.

As they walked on, back over the bridge and around the turn, they hurried towards the shade of the tall trees that grew on either side of the road, the branches meeting overhead. Here they lingered, feeling kinder towards each other. The river slurped against the arch of the bridge and when they moved on they could hear inside the walls of the estate the sharp rap back and forth of a tennis ball. They followed the staccato rhythm of the game and heard the voices of the Corbetts and their friends who were spending the summer there. As they passed the green door in the wall through which they might see the lawns, the tennis court, the shrubbery and the glasshouses, Mrs Flynn winked at Sara to come and peep, too, but her mother had turned around and was beckoning her to come on. They were out on the open road again, with low banks on either side topped by barbed wire fences, when they heard the distant sound of an engine on the road behind them. Sara's mother and Mrs Martin looked at each other.

'They're coming back,' Mrs Flynn said. 'Come on, quick, we'll be as far as your house.'

'Oh, it might not be them at all,' Sara's mother said. But she reached back and grabbed Jamie's hand and he trotted along beside her, looking back, and stumbling. 'Sara!' She turned to her and smiled. 'That dog, is he gone again? Oh well, he's probably home by now.'

They were hurrying towards Martin's house when the truck came roaring down the road behind them and Captain reappeared, darting out under the wire. They had just reached the front of the house from the road and were walking in single file on the grassy margin.

The truck drove up beside them, the wheels spewing clouds of dust, and Captain came running after it, barking at the rolling wheels and at the men in the back of the truck who were yelling at him. Mrs Flynn called Captain to come back. The truck braked suddenly and Captain too skidded to a halt behind it. He crouched there, yapping at the jeering men as they pelted him with small stones and pellets of hardened mud they picked off the floor of the truck. He whimpered when they hit him and would cower for a moment. But he would not stay away. Mrs Flynn and Sara caught him between them and tried to coax him and lead him away. And all the time the engine churned the stillness of the day to shreds. Mrs Flynn held him back, her arms binding him against her legs while he struggled, quivering and panting with excitement, to escape. Mrs Martin whispered to Sara's mother that they should all go into the house. 'Maybe they won't mind us,' she said. But her mother shook her head and stayed there. She was trying to soothe Jamie and Mrs Flynn's child who had begun to cry.

'Come on, let him out, Missus,' one of the men shouted to Mrs Flynn. He was sitting nearest to the opening, facing them. He held his rifle across his knees. Mrs Flynn tightened her arms around the dog and looked to the other women. 'Come on, Missus, let him off.' He swivelled around, resting on one knee, the rifle against his shoulder. The other soldiers looked on, and the driver rested his elbow on the ledge of the window and adjusted the mirror.

Then another soldier poised his rifle, grinned and said, 'Leave him to me, I can take him where he is.' But the first soldier pushed him aside with his elbow. He shrugged his shoulders and sat back. Sara searched all their faces. There was one soldier, a thin pale man with a dark moustache, who sat there with his hands clasped between his knees. He looked on with none of the anticipation of the others, but neither with impatience, as if all this had been bound to occur and he must bide while it lasted. 'Ah, what do you want with the poor dog,' Mrs Flynn said. She smirked as she glanced at the other women to see what they thought, and to blame their presence if her tactics were not the most effective she might have used. 'He belongs to the little one here. Sure you wouldn't harm him.'

The soldier with the moustache stretched his leg, turned away and looked across the flat countryside. It was to him Sara felt they should have appealed to stop it. Now she too turned away. She stood there waiting, her head bowed, her fingers twisting the fringe of the baby's sunshade. She heard the soldier saying, in his alien accent, 'Maybe you'd rather I'd shoot him where he is . . . take two birds. . . .' She heard them whispering and someone laughed, 'Three birds, aye. What do you say, Missus?'

Mrs Flynn's arms went limp. The truck began to trundle away from them. Captain slipped from her arms. He stood still for a moment, unsure of his freedom. But as the truck picked up speed, he streaked away after it again, barking excitedly, flurries of dust in his wake. The soldier aimed and fired, and fired and fired again until the barking stopped. And when Sara looked up, the truck was near the top of the hill, clouded in dust as it gathered speed. The soldier was still shooting, into the air now, every shot puncturing the fragile blue shell of the day. Frightened birds flew squawking out of the hedges and trees, and in Martin's paddock a mare and her foal left their grazing and ran to the far side and the stamping of their hooves vibrated along the hard ground. And when the noise had stopped and the dust cleared she saw Captain lying on the road at the foot of the hill, unbelievably still as they approached him. Blood oozed through his brown and white coat in darkening patches and trickled onto the road and was absorbed in the dust.

Group discussion

- Working in pairs, decide on a title for the story. Share your title with the rest of the group and try to decide on a consensus title. Then check Appendix 3 for the title that was given to the story by the author.
- Discuss how language is used to tell the story from the perspective of the women and not the soldiers in the truck.
- Discuss how this use of perspective in the story affects meaning and whether the reader is invited to identify with one group more than the other.
- Discuss what the women are shown to do and say, and then compare that with what the soldiers are given to do and say. Discuss how this may affect interpretation.
- On the surface, the narrative describes an encounter between the women and the soldiers. Considering the wider context of the story, however, does it have wider significance?

Writing ☛

Rewrite a version of the story that narrates the incident from the point of view of the soldiers.

Then write a brief commentary on how you tackled this assignment, commenting particularly on the perspective from which the narrative is seen and the contrast this creates with the original story.

4.4   A minority voice

African-Americans comprise a significant minority of the population in the United States. The African-American experience of the 'American way of life' has been the subject matter of the writings of many well-known writers such as Richard Wright, James Baldwin, Maya Angelou, Alice Walker and Toni Morrison. These writers have inevitably portrayed the 'American dream' in a different light from writers who have not shared their culture and heritage.

Below is an extract from Toni Morrison's novel *Jazz*. The extract tells of the experience of a young couple, Violet and Joe, who in 1906, in common with thousands of other African-Americans, leave the oppressive southern state they were born in and move to a northern city where they hope to find a new life and freedom.

'Breakfast in the dining car. Breakfast in the dining car. Good morning. Full breakfast in the dining car.' He held a carriage blanket over his arm and from underneath it drew a pint bottle of milk, which he placed in the hands of a young woman with a baby asleep across her knees. 'Full breakfast.'

He never got his way, this attendant. He wanted the whole coach to file into the dining car, now that they could. Immediately, now that they were out of Delaware and a long way from Maryland there would be no green-as-poison curtain separating the colored people eating from the rest of the diners. The cooks would not feel obliged to pile extra helpings on the plates headed for the curtain; three lemon slices in the iced tea, two pieces of coconut cake arranged to look like one – to take the sting out of the curtain; homey it up with a little extra on the plate. Now, skirting the City, there were no green curtains; the whole car could be full of colored people and everybody on a first-come first-serve basis. If only they would. If only they would tuck those little boxes and baskets underneath the seat; close those paper bags, for once, put the bacon-stuffed biscuits back into the cloth they were wrapped in, and troop single file through the five cars ahead on into the dining car, where the table linen was at least as white as the sheets they dried on juniper bushes; where the napkins were folded with a crease as stiff as the ones they ironed for Sunday dinner, where the gravy was as smooth as their own, and the biscuits did not take second place to the bacon-stuffed ones they wrapped in cloth. Once in a while it happened. Some well-shod woman with two young girls, a preacherly kind of man with a watch chain and a rolled-brim hat might stand up, adjust their clothes and weave through the coaches toward the tables, foamy white with heavy silvery knives and forks. Presided over and waited upon by a black man who did not have to lace his dignity with a smile.

They met in Vesper County, Virginia, under a walnut tree. She had been working in the fields like everybody else, and stayed past picking time to live with a family twenty miles away from her own. They knew people in common; and suspected they had at least one relative in common. They were drawn together because they had been put together, and all they decided for themselves was when and where to meet at night.

Violet and Joe left Tyrell, a railway stop through Vesper County, in 1906, and boarded the colored section of the Southern Sky. When the train trembled approaching the water surrounding the City, they thought it was like them: nervous at having gotten there at last, but terrified of what was on the other side. Eager, a little scared, they did not even nap during the fourteen hours of a ride smoother than a rocking cradle. The quick darkness in the carriage cars when they shot through a tunnel made them wonder if maybe there was a wall ahead to crash into or a cliff hanging over nothing. The train shivered with them at the thought but went on and sure enough there was ground up ahead and the trembling became the dancing under their feet. Joe stood up, his fingers clutching the baggage rack above his head. He felt the dancing better that way, and told Violet to do the same.

They were hanging there, a young country couple, laughing and tapping back at the tracks, when the attendant came through, pleasant but unsmiling now that he didn't have to smile in this car full of colored people.

Joe and Violet wouldn't think of it – paying money for a meal they had not missed and that required them to sit still at, or worse, separated by, a table. Not now. Not entering the lip of the City dancing all the way. Her hip bones rubbed his thigh as they stood in the aisle unable to stop smiling. They weren't even there yet and already the City was speaking to them. They were dancing. And like a million others, chests pounding, tracks controlling their feet, they stared out the windows for first sight of the City that danced with them, proving already how much it loved them. Like a million more they could hardly wait to get there and love it back.

Some were slow about it and travelled from Georgia to Illinois, to the City, back to Georgia, out to San Diego and finally, shaking their heads, surrendered themselves to the City. Others knew right away that it was for them, this City and no other. They came on a whim because there it was and why not? They came after much planning, many letters written to and from, to make sure and know how much and where. They came for a visit and forgot to go back to tall cotton or short. Discharged with or without honor, fired with or without severance, dispossessed with or without notice, they hung around for a while and then could not imagine themselves anywhere else. Others came because a relative or hometown buddy said, Man, you best see this place before you die; or, We got room now, so pack your suitcase and don't bring no high-top shoes.

- Read the first two paragraphs of the extract again. What clues are given there to tell the reader that Violet and Joe are African-Americans?
- ... when the attendant came through, pleasant but unsmiling now that he didn't have to smile in this car full of colored people.
  What meaning does this description have for you?
- In paragraph six of the extract, what evidence is supplied to tell the reader that the train has travelled through the states which have more discriminatory policies towards African-Americans and is now in a more 'liberal' region?
- What is the effect of the writer not mentioning the name of the city the train is headed for, but merely referring to it as the 'City'?
- How does the writer use the metaphor of dancing in the extract?
- How is language used to suggest that Violet and Joe's experience is shared by many other African-Americans?

Writing

Write an essay about the extract discussing how the writer represents a picture of the 'African-American experience' through her use of language.

4.5   Vernacular and standard English

The conventional language of narrative fiction is 'standard English'. What is standard English? It has come to mean the accepted norm of oral and written use of the English language, the kind of English that is used in official communications, in television and radio news bulletins, in business affairs and negotiations of all kinds. It is the language of government and education as well. This book is mostly written in standard English, for example.

Most English-speaking people, however, are familiar with, and use, a vernacular form of English. Vernacular (sometimes called 'dialect') is different from accent. Standard English can be spoken with a regional accent and remain standard English. Each vernacular variation or dialect of English, however, has its differences of vocabulary and grammar. Most people for whom English is their first language are 'bilingual': they use standard or vernacular English as appropriate to the situation.

Here is a short story by James Kelman, an author who writes about working-class life in the city of Glasgow. Kelman is a writer who uses Glaswegian vernacular for the utterances his narrative figures make and mostly standard English in his telling of the tale.

Sunday papers

Tommy had lain awake for almost ten minutes before the alarm finally shattered the early Sunday morning peace. He switched it off and jumped out of bed immediately, dressing in seconds. He opened the bedroom door, padded along the lobby into the kitchenette. A plate of cornflakes lay beside a bottle of milk and bowl of sugar from which he poured and sprinkled.

When he had finished eating the door creaked open and his mother blinked around it: 'Are you up?' she asked.

'Aye mum. Had my cornflakes.' He could not see her eyes.

'Washed yet?'

'Aye mum, it's a smashing day outside.'

'Well you better watch yourself. There's an orange somewhere.'

'Aye mum.'

'It's yes.'

He nodded and stood up, screeching the chair backwards.

'Sshh . . .' whispered his mother, 'you'll waken your dad.'

'Sorry,' whispered Tommy. 'See you later mum.'

'At eight?'

'Don't know,' he said, stooping to pick up the canvas paper-bag.

'John's always in at eight for something to eat,' said his mother.

'Okay!' He swung the bag onto his shoulder the way his brother did.

'Don't say okay,' said his mother frowning a little, eyes open now, becoming accustomed to the morning light.

'Sorry mum.'

'Alright. You better go now. Cheerio!'

'Cheerio!' he called as she disappeared into the dark curtain-drawn bedroom.

Immediately her head reappeared around the door: 'SHH!'

'What's going on,' grunted a hoarse voice from the depth.

'Sorry mum!' Tommy could hear his father coughing as the bedroom door closed. He washed his face before quietly opening the outside door. He stepped out onto the landing and kicked over an empty milk-bottle but managed to snatch it up before the echo had died away. A dog barked somewhere. Hurrying downstairs not daring to whistle he jumped the last half flight of steps then halted, hardly breathing, wondering if he could have wakened the neighbours by the smack of his sandshoes on the solid concrete.

Out the close he clattered down the remaining steps to the pavement, not caring how much noise he made now that he was out in the open. Crossing the road he leaned against the spiked wooden fence looking far across the valley. So clear. He could see the Old Kilpatricks and that Old Camel's Hump linking them with the Campsies. He whistled as loudly as he could with two fingers, laughing as the echoes pierced across the burn and over to Southdeen. He turned and waved the paper-bag round and round over his head; then he began trotting along the road, swinging it at every passing lamp-post. He kept forgetting the time and day. It was so bright. He felt so good.

At the top of Bellsyde Hill he slowed down and stared at the view. What hills away over there? The Renfrews maybe. Or it could still be the Old Kilpatricks? Rather than use the tarred pathway he ran downhill across the grass embankment. He had seen nobody since leaving the house more than ten minutes ago. A truck nearly killed him as he came dashing out onto Drumchapel Road from the blind-spot exit.

The truck jammed to a halt and the driver peered out the window. 'Wee bastard!' he roared. 'You daft wee bastard!'

But Tommy never stopped running. He flew on down Garscadden Road and up through the goods' entrance into Drumchapel Railway Station. The paper-hut stood by itself on the adjacent waste ground, parked beside it were a couple of cars. Half a dozen bicycles were propped against the wooden hut walls. He pushed open the door. The thick blue air made his eyes smart. The place was crowded. It seemed as if everybody was shouting, swearing and joking. Tommy joined at the end of the queue of boys waiting to receive their papers. The boy standing in front of him was a man with a beard. Tommy gazed at him. Behind the wide counter three men assisted by two youths were distributing the Sunday newspapers. The big man and the thin man were laughing uproariously at something the crew-cut man was saying. Some of the boys were also grinning and it was obviously very funny.

Each boy's bag was being packed tight with newspapers and one large boy had so many that he needed two bags. When Tommy's turn came he stepped forwards and cried: 'Six run!'

'Six run?' repeated the crew-cut man gaping at him.

'Aye!'

'Where's MacKenzie?'

'He's away camping. I'm his wee brother.'

'What's that?' called the thin man.

'Says he's MacKenzie's wee brother,' said the crew-cut man over his shoulder.

'Hell of a wee!' frowned the big man.

'What age are you kid?' asked the crew-cut man.

'Twelve and a half. I've been round with my brother before. Three times.'

'Ach he'll be okay,' said the crew-cut man when the big man's eyes widened.

'MacKenzie be back next Sunday?' asked the thin man.

'Aye,' replied Tommy. 'he's only away for a week. He's down at Arran with the B.B.'

The thin man nodded to the other two.

'Aye okay,' agreed the big man.

'Right then Wee MacKenzie, pass me your bag!' The crew-cut man began packing in *Post*, *Express* and *Mail*; as he worked he called out to the two youths who collected other newspapers from the shelves which ran along the length of the wall behind them. When the bag was filled and all the newspapers in order the man bumped the bag down twice on the counter and told Tommy to listen. 'Right son,' he said, 'they're all in order.' He counted on his fingers. '*Post*, *Express*, *Mail*. That's easy to remember eh? Then *People*, *World*, *Pictorial*, *Reynolds* and *Empire*. Okay?'

Tommy hesitated and the crew-cut man repeated it. Tommy nodded and he continued: '*Telegraph*, *Observer* and *Times*. You got that?'

'Aye.'

'Right kid, then off you go, and we close at two remember.'

'At two?'

'Aye, two. Remember!'

'But John's always home before eleven.'

'Aye that's John kid.' The crew-cut man grinned. 'Anyhow, take it away.' He pushed the bag along the counter and Tommy walked after it. One of the youths held the strap out and he ducked his right arm and head through. The youth helped him to manoeuvre it to the edge of the counter and then he looked down at him rather worriedly.

'Okay son?' he asked.

Tommy nodded and straining he heaved it off from the counter. The bag of papers plummeted to the floor like a boulder, carrying him with it. Everybody in the hut roared with laughter as he lay there unable to extricate himself. Eventually the thin man cried, 'Give him a hand!'

Three boys jumped forward. They freed him and hoisted the bag back up onto the counter. Tommy gazed at the men. After a moment the thin man said to the crew-cut man, 'Well Jimmy, what do you think now?'

'Ach the kid'll be okay.'

'Give him a weer run,' suggested the big man, 'that six is a big bastard. Somebody else can do it.'

'No mister,' said Tommy, 'I can do it. I've helped my brother before.'

The crew-cut man nodded then smiled. 'Right Wee MacKenzie. Put the strap over one shoulder just. The left's the best. Don't put you head under either, that's how that happened. It's a question of balance. Just the one shoulder now. Okay?'

Tommy nodded, pulled the strap on, and the crew-cut man pushed the bag to the edge of the counter. 'Ready?'

'Aye.'

'Right you are kid, take it away.'

Tommy breathed in deeply and stepped away from the counter, bending almost horizontal beneath the weight. He struggled to the door, seeing only the way as far as his feet.

'Open it!' shouted the thin man.

As the door banged shut behind him he could hear the big man say: 'Jesus Christ!'

Tommy reached the top of Garscadden Road and turned into Drumchapel Road by the white church. His chest felt tight under the burden and the strap cut right into his shoulder but he was not staggering so often now. It was getting on for 5.30 a.m. When he looked up he saw the blue bus standing at Dalsetter Terminus. About fifty yards from it he looked again, in time to see the driver climb up into the cabin. Tommy tried to run but his knees banged together. The engine revved. He half trotted in a kind of jerking motion. The bus seemed to roll up the small incline to the junction. Fifteen yards now and Tommy was moving faster on the downhill towards it. An oil-tanker passing caused the bus to stay a moment and Tommy went lunging forwards and grabbed at the pole on the rear platform. The bus turned into the main road and he swung aboard with his right foot on the very edge, managing to drag on his left, but he could not pull up the bag. The weight strained on his shoulder. It was pulling him backwards as the bus gathered speed. Nobody was downstairs. His chest felt tighter and his neck was getting really sore. The strap slipped, it slipped down, catching in the crook of his elbow. he clenched his teeth and hung onto the pole.

Then a cold hand clutched him.

'PULL!' screamed the old conductress.

He gasped with the effort. She wrenched him up onto the platform where he stood trembling, the paper-bag slumped between his legs, unable to speak.

'Bloody wee fool!' she cried. 'Get inside before you fall off!' She helped him and the bag up the step and he collapsed onto the long side-seat with the bag staying on the floor. 'I don't know what your mother's thinking about!' she said.

He got the money out of his trouser pocket and said politely, 'Tuppny-half please.'

At the foot of Achamore Road he got down off the platform first and then got the paper-bag over his left shoulder again and he dragged if off. He heard the ding ding as the conductress rang the bell for the driver. On the steep climb up to Kilmuir Drive he started by resting every twenty or so yards but by the time he had reached halfway it was every eight to ten yards. Finally he stopped and staggered into the first close and he straightened up and the bag crashed to the concrete floor. He waited a moment but nobody came out to see what had happened. A lot of the papers had shifted inside the bag and he heaved it up and bumped it down a bit, trying to get them settled back, but they did not move. His body felt strange. He began doing a funny sort of walk about the close, as if he was in slow motion. He touched himself on the shoulder, his left arm hanging down. Then he walked to the foot of the stairs and sat on the second bottom one. He got up and picked out a *Sunday Post* but it stuck halfway it was so tightly wedged; when he tugged, the pages ripped. Eventually he manoeuvred it out and he read the football reports sitting on the step. Then he did the same with the *Sunday Mail*. A long time later he returned the *Reynolds News* and stood up, rubbing his ice-cold bottom.

He completed the first close in five minutes then dragged the bag along the pavement to the next. At the faraway flat on the top landing, as he pushed through the rolled up *Post*, *Mail* and *World*, the dog jumped up snapping and yelping and he jammed three fingers in the letter-flap. He sucked them walking downstairs. At the third close he left the newspapers sticking halfway out. At the fourth he dragged the bag on to a point between it and the fifth and he delivered both sets of papers at once. He was down to about two to three minutes a close now.

About three quarters of the way through the delivery he noticed the dairy had opened at the wee block of shops. Some of his customers had paid him at the same time as he was giving in the papers so he had enough for an individual fruit pie and a pint of milk. In the newsagents he bought a packet of five Capstan and a book of matches. After the snack and a smoke he raced around the rest of Kilmuir and finished the first part. He had twelve *Sunday Mail* extra and was short of eight *Sunday Post* plus he had different bits of the *Observer* and the *Times*.

On the long road home he had to hide up a close at one point when he saw Mrs Johnstone the Sunday school teacher passing by on her way to church. As soon as he got into the house he rushed into the bathroom. He brushed his teeth to get rid of the smell of smoke then sat down to toast and egg. His father was still in bed. At about this time John would usually have finished the run completely and be in the process of cashing in down at the paper-hut. His mother did not make any comments about it. Shortly after eleven he made the return journey to Kilmuir Drive and began collecting the money. There were also some outstanding sums to collect which John had left notes on. One family owed nine weeks' money. Tommy had delivered papers to them in error, against his brother's instructions and they never answered the door when he rang and rang the bell. Other people were not in either. Some of them he managed to get in when he went back but by the end of it all he still had a few to collect. He got a bus back to Dalsetter Terminus. The conductor told him it was quarter past three.

He walked slowly up to the junction at the white church. He had money in three of his four jeans' pockets. One of the ones at the front had a hole in it. In the other front one he had a pile of pennies and ha'pennies and three-penny bits; all his tips. In the two back pockets he was carrying the sixpences, shillings, two-bob bits and half crowns. He had the 10/- notes folded inside the Capstan packet which he held in his left hand. There were three fags and a dowp left in it.

The three men were alone in the hut. They were sitting up on the counter smoking and drinking lemonade. The big man stood down. 'You made it!' he cried.

Tommy looked at him but did not reply.

'Right,' said the crew-cut man coming over with a wooden tray, 'pour the cash on and we'll get it counted.'

Both men stacked and quickly double-checked the money while the thin man marked up the pay-in-chit for £7/5/4.

'Much did you say?' echoed the big man.

'Seven pound five and four.'

'Well he's only got four and a half here!'

'What?'

'Four and a half.'

'Christ sake!'

The crew-cut man shook his head. 'No more money kid?'

'No. Just my tips.'

'Your tips!'

'His tips,' said the big man.

The thin man smiled. 'Get them out,' he said.

Tommy hesitated but then lifted out all the change from his right front pocket, dumped it onto the counter. The crew-cut man counted it rapidly. 'Twenty-two and seven,' he said 'plus it's a twenty-five bob run.'

The thin man nodded.

'Seven and nine short,' said the crew-cut man. He looked at Tommy. 'You're seven and nine short kid.'

Tommy frowned.

'You still got money to collect?'

'Aye.'

The crew-cut man nodded. 'Good, you'll get it through the week then eh?'

'Aye.' Tommy gazed across at the big man who had taken the wooden tray of money over to a desk. The thin man was also over there and writing into a large thick book.

'Okay kid,' said the crew-cut man, 'that's us locking up now . . .' He lifted a key from a hook on the wall and came to the counter, vaulted across it, landing with a thump nearby the door. He opened the door, ushering

Tommy out. 'MacKenzie'll be back next week, eh?'

'Aye.'

'Good, good.'

The thin man called, 'Is he looking for a run?'

The crew-cut man nodded and said, 'You looking for a run yourself?'

'Aye!'

'Okay then son, as soon as one falls vacant I'll tell your brother, eh? How's that?'

'Great, that's great mister.'

'Right you are,' answered the crew-cut man and he shut the door behind him. Tommy heard the key turning in the lock.

His mother opened the door when he arrived home. She cried, 'It's nearly four o'clock Tommy where've you been? What happened?'

'Nothing mum, I was just late, honest.'

'Just late!'

'Aye, honest.'

'Tch! Away and take off these old trousers then and I'll make you a piece on cheese! And go and wash yourself in the bathroom you're filthy! Look at your face! Where did you get dirt like that?

When he came through to the living room after his piece was on a plate on the sideboard and there was a cup of milk. His father was sitting on his armchair reading the *Mail* and drinking tea, a cigarette smouldering on the ashtray. 'How did you get on?' he asked over his spectacles.

'Okay dad.'

'What a time he took!' said his mother.

'Any problems?' asked his father.

'Some but it was okay really. I've to collect people through the week.'

His father nodded.

'Were they not in to pay the money?' asked his mother.

'No, and I went back.'

'That's terrible.'

'The man said I might get a run soon. He'll tell John.'

His father nodded, his gaze returning to the paper.

'That's good son,' replied his mother.

Then his father murmured, 'See and save something.'

Tommy nodded, biting into the piece on cheese.

Group discussion

- Working in pairs, make a list of words and phrases from the story that you consider to be examples of vernacular. Then as a group compare the various lists.
- Consider the balance between the use of utterances (dialogue) and narrative in the story. What roughly is the proportion of dialogue to narrative? Does this have an effect on you as a reader?

- In unit 3, we discussed realism in fiction. Could this story justifiably be described as an attempt to represent 'reality'? Does the term 'realism' have much validity?
- Discuss whether the story is told from the perspective of any particular narrative figure.
- Discuss the use of dialect in the story. Does its use 'enhance' the story for you as a reader or provide any difficulties? What other examples of the use of dialect in fiction come to mind?

Writing ☛ Choose a vernacular form of English you are familiar with and write a story using the vernacular frequently or entirely. If you decide to use vernacular all the way through the story, that means you have to use it in the narrative sections as well as in the utterances.

Then write a commentary on how you did it, mentioning any difficulties you had, for example, writing vernacular words rather than speaking them. If you decided to use standard English in some sections, mention how and why you did so.

4.6 Social class and the reader: the English middle-class abroad

Very often class distinctions among the British become very apparent when they live or travel abroad. Olivia Manning wrote a series of novels about two English people, a wife and her husband, Harriet and Guy Pringle, who find themselves in the Balkans and the Middle East during the early years of the Second World War. In this extract from *The Great Fortune*, the first novel of Manning's *Balkan Trilogy*, we find Guy Pringle working in the English department of the University of Bucharest in Rumania. Harriet has married him during the summer vacation and they have returned to Bucharest. Britain is at war with Germany and German troops are massing on the Rumanian frontier and threatening to invade.

> Near the end of the road, near the cross roads where the turbaned boyar, Cantacuzino, pointed the way to the Chicken Market, a row of open *trǎsurǎs* waited to be hired. Guy suggested they drive up the Chaussée. Harriet peered at the horses, whose true condition was hidden by the failing of the light.
> 'They look wretchedly thin,' she said.
> 'They're very old.'
> 'I don't think we should employ them.'
> 'If no one employed them, they would starve to death.'

Choosing the least decrepit of the horses, the Pringles climbed into the carriage, which was about to start when commanded to a halt. A tall, elderly man was holding out his walking-stick with an imperious air.

Guy recognised the man with surprise. 'It's Woolley,' he said. 'He usually ignores "the culture boys."' Then his face lit with pleasure: 'I expect he wants to meet you.' Before Woolley could state his business, Guy introduced him to Harriet: 'The leading English businessman, the chairman of the Golf Club', enhancing from sheer liberality of spirit such importance as Woolley had; then, turning with tender pride towards Harriet, he said: 'My wife.'

Woolley's cold nod indicated that duty not frivolity had caused him to accost them. 'The order is,' he announced in a nasal twang, 'the ladies must return to England.'

'But,' said Guy, 'I called at the Legation this morning. No one said anything about it.'

'Well, there it is,' said Woolley in a tone that implied he was not arguing, he was telling them.

Harriet, exasperated by the mildness of Guy's protest asked: 'Who has given this order? The Minister?'

Woolley started, surprised, it seemed, not only by the edge on her voice but by the fact she had a voice at all. His head, hairless, with toad-mottled skin, jerked round and hung towards her like a lantern tremulous on a bamboo: 'No, it's a general order, like. I've sent me lady wife as an example. That was enough for the other ladies.'

'Not for me, I'm afraid. I never follow examples.'

Woolley's throat moved several times before he said: 'Oh, don't you? Well, young woman, I can tell you this: if trouble starts here, there'll be a proper schemozzle. The cars and petrol will be requisitioned by the army and the trains'll be packed with troops. I doubt if anyone'll get away, but if you do, you'll go empty-handed, and it won't be no Cook's tour. Don't say I haven't warned you. What I say is, it's the duty of the ladies to go back home and not to be a drag on the gents.'

'You imagine they'll be safer in England? I can only say, you don't know much about modern warfare. I think, Mr Woolley, it would be better if you set an example by not getting into a panic.'

Harriet poked at the coachman and the *trăsură*, seeming about to break fore from aft, heaved itself to a start. As it went, Harriet looked back to give a regal nod and saw that Woolley's face, under a street lamp, had lost what colour it had. He shouted after them, his voice passing out of control: 'You young people these days have no respect for authority. I'd have you know, the Minister described me as the leader of the English colony.'

They were under way. Guy, his brows raised, gazed at Harriet, having seen an extra dimension added to the woman he had achieved. 'I never dreamt you could be so grand,' he said.

Pleased with herself, she said: 'He's an impossible old ass. How could you let him bully you?'

Guy laughed. 'Darling, he's pathetic.'

'Pathetic? With all that self-importance?'

'The self-importance is pathetic. Can't you see?'

For a sudden moment she could see, and her triumph subsided. His hand slipped into hers and she raised to her lips his long, unpractical fingers. 'You're right, of course. Still . . .' She gave his little finger a bite that made him yelp. 'That,' she said, 'is in case you get too good to be true.'

Group discussion

- How is Harriet represented as being a 'caring' person in the first dozen lines of the extract?
- Discuss how Woolley is introduced to us as readers. Select examples of language use that attempt to fix an image of this narrative figure in our minds. You need to consider language use that provides details of his appearance and his manner, as well as the things that the other narrative figures say about him.
- Does the author 'judge' her own narrative figure of Woolley? Does she, by her choice of language, indicate what she feels about this 'character'?
- Judging by this extract, what kind of 'character' is the author intending to create for the narrative figures of Harriet and Guy respectively in the remainder of the novel?
- Discuss whether this extract could be fairly described as representing 'middle-class' people talking in a 'middle-class' way about 'middle-class' things? Is the social background of the narrative figures at all relevant to your reading of the text?
- Compare this extract with the James Kelman short story. Would you say there are any examples of vernacular in the Manning extract or is it all in standard English? Do you find one extract more 'accessible' than the other? Consider the following factors: language use; the social class of the characters represented; the period in which the narratives are set; the age of the narrative figures; the type of narrative incident that is described?

Writing ☛

'The British abroad': write a short story with this title, based on the idea of two groups of British people from different social backgrounds encountering one another on foreign soil.

5 Further texts for analysis and comparison

This unit consists of more prose passages for further practice in reading of text. Each section includes suggestions for written responses to the given texts.

5.1 Two journalistic discourses

George Orwell, the author of the novels *1984* and *Animal Farm*, also wrote a considerable amount of journalism. Below is an extract from a regular weekly feature 'As I please' which he used to write for a periodical. This particular piece first appeared in February 1944, so the events of the Second World War mentioned in the piece must have been very present in his readers' minds. Orwell had also taken part in the Spanish Civil War alongside the Republicans when General Franco took up arms against the elected government of Spain.

When Sir Walter Raleigh was imprisoned in the Tower of London, he occupied himself with writing a history of the world. He had finished the first volume and was at work on the second when there was a scuffle between workmen beneath the window of his cell, and one of the men was killed. In spite of diligent enquiries, and in spite of the fact that he had actually seen the thing happen, Sir Walter was never able to discover what the quarrel was about: whereupon, so it is said – and if the story is not true it certainly ought to be – he burned what he had written and abandoned his project.

This story has come into my head I do not know how many times during the past ten years, but always with the reflection that Raleigh was probably wrong. Allowing for all the difficulties of research at that date, and the special difficulty of conducting research while in prison, he could probably have produced a world history which had some resemblance to the real course of events. Up to a fairly recent date, the major events recorded in the history books probably happened. It is probably true that the battle of Hastings was fought in 1066, that Columbus discovered America, that Henry VIII had six wives, and so on. A certain degree of truthfulness was possible so long as it was admitted that a fact may be true even if you don't like it. Even as late as the last war it was possible for the *Encyclopaedia Britannica*, for instance, to compile its articles on the various campaigns partly from German sources. Some of the facts – the casualty figures, for instance – were regarded as neutral and in substance accepted by everybody. No such thing would be possible now. A Nazi and a non-Nazi version of the present war would have no resemblance to one another, and which of them finally gets into the history books will be decided not by evidential methods but on the battlefields.

During the Spanish Civil War I found myself feeling very strongly that a true history of this war never would or could be written. Accurate figures, objective accounts of what was happening, simply did not exist. And I felt that even in 1937, when the Spanish Government was still in being, and the lies which the various Republican factions were telling about each other and about the enemy were relatively small ones, how does the case stand now? Even if Franco is overthrown, what kind of records will future historians have to go upon? And if Franco and anyone at all resembling him remains in power, the history of the war will consist quite largely of 'facts' which millions of people now living know to be lies. One of these 'facts', for instance, is that there was a considerable Russian army in Spain. There exists the most abundant evidence that there was no such army. Yet if Franco remains in power, and if Fascism in general survives, that Russian army will go into the history books and future schoolchildren will believe in it. So for practical purposes the lie will have become truth.

This kind of thing is happening all the time. Out of the millions of instances which must be available, I will choose one that happens to be verifiable. During part of 1941 and 1942, when the Luftwaffe was busy in Russia, the German radio regaled its home audience with stories of devastating air raids on London. Now, we are aware that these raids did not happen. But what use would be our knowledge if the Germans conquered Britain? For the purpose of future historians, did these raids happen or didn't they? The answer is: if Hitler survives, they happened, and if he falls, they didn't happen. So with innumerable other events of the past ten or twenty years. Is the Protocols of the Elders of Zion a genuine document? Did Trotsky plot with the Nazis? How many German aeroplanes were shot down in the Battle of Britain? Does Europe welcome the New Order? In no case do you get one answer which is universally accepted because it is true: in each case, you get a number of totally incompatible answers, one of which is finally adopted as the result of a physical struggle. History is written by the winners.

Writing ☞ By reference to the language used, analyse in detail how the author builds up to the final sentence 'History is written by the winners'. Then discuss how the overall tone of the passage strikes you, again referring in detail to the language used.

* * *

In the sixties, principally in America, there grew up a style of journalism which was dubbed the 'new journalism'. The aim of new journalism was said to be to communicate a highly personal, idiosyncratic impression of current issues and society. The writing was much more personal in tone and subject; often the subject matter was pop culture, celebrities or 'unusual' experiences undergone by the individual writer. Below is an extract from a piece, 'The shockkkkk of recognition', by Tom Wolfe, the American journalist and novelist.

This could be so perfect. Clarence, or 'Clancy', as he wants to be called, a 23-year-old-boy from Woodhaven, Queens, with tractor-tread shoes on a charcoal raincoat that shines and an unsqueezed purple goober on his chin and a mother who gives him such a look when he comes home at night from wherever it is he goes – he, Clancy, will have Natalie Wood all to himself. *Shock* – the real Natalie Wood will be... *his in the dark.* None of these idiots like Penner, with his Leica, what a joke, $400 for a camera when what he needs is a complete brain jòb – but Penner and none of them are out here and Clancy will have Natalie Wood all to himself, if only she will come out of the hotel. Make her come out!

Because this could be so perfect! There were six photograph hounds out here in front of the Sherry-Netherlands waiting for Natalie Wood. The photograph hound is the new version of the autograph hound. Instead of getting autographs of the stars, they take pictures. Clarence, and all of them, they read the newspapers in such a way, like an old man picking around in the bottom of a Ritz cracker box, to find out who is in town. Pretty soon one learns that Natalie Wood always stays at the Sherry-Netherlands Fifth Avenue and 59th Street, One waits and waits with a Nikon around his neck and finally this little, girlish figure will come out of that great burst of brass facings at the revolving door – *Natalie*! – it will be the *actual, real Natalie Wood*, and one will have her in the viewer and – *shock* – suddenly in that instant, one will have her. Nobody understands this, it's comical, they don't get the point – you have your face all pressed into the back of the camera and your eye, your...*self,* engulfs her like a lava-Jello amoeba, her marvellous great eyes open – little girl! – like they did in *West Side Story* and *Splendor in the Grass,* and when you press the button it makes this sound in your head, *shock,* and with a flashgun it is even better, the whole...feeling runs down your body like electricity, so that Clancy keeps the flashgun on even in the daytime – *shockkkkk* – *that feeling*! Make her come out here.

Natalie Wood and some magazine writer in a striped green suit leave all the people in her suite on the 12th floor and get on the elevator. One floor a man gets on and stares straight ahead and then he cuts a glance at Natalie Wood, and that's Natalie Wood, all right, that same trim little figure that turned everybody on in *Rebel Without a Cause* eleven years ago, the great big marvellous mothering brown eyes, looking a little more mature, of course, but very lively looking in this pink plaid suit and white textured stockings, it's Natalie Wood, all right – so he looks away and a runny smile starts to work its way over his face and then he turns to her, beaming, and says, 'I saw you on television in Montreal last night'.

Natalie Wood smiles, but she doesn't say anything. Uh, yes, TV, Montreal – man, this elevator moves slow. Ten, 9, 8, 7, 6 – silence is blowing up in here like a balloon. 'Well, you see,' he says, 'I was in Montreal on business, and I happened to be in my room, usually I'm not up in my room much, but I was in my room, and I turned on the television set.' Whew, boy, they make it to the bottom. Green Suit and Natalie Wood head through the lobby toward the revolving door.

I saw you on TV in Montreal. The thing is, Natalie Wood has been through the whole course in Hollywood, even more thoroughly than Elizabeth Taylor or Marilyn Monroe or any of them. She started in the movies at the age of six. She was a child star at eight in *Miracle on 34th Street*, an adult star at 16 in *Rebel Without A Cause*. She went through a highly publicised Hollywood marriage, to Robert Wagner, from 1957 to 1961, had the full Hollywood movie queen treatment, including a marble bathtub on the second floor of her home that was so heavy the ceiling below started collapsing about the time her marriage did. By the end of 1961, when she was 23, she had made 33 movies, including two great ones that year, *West Side Story* and *Splendor in the Grass*. She had pushed the publicity mill as hard as it would go, then had withdrawn from it almost like Garbo. She was known as one of the better actresses of Hollywood, was ambitious and aggressive about her career but was well liked, co-operative – and today, at 27, is a rather natural, thoughtful person emerging from twenty-one solid years inside of the Hollywood Petri dish.

One thing she has discovered is the Restrained Polite solution for responding to strangers who saw her on TV in Montreal. To be aloof is to have everybody hate you as an egomaniac. To be too responsive, specially for a female actress, is to egg on the kind of fan who hangs on; *waiting* for something. God knows what. So Natalie Wood smiles.

Writing 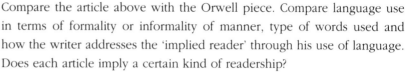 Compare the article above with the Orwell piece. Compare language use in terms of formality or informality of manner, type of words used and how the writer addresses the 'implied reader' through his use of language. Does each article imply a certain kind of readership?

Write an article for a magazine of today about a topic that interests you. Create two versions of the article – one for a 'quality' weekly with an older readership and the other for a magazine that aims to appeal to young people of your own age. After writing both versions, write a brief commentary on how you found you had to vary the kind of language you used according to the context for which you were writing.

5.2   Openings to novels

Below is an extract from the opening to a late nineteenth-century novel, *The Mayor of Casterbridge* by Thomas Hardy.

One evening of late summer, before the nineteenth century had reached one-third of its span, a young man and woman, the latter carrying a child, were approaching the large village of Weydon-Priors, in Upper Wessex, on foot. They were plainly but not ill clad, though the thick hoar of dust which had accumulated on their shoes and garments from an obviously long journey lent a disadvantageous shabbiness to their appearance just now.

The man was of a fine figure, swarthy, and stern in aspect; and he showed in profile a facial angle so slightly inclined as to be almost perpendicular. He wore a short jacket of corduroy, newer than the remainder of his suit, which was a fustian waistcoat with white horn buttons, breeches of the same, tanned leggings, and a straw hat overlaid with black glazed canvas. At his back he carried by a looped strap a rush basket, from which protruded at one end the crutch of a hay-knife, a wimble for hay-bonds being also visible in the aperture. His measured springless walk was the walk of a skilled countryman as distinct from the desultory shamble of the general labourer; while in the turn and plant of each foot there was, further, a dogged and cynical indifference personal to himself, showing itself even in the regularly interchanging fustian folds, now in the left leg, now in the right, as he paced along.

What was really peculiar, however, in this couple's progress, and would have attracted the attention of any casual observer disposed to overlook them, was the perfect silence they preserved. They walked side by side in such a way as to suggest afar off the low, easy, confidential chat of people full of reciprocity; but on closer view it could be discerned that the man was reading, or pretending to read, a ballad sheet which he kept before his eyes with some difficulty by the hand that was passed through the basket strap.

Whether this apparent cause was the real cause, or whether it was an assumed one to escape an intercourse that would have been irksome to him, nobody but himself could have said precisely; but his taciturnity was unbroken, and the woman enjoyed no society whatever from his presence. Virtually she walked the highway alone, save for the child she bore. Sometimes the man's bent elbow almost touched her shoulder, for she kept as close to his side as was possible without actual contact; but she seemed to have no idea of taking his arm, nor he of offering it; and far from exhibiting surprise at his ignoring silence she appeared to receive it as a natural thing. If any word at all were uttered by the little group, it was an occasional whisper of the woman to the child – a tiny girl in short clothes and blue boots of knitted yarn – and the murmured babble of the child herself.

The chief – almost the only – attraction of the young woman's face was its mobility. When she looked down sideways to the girl she became pretty, and even handsome, particularly that in the action her features caught slant-wise the rays of the strongly coloured sun, which made transparencies of her eyelids and nostrils and set fire on her lips. When she plodded on in the shade of the hedge, silently thinking, she had the hard, half-apathetic expression of someone who deems anything possible at the hands of Time and Chance except, perhaps, fair play. The first phase was the work of Nature, the second probably of civilisation.

That the man and woman were husband and wife, and the parents of the girl in arms, there could be little doubt. No other than such relationship would have accounted for the atmosphere of stale familiarity which the trio carried along with them like a nimbus as they moved down the road.

Writing ▶ Write an essay commenting on the kind of language used in this extract. These are some of the aspects of language you might consider:
- words that identify this passage as an extract from a novel of the nineteenth century rather than a novel written in the last fifty years
- how the author creates 'character' through a deliberate choice of words
- how the author uses words to communicate his attitude to the narrative figures and the situation he has created for them.

✳   ✳   ✳

Below is another extract from the opening pages of a novel. The extract is from *The Accidental Tourist* by the American novelist, Ann Tyler. It was first published in 1985.

They were supposed to stay at the beach a week, but neither of them had the heart for it and they decided to come back early. Macon drove. Sarah sat next to him, leaning her head against the side window. Chips of cloudy sky showed through her tangled brown curls.

Macon wore a formal summer suit, his travelling suit – much more logical for travelling than jeans, he always said. Jeans had those stiff, hard seams and those rivets. Sarah wore a strapless terry beach dress. They might have been travelling from two entirely different trips. Sarah had a tan but Macon didn't. He was a tall, pale, gray-eyed man with straight fair hair cut close to his head, and his skin was of that thin kind that easily burns. He'd kept away from the sun during the middle part of every day.

Just past the start of the divided highway, the sky grew almost black and several enormous drops spattered the windshield. Sarah sat back up again, but she kept her eyes on the road.

It was a Thursday morning. There wasn't much traffic. They passed a pick-up truck, then a van all covered with stickers from a hundred scenic attractions. The drops on the windshield drew closer together. Macon switched his wipers on. Tick-*swoosh* they went – a lulling sound; and there was a gentle patter on the roof. Every now and then a gust of wind blew up. Rain flattened the long, pale grass at the sides of the road. It slanted across the boat lots, lumberyards, and discount furniture outlets, which already had a darkened look as if there it might have been raining for some time.

'Can you see all right?' Sarah asked.

'Of course,' Macon said. 'This is nothing.'

They arrived behind a trailer truck whose rear wheels sent out arcs of spray. Macon swung to the left and passed. There was a moment of watery blindness till the truck had dropped behind. Sarah gripped the dashboard with one hand.

'I don't know how you can see to drive,' she said.

'Maybe you should put on your glasses.'

'Putting on my glasses would help you to see?'

'Not me; you,' Macon said. 'You're focused on the windshield instead of the road.'

Sarah continued to grip the dashboard. She had a broad, smooth face that gave an impression of calm, but if you looked closely, you'd notice the tension at the corners of her eyes.

The car drew in around them like a room. Their breaths fogged the windows. Earlier the air conditioners had been running and now some artificial chill remained, quickly turning dank, carrying with it the smell of mildew. They shot through an underpass. The rain stopped completely for one blank, startling second. Sarah gave a little gasp of relief, but even before it was uttered, the hammering on the roof resumed. She turned and gazed back longingly at the underpass. Macon sped ahead, with his hands relaxed on the wheel.

'Did you notice that boy with the motorcycle?' Sarah asked. She had to raise her voice; a steady, insistent roaring sound engulfed them.

'What boy?'

'He was parked beneath the underpass.'

'It's crazy to ride a motorcycle on a day like today,' Macon said. 'Crazy to ride one any day. You're so exposed to the elements.'

'We could do that,' Sarah said. 'Stop and wait it out.'

'Sarah, if I felt we were in the slightest danger I'd have pulled over long ago.'

'Well, I don't know that you would have,' Sarah said.

They passed a field where the rain seemed to fall in sheets, layers and layers of rain beating down the cornstalks, flooding the rutted soil. Great lashings of water flung themselves at the windshield. Macon switched his wiper blades to high.

'I don't know that you really care that much,' Sarah said. 'Do you?'

Macon said, 'Care?'

'I said to you the other day, I said, Macon, now that Ethan's dead I sometimes wonder if there's any point to life. Do you remember what you answered?'

'Well, not offhand,' Macon said.

'You said, honey, to tell the truth, it never seemed to me there was all that much point to begin with. Those were your exact words.'

'Um...'

'And you don't even know what was wrong with that.'

'No, I guess I don't,' Macon said.

Writing Compare the above extract with the extract from the Thomas Hardy novel, drawing attention to any similarities and differences of subject matter and language use between the two passages. In your judgement, which of the two is the more effective as the opening to a novel? Give your reasons.

5.3 An article about language

The passage on page 130 is an extract from *The Language Instinct* by Steven Pinker. This extract was printed in a 'quality' weekly magazine in its regular section headed *Science and Environment*. The magazine largely deals with current social, political and environmental issues.

Language is obviously as different from other animals' communication systems as the elephant's trunk is different from other animals' nostrils. Some psychologists, however, believe that changes in the vocal organs and in the neural circuitry that produces and perceives speech sounds are the *only* aspects of language that evolved in our species. On this view, there are a few general learning abilities found in animals, and they work most efficiently in humans. Thus chimpanzees, the second-best learners in the animal kingdom, should be able to acquire a language too, albeit a simpler one. All it takes is a teacher.

In the 1930s and 1940s, two psychologist couples adopted baby chimpanzees. The chimps became part of the family and learned to dress, use the toilet, brush their teeth, and wash the dishes. One of them, Gua, was raised alongside a boy of the same age but never spoke a word. The other, Viki, was given arduous training in speech, mainly by the foster parents' moulding the puzzled chimp's lips and tongue into the right shapes. With a lot of practice, and often with the help of her own hands, Viki learned to make three utterances that charitable listeners could hear as *papa*, *mama*, and *cup*, though she often confused them when she got excited. She could respond to some stereotyped formulas, like *Kiss me* and *Bring me the dog*, but stared blankly when asked to act out a novel combination like *Kiss the dog*.

But Gua and Viki were at a disadvantage: they were forced to use their vocal apparatus, which was not designed for speech and which they could not voluntarily control. Beginning in the late 1960s, several famous projects claimed to have taught language to baby chimpanzees with the help of more user-friendly media. One, Sarah, learned to string magnetised plastic shapes on a board. Lana and Kanzi learned to press buttons with symbols on a large computer console or point to them on a portable tablet. Washoe and Koko (a gorilla) were said to have acquired American Sign Language (ASL). According to their trainers, these apes learned hundreds of words, strung them together in meaningful sentences, and coined new phrases, like 'water bird' for a swan and 'cookie rock' for a stale Danish.

These claims quickly captured the public's imagination and were played up in popular science books and magazines and television programmes. Many scientists have also been captivated, seeing the projects as a healthy deflation of our species' arrogant chauvinism. I have seen popular science columns that list the acquisition of language by chimpanzees as one of the major scientific discoveries of the century. In a recent, widely excerpted book, Carl Sagan and Ann Druyan have used the ape language experiments as part of a call for us to reassess our place in nature.

This well-meaning but misguided reasoning could only have come from writers who are not biologists. To begin with, the apes did *not* 'learn American Sign Language'. This preposterous claim is based on the myth that ASL is a crude system of pantomimes and gestures, rather than a full language with complex phonology, morphology, and syntax. In fact, the apes had not learned any true ASL signs. The one deaf native signer on the Washoe team later remarked candidly:

Every time the chimp made a sign, we were supposed to write it down in the log . . . They were always complaining because my log didn't show enough signs. All the hearing people turned in logs with long lists of signs. They always saw more signs than I did . . . I watched really carefully. The chimp's hands were moving constantly. Maybe I missed something, but I don't think so. I just wasn't seeing any signs. The hearing people were logging every movement the chimp made as a sign. Every time the chimp put his finger in his mouth, they'd say, 'Oh, he's making the sign for drink,' and they'd give him some milk . . . When the chimp scratched itself, they'd record it as the sign for scratch . . . When (the chimps) want something, they reach. Sometimes (the trainers would) say, 'Oh, amazing, look at that, it's exactly like the ASL sign for give!' It wasn't.

To arrive at their vocabulary counts in the hundreds, the investigators would also 'translate' the chimps' pointing as a sign for *you*, their hugging as a sign for *hug*, their picking, tickling, and kissing as signs for *pick*, *tickle*, and *kiss*. Often the same movement would be credited to the chimps as different 'words', depending on what the observers thought the appropriate word would be in the context. In the experiments in which the chimps interacted with a computer console, the key that the chimp had to press to initialise the computer was translated as the word *please*. One observer estimates that, with more standard criteria, the true vocabulary count would be closer to 25 than 125.

Writing ▶ Write an essay in response to your reading of this text, commenting specifically on these aspects:

– the 'implied reader' the article is aimed at
– the type of discourse the text offers
– the level of formality, or otherwise, of the language used.

5.4 An incomplete short story

Below is the first half of a short story by Jamaica Kincaid.

What I have been doing lately

What I have been doing lately: I was lying in bed and the doorbell rang. I ran downstairs. Quick. I opened the door. There was no one there. I stepped outside. Either it was drizzling or there was a lot of dust in the air and the dust was damp. I stuck out my tongue and the drizzle or the damp dust tasted like government school ink. I looked north. I looked south. I decided to start walking north. While walking north, I noticed that I was barefoot. While walking north, I looked up and saw the planet Venus. I said, 'It must be almost morning.' I saw a monkey in a tree. The tree had no leaves. I said, 'Ah, a monkey. Just look at that. A monkey.' I walked for I don't know how long before I came up to a big body of water. I wanted to get across it but I couldn't swim. I wanted to get across it but it would take me years to build a boat. I wanted to get across it but it would take me I didn't know how long to build a bridge. Years passed and then one day, feeling like it, I got into my boat and rowed across. When I got to the other side, it was noon and my shadow was small and fell beneath me. I set out on a path that stretched out straight ahead. I passed a house, and a dog was sitting on the verandah but it looked the other way when it saw me coming. I passed a boy tossing a ball in the air but the boy looked the other way when he saw me coming. I walked and I walked but I couldn't tell if I walked a long time because my feet didn't feel as if they would drop off. I turned around to see what I had left behind me but nothing was familiar. Instead of the straight path, I saw hills. Instead of the boy with his ball, I saw tall flowering trees. I looked up and the sky was without clouds and seemed near, as if it were the ceiling in my house and, if I stood on a chair, I could touch it with the tips of my fingers. I turned around and looked ahead of me again. A deep hole had opened up before me. I looked in. The hole was deep and dark and I couldn't see the bottom. I thought, What's down there?, so on purpose I fell in. I fell and I fell, over and over, as if I were an old suitcase. On the sides of the deep hole I could see things written, but perhaps it was in a foreign language because I couldn't read them. Still I fell, for I don't know how long. As I fell I began to see that I didn't like the way falling made me feel. Falling made me feel sick and I missed all the people I had loved. I said, I don't want to fall anymore, and I reversed myself. I was standing again on the edge of the deep hole. I looked at the deep hole and said, You can close up now, and it did. I walked some more without knowing distance. I only knew that I passed through days and nights, I only knew that I passed through rain and shine, light and darkness. I was never thirsty and I felt no pain. Looking at the horizon, I made a joke for myself: I said, 'The earth has thin lips,' and I laughed.

Looking at the horizon again, I saw a lone figure coming toward me, but I wasn't frightened because I was sure it was my mother. As I got closer to the figure, I could see that it wasn't my mother, but still I wasn't frightened because I could see that it was a woman.

When this woman got closer to me, she looked at me hard and then she threw up her hands. She must have seen me somewhere before because she said, 'It's you. Just look at that. It's you. And just what have you been doing lately?'

I could have said, 'I have been praying not to grow any taller.'

I could have said, 'I have been listening carefully to my mother's words, so as to make a good imitation of a dutiful daughter.'

I could have said, 'A pack of dogs, tired from chasing each other all over town, slept in the moonlight.'

Writing ▶ Continue the story from where it leaves off. As far as possible, imitate the kind of language use the author has employed, but developing the narrative as you wish.

When you have completed the task, write a commentary on how you achieved it, mentioning any aspects of the original that influenced your writing and any problems you had to solve to complete the story.

(See Appendix 4 for completion of the original story.)

Poetry

We have discussed how literature may be perceived as a particular way of arranging language often within the 'compartments' of specific genres, such as novels, short stories, autobiography, essays and other text types. Poetry is another literary form for patterning language in specific ways.

Just as we interpret pieces of prose writing in relation to other prose pieces of a similar kind (intertextuality), we interpret poems in relation to other poems. We learn a way of 'decoding' poetry just as we learn to decode other uses of language in particular contexts.

A well-known linguist has referred to the 'prison-house of language' which we inhabit. By this, he means that language forms our ideas, our picture of ourselves and others, our view of the world in general. But literature may be a way of breaking out of this 'prison' by forcing us to look at words in a concentrated and fresh way, rather than just taking language for granted and allowing it to form our view of reality. Poetry, in particular, because of its very concentrated form, may compel us to reassess words and their meanings (including their associations and connotations) and through that our view of familiar reality.

6 The distinctive features of poetry

The term 'poetry' encompasses a wide range of expressive language and forms. In this unit we will be looking at a variety of poetic forms from the 'tight', generic forms of the sonnet, ode and haiku to the looser, more elastic forms of the twentieth-century song lyric.

6.1 A novel in verse

But what is poetry? How is it different from prose? Are the boundaries between prose and poetry always easy to define?

Below is an extract from the beginning of *The Golden Gate*, a novel by Vikram Seth. This novel is written in verse, in separate stanzas that follow the same pattern throughout the 300 pages of its length. The narrative setting is San Francisco; the time 1980.

> 1.1
> To make a start more swift than weighty,
> Hail Muse. Dear Reader, once upon
> A time, say, circa 1980,
> There lived a man. His name was John.
> Successful in his field though only
> Twenty-six, respected, lonely,
> One evening as he walked across
> Golden Gate Park, the ill-judged toss
> Of a red frisbee almost brained him.
> He thought, 'If I died, who'd be sad?'
> Who'd weep? Who'd gloat? Who would be glad?
> Would anybody?' As it pained him,
> He turned from this dispiriting theme
> To ruminations less extreme.

1.2

He turned his thoughts to electronic
Circuitry. This soothed his mind.
He left irregular (moronic)
Sentimentality behind.
He thought of or-gates and of and-gates,
Of ROMs, of nor-gates, and of nand-gates,
Of nanoseconds, megabytes,
And bits and nibbles... but as flights
Of silhouetted birds move cawing
Across the pine-serrated sky,
Dragged from his cove, not knowing why,
He feels an urgent riptide drawing
Him far out, caught in the kelp
Of loneliness, he cries for help.

1.3

John's looks are good. His dress is formal.
His voice is low. His mind is sound.
His appetite for work's abnormal.
A plastic name tag hangs around
His neck like a votive necklace.
Though well-paid, he is far from reckless,
Pays his rent promptly, jogs, does not
Smoke cigarettes, and rarely pot,
Eschews both church and heavy drinking,
Enjoys his garden, likes to read
Eclectically from Mann to Bede.
(A surrogate, some say, for thinking.)
Friends claim he's grown aloof and prim.
(His boss, though, is well-pleased with him.)

1.4

Gray-eyed, blond-haired, aristocratic
In height, impatience, views and face,
Discriminating though dogmatic,
Tender beneath a carapace
Of well-groomed tastes and tasteful grooming,
John, though his corporate stock is booming,
For all his mohair, serge and tweed,
Senses his life has run to seed.
A passionate man with equal parts of
Irritability and charm,
Without as such intending harm,
His flaring temper singed the hearts of
Several women in the days
Before his chaste, ambitious phase.

Group discussion
- There are variations in the use of tense in these stanzas. In pairs, discuss these variations. Note where one tense is used predominantly and where another is the ***dominant tense***. Then as a group discuss how these variations alter meaning.
- or-gates   and-gates   ROMs   nor-gates   nand-gates
  Words are associated with other words and particular contexts. These words from stanza 1.2 have associations with computer technology. Discuss whether these associations are in any way altered by the words appearing in a poem, or by your expectations of the kind of language that is 'normally' used in poetry.
- Pick out examples of informal language from these stanzas. Then pick out examples of formal language. Which dominates – formal or informal language?
- Words are known by the company they keep. ***Collocation*** is the term we use to describe the placing together of two or more words or phrases. There is collocation that is entirely familiar and predictable, for example, as white as snow, bad weather, gloomy night. However, collocation may be unpredictable and unexpected, for example, the Ambrosia rice-coloured snow, the grungy weather, impenetrable night. Unexpected collocation can force us, the readers, to reassess the meaning of words and, thus, our view of reality.

  Working in pairs, make a list from the extract of any combinations of words that are examples of conventional and familiar collocation. Then make a list of examples of unexpected collocation. As a group compare lists and discuss how the unexpected collocation affects meaning.
- Here is the first stanza of the verse-novel written out as prose. The same language is retained, but it is not written in separate lines and the word order has been changed in some cases.

  > To make a more swift than weighty start, hail Muse. Dear Reader, once upon a time, say circa 1980, there lived a man. His name was John; he was respected, lonely, successful in his field though only twenty-six. One evening as he walked across Golden Gate Park, the ill-judged toss of a red frisbee almost brained him. He thought, 'If I died, who'd be sad? Who'd weep? Who'd gloat? Who would be glad? Would anybody?' As it pained him, he turned from this dispiriting theme to less extreme ruminations.

  Discuss how this change from 'poetry' to 'prose' alters meaning. Do rhyme and rhythm become less obvious? If so, how does this affect meaning? If we describe the version immediately above as prose and the original stanza 1.1 as poetry, what is it about the arrangement of the language that differentiates one from the other?

- Each stanza uses the same patterning of language: the basic structure consists of: a *quatrain* (four lines rhyming alternately), two *rhyming couplets* (two pairs of two lines that rhyme), four lines in which the first line rhymes with the fourth line and the second and third lines form a rhyming couplet, followed by a closing rhyming couplet. The rhyming scheme can be denoted like this:

a
b
a
b
c
c
d
d
e
f
f
e
g
g

Check this pattern in relation to the four stanzas and discuss how this arrangement of language affects meaning.

Writing Write a piece on your thoughts about poetry as a particular way of arranging language. Discuss what are, if any, the distinctive features of poetry for you. You might also discuss what poetry has had particular meaning for you and why.

GLOSSARY

Dominant tense: the main tense in a piece of writing, although other tenses may also be used.

Quatrain: four lines of verse with rhyming alternate lines (the heroic quatrain).

Rhyming couplet: two consecutive lines of verse that rhyme, often used to make a witty point or to emphasise an idea or image.

6.2 A particular poetic genre

If poetry is a particular way of patterning language, within that 'patterning' there are certain recognisable 'patterns' or forms. One such is the sonnet, which usually consists of fourteen lines arranged according to fairly strict conventions.

Shakespeare (1564-1616) wrote many sonnets of a particular pattern that came to be known as the 'Shakespearian sonnet'. Below is one of his best known sonnets.

Sonnet CXVI

Let me not to the marriage of true minds
Admit impediments. Love is not love
Which alters when it alteration finds,
Or bends with the remover to remove:
O, no! it is an ever-fixed mark,
That looks on tempests and is never shaken;
It is the star to every wandering bark,
Whose worth's unknown, although his height be taken.
Love's not Time's fool, though rosy lips and cheeks
Within his bending sickle's compass come;
Love alters not with his brief hours and weeks,
But bears it out even to the edge of doom.
If this be error and upon me proved,
I never writ, nor no man ever loved.

Group discussion
- This sonnet consists of three quatrains and a closing rhyming couplet. A quatrain consists of four lines; usually it rhymes *abab*, but there are several variations that can be used. Working in pairs, study the sonnet and discuss whether the poem does break down into these component parts.
- How does the poet use the structure of the three quatrains and the closing couplet to affect meaning?
- *Poetic diction* is a term used to describe language that is divorced from everyday speech and reserved for use in poetry or ornate prose. Again working in pairs, select examples of language use that strike you as belonging to a poetic diction.
- Select examples of language that a twentieth-century poet would not have used.
- *Metaphor* is defined in section 1.6 of this book. It is the giving of the

qualities of one 'thing' to another 'thing', and is used for illustration and comparison. For example, 'Greta Garbo was a queen of the silver screen': in this example, a film star is given the qualities of a queen with all the associations which that word has.

Discuss any use of metaphor in the poem and comment on meaning produced by such usage.

- Love's not Time's fool, though rosy cheeks and lips
  Within his bending sickle's compass come;

Shakespeare uses **personification** here: the abstract concept of time is given human qualities. How is language used in these lines to give 'Time' these human qualities?

- Some lines in the sonnet do not 'pause' at the end but 'run on' into the next line. For example, look at the first two lines of the poem and read them aloud. See how the 'sense' leads you to read without stopping at the end of line 1. This feature of verse is called **enjambement** or **run-on lines**. Select other examples of enjambement from the poem.

- There are also examples of **end-stopped lines** in the sonnet. This is when there is a pause at the end of a line usually marked by a comma, full stop or other punctuation mark. Line 4 is an end-stopped line. What other examples of end-stopped lines are there in the poem?

- Compare Shakespeare's use of the sonnet form with Vikram Seth's in the previous section. Discuss matters such as rhyme, enjambement and end-stopped lines, the kind of language used and the overall meaning the language produces for you.

Writing ☞ Write a critical appreciation of this Shakespearian sonnet, in which you comment on the poet's use of the sonnet form, his language use, the meaning that is produced and the value you attach to the poem.

GLOSSARY

Poetic diction: the language used in poetry. This term is often used to mean language that is largely reserved for use in verse and seldom heard in everyday usage.

Personification: the giving of human qualities to inanimate objects or abstract concepts.

Enjambement: the running on of the sense of one line of poetry into the line that follows.

End-stopped lines: where the sense of a line 'pauses' at the end of that line.

6.3 Performance poetry

Most poetry is read by individuals on their own, rather than listened to by a group of people. In other words, poetry is only occasionally 'performed' nowadays. There are poetry readings where poets read their own work, but generally when we think of poetry, we have an image of a solitary person reading a book or of a poem being discussed in a school or college.

However, the origins of poetry were in the speech mode rather than the written mode. Before the invention of the printing press, most people's experience of poetry was through hearing travelling minstrels performing song ballads that became well-known through repetition.

A ballad tells a story in song. As well as professional balladeers, it is very likely that, before the spread of printed material, each community would have had its share of people who participated in telling tales in verse and song. These occasions were communal and did not depend on written texts.

Some of the ballads that were performed centuries ago have been preserved in print for us to enjoy today. Characteristics of the ballad include the telling of a story through dramatic incident and dialogue, a repetitive ***refrain*** and a simple use of language. These features of the ballad arose from the circumstances in which they were performed: balladeers had to hold the attention of their audience by concentrating on a single dramatic incident, the song had to be immediately understandable to people who were not literate, there had to be plenty of melodrama and intensity to the narrative, and unnecessary elaboration of language in terms of detail of description or character was excised.

Most of the ballads that have come down to us from the fourteenth century on are 'anonymous'. We do not know the identity of the 'author', nor do we need to know. Individual poets have written in the ballad style (Coleridge's 'Rime of the Ancient Mariner', Keats' 'La Belle Dame Sans Merci'), but these are referred to as *literary* ballads.

Opposite is an example of an eighteenth-century ballad from Scotland.

Group discussion
- Each stanza of the ballad has four lines. Working in pairs, discuss the rhyming scheme and its effect on meaning, the number of stresses in each line and any other feature of the stanza structure employed in the poem. Then share your findings with the group.
- Consider 'Thomas the Rhymer' in terms of these characteristics of the genre: repetition of language, simplicity of diction, the telling of a dramatic incident, the use of dialogue and a limitation of physical description.

Thomas the Rhymer

I   True Thomas lay on Huntlie bank;
A ferlie he spied wi' his e'e;
And there he saw a ladye bright
Come riding down by the Eildon Tree.

II   Her skirt was o' the grass-green silk,
Her mantle o' the velvet fyne;
At ilka tett o' her horse's mane
Hung fifty siller bells and nine.

III   True Thomas he pu'd aff his cap
And louted low down on his knee:
'Hail to thee, Mary, Queen of Heaven!
For thy peer on earth could never be.'

IV   'O no, O no, Thomas,' she said,
That name does not belang to me;
I'm but the Queen o' fair Elfland,
That am hither come to visit thee.

V   'Harp and carp, Thomas,' she said;
'Harp and carp along wi' me;
And if ye dare to kiss my lips,
Sure of your bodie I will be.'

VI   'Betide me weal, betide me woe,
That weird shall never daunten me.'
Syne he has kiss'd her rosy lips,
All underneath the Eildon Tree.

VII   'Now ye maun go wi' me,' she said,
'True Thomas, ye maun go wi' me;
And ye maun serve me seven years,
'Thro weal or woe as may chance to be.'

VIII   She's mounted on her milk-white steed,
She's ta'en true Thomas up behind;
And aye, whene'er her bridle rang,
The steed gaed swifter than the wind.

IX   O they rade on, and farther on,
The steed gaed swifter than the wind;
Until they reach'd a desert wide,
And living land was left behind.

X   'Light down, light down now, true Thomas,
And lean your head upon my knee;
Abide ye there a little space,
And I will show you ferlies three.

XI   'O see ye not yon narrow road,
So thick beset wi' thorns and briers?
That is the Path of Righteousness,
Though after it but few inquires.

XII   'And see ye not yon braid, braid road,
That lies across the lily leven?
That is the Path of Wickedness,
Though some call it the Road to Heaven.

XIII   'And see ye not yon bonny road
That winds about the fernie brae?
That is the Road to fair Elfland,
Where thou and I this night maun gae.

XIV   'But, Thomas, ye sall haud your tongue,
Whatever ye may hear or see;
For speak ye word in Elflyn-land,
Ye'll ne'er win back to your ain countrie.'

XV   O they rade on, and farther on,
And they waded rivers abune the knee;
And they saw neither sun nor moon,
But they heard the roaring of the sea.

XVI   It was mirk, mirk night, there was nae starlight,
They waded thro' red blude to the knee;
For a' the blude that's shed on the earth
Rins through the springs o' that countrie.

XVII   Syne they came to a garden green,
And she pu'd an apple frae a tree:
'Take this for thy wages, true Thomas;
It will give thee tongue that can never lee.'

XVIII   'My tongue is my ain,' true Thomas he said;
'A gudely gift ye wad gie to me!
I neither dought to buy or sell
At fair or tryst where I might be.

XIX   'I dought neither speak to prince or peer,
Nor ask of grace from fair ladye!'—
'Now haud thy peace, Thomas,' she said,
'For as I say, so must it be.'

XX   He has gotten a coat of the even cloth
And a pair o' shoon of the velvet green;
And till seven years were gane and past,
True Thomas on earth was never seen.

- Make a list of vernacular (dialect) words from the ballad. Some of these might be unfamiliar to you. Discuss whether the surrounding context helps you interpret the meaning despite this unfamiliarity.
- This ballad, like all traditional ballads, would have been performed in song in the eighteenth century. Discuss whether we lose anything by reading it on the page rather than listening to it in a performance.

Writing ☛ Choose a literary ballad that you know and compare its general characteristics with the features you have noted about 'Thomas the Rhymer'.

☛ There are many contemporary singers who create and perform songs that resemble ballads (Bob Dylan and Joan Baez are two examples). Choose some examples of modern ballads from the sphere of contemporary popular, rock or folk music and analyse what characteristics they share with traditional ballads.

☛ Write a poem in the ballad manner dealing with a dramatic incident set in the present day. The language you employ should be 'simple', perhaps with some use of a vernacular you are familiar with. There should be little elaboration of setting or 'character'. Use repetition of language, including a refrain. The ballad should be suitable for oral performance.

GLOSSARY

Refrain: words repeated at intervals in a poem or song. Usually, a refrain is an exact repetition, but it may undergo slight changes through the poem.

6.4 Singing 'the blues'

'The blues' emerged from the African-American experience of slavery and oppression. The blues are songs that had a communal origin, like the traditional ballads, and they usually express feelings of despair about mistreatment, exploitation and relationships that have gone sour.

The blues have been incorporated by the music industry and now are an integral part of commercialised popular music and jazz. Individual African-American artists such as Bessie Smith and Billie Holliday became famous for their performance of the blues. Despite the fact that the blues have been 'taken over' by mainstream popular music, it should be remembered what their origins were and how they continue to be an important feature of the artistic expression of African-Americans who are not professional entertainers.

Bessie Smith (1898-1937) was one of the most famous of blues singers. Here is the lyric of one of the blues songs she herself wrote.

Dirty no gooder blues

Did you ever fall in love with a man that was no good
Did you ever fall in love with a man that was no good
No matter what you did for him he never understood
The meanest things he could say would thrill you
    through and through

The meanest things he could say would thrill you
    through and through
And there was nothing too dirty for that man to do

He'd treat you nice and kind 'til he'd win your heart
    in hand
He'd treat you nice and kind 'til he'd win your heart
    in hand
Then he'd get so cruel that man you just could not stand

Lord, I really don't think no man love can last
Lord, I don't think no man love can last
They love you to death then treat you like a thing of
the past

There's nineteen men living in my neighborhood
There's nineteen men living in my neighborhood
Eighteen of them are fools and the one ain't no doggone
    good

Lord, lord, lord, lord, lord, oh lord, lord lord
That dirty no-good man treats me just like I'm a dog

Group discussion
- Working in pairs, discuss the repetition of language employed in the song lyric and how this affects meaning.
- Working in pairs, consider the language used and make a judgement about how formal or informal, simple or elaborate, it is.
- Discuss any features this blues lyric has in common with ballads.
- Which aspects of the language used identify the song as an expression of the African-American experience?
- Discuss what other features of this song qualify it as an example of 'the blues'.

Writing

Many contemporary singers and groups employ blues and variations of the blues in their repertoire (for example, rhythm 'n blues bands such as the Rolling Stones). Make a small collection of these contemporary blues songs and compare them with 'Dirty no gooder blues' and other blues songs that emerged directly from the African-American experience.

Write a blues lyric of your own. Use repetition of language, refrains and contemporary 'street' vocabulary.

6.5 A contemporary song lyric

The world of the twentieth-century entertainment industry is very different from the artistic environment in which the itinerant balladeers performed several centuries ago. The contemporary music industry sells its products in the form of CDs and tapes to millions of people across the world. Songs are produced for mass consumption.

The term 'for mass consumption' usually has pejorative overtones. Received wisdom often suggests that anything produced for millions of people to 'consume' is necessarily going to be inferior and uniform. However, amidst the plethora of 'musical product' that is produced by the popular music industry, there are numerous examples of work that has some obvious worth and perhaps some lasting significance.

Opposite is the lyric of a song by the group Talking Heads.

(Nothing but) Flowers

Here we stand
Like an Adam and an Eve
Waterfalls
   The Garden of Eden
Two fools in love
So beautiful and strong
The birds in the trees
Are smiling upon them
From the age of the dinosaurs
Cars have run on gasoline
Where, where have they gone?
Now, it's nothing but flowers

This used to be real estate
Now it's only fields and trees
Where, where is the town
Now, it's nothing but flowers
The highways and cars
Were sacrificed for agriculture
I thought that we'd start over
But I guess I was wrong
Once there were parking lots
   Now it's a peaceful oasis
      YOU GOT IT, YOU GOT IT
   This was a Pizza Hut
Now it's all covered with daisies
      YOU GOT IT, YOU GOT IT
   I miss the honky tonks,
Dairy Queens and 7-Elevens
   YOU GOT IT, YOU GOT IT
And as things fell apart
   Nobody paid much attention
      YOU GOT IT, YOU GOT IT

There was a factory
Now there are mountains and rivers
      YOU GOT IT, YOU GOT IT
   We caught a rattlesnake
Now we got something for dinner
      WE GOT IT, WE GOT IT
   There was a shopping mall
Now it's all covered with flowers
      YOU'VE GOT IT, WE'VE GOT IT
   If this is paradise
I wish I had a lawnmower
      YOU'VE GOT IT, WE'VE GOT IT
      Years ago
   I was an angry young man
   I'd pretend
   That I was a billboard
   Standing tall
   By the side of the road
   I fell in love
   With a beautiful highway

   I dream of cherry pies,
Candy bars and chocolate chip cookies
      YOU GOT IT, YOU GOT IT
   We used to microwave,
   Now we just eat nuts and berries
      YOU GOT IT, YOU GOT IT
   This was a discount store,
Now it's turned into a cornfield
   YOU GOT IT, YOU GOT IT
Don't leave me stranded here,
   I can't get used to this lifestyle

- Working in pairs, read through the first twelve lines of the lyric. Discuss the way in which the lines are linked or not linked with one another. Is there a clear flow of sense through these twelve lines? Then share the points that come up from your discussion with the rest of the group.
- There is a refrain that runs through the song. Pick it out and comment on how this affects meaning.
- Talking Heads were an American group. Select any examples of American English from the lyric.
- Discuss whether the lyric is ironic in tone: is its actual meaning different from its literal meaning?
- Make a list of the images of contemporary society that the lyric-writer has used, and then make another list of the images of 'natural life' he uses. What meaning is produced by these contrasting images?
- This is a song lyric. Make a value judgement about whether it has worth as a lyric or poem in itself. If you had not been informed that it was the lyric of a song, what features of the language might have suggested to you that this is the case?

Writing ▶

Make a collection of contemporary song lyrics that you consider to be of some worth. Analyse their use of language and discuss why you think they have merit.

▶

The lyric 'Flowers' deals with a contemporary issue. Write a song lyric of your own that takes as its theme some contemporary social issue.

6.6 Concrete poetry

Concrete poetry or 'shape' poems attempt to integrate pictorial typography with words to produce 'visual poetry'. The shape of the poem, the manner in which words and letters are placed on the page, produces in itself a sign that communicates meaning. Concrete poetry can be on paper, sand, glass, fabric, wood or almost any surface.

Opposite is a shape poem by Mary Ellen Solt.

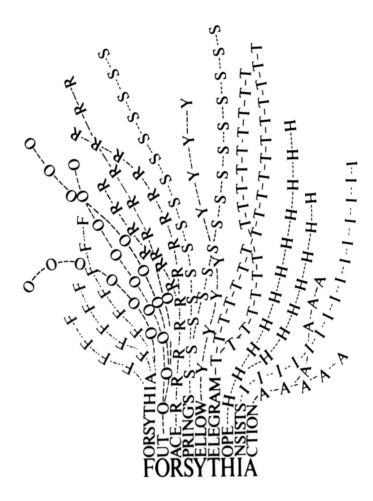

FORSYTHIA

Group discussion

- Working in pairs, describe in straightforward terms how the poem is actually constructed on the page. Then discuss your analysis with the rest of the group.

- Consider the word element of the poem:

  FORSYTHIA

  OUT

  RACE

  SPRING'S

  YELLOW

  TELEGRAM

  HOPE

  INSISTS

  ACTION

  If the entire poem had been laid out as above, how would that affect meaning compared to the original?

- Consider the pictorial elements of the poem. Discuss what these add, if anything, to any meaning produced.
- We have called this poem an example of concrete or shape poetry. Another way of describing it would be 'pattern poetry'. Discuss which term best describes it.

Writing ✏️ Create a shape poem of your own, trying to integrate pictorial elements with the language you choose to use. The shape of the poem itself must express meaning.

6.7 Haiku and tanka

Haiku and tanka are two Japanese verse forms that impose a rigid discipline on poets by regulating the number of syllables that can be used in a line and the number of lines each poem consists of.

A haiku, in its pure form, consists of 17 syllables comprising three lines of 5, 7 and 5 syllables respectively. A haiku is meant to communicate a single idea, image or feeling. Below are some examples.

> Hardly Spring, with ice
> still upon the rocks, and yet
> the kisses are bitter
>
> CHIYO

> *Loneliness*
>
> A flitting firefly
> 'Look! Look there! I start to call –
> But there's no one by.
>
> TAIGI

> *City people*
>
> Townsfolk, it is plain
> carrying red maple leaves
> in the homebound train
>
> MEISETSU

> In the amber dusk
> Each island dreams its own night.
> The sea swarms with gold.
>
> JAMES KIRKUP

Tanka are a verse form consisting of 31 syllables in lines of 5, 7, 5, 7 and 7 syllables. Here is an example.

> The blossoms have fallen.
> I stare blankly at a world
> Bereft of colour:
> In the wide vacant sky
> The spring rains are falling.
>
> PRINCESS SHIKISHI
> TRANS. BY DONALD KEENE

Group discussion
- Examine the examples of the haiku and tanka and discuss how they conform to the discipline of the respective poetic forms as outlined in the introduction to this section.
- Pick out examples of enjambement and end-stopped lines from each example above and discuss how the use of either affects meaning.
- In the first haiku by Chiyo, there is a comma after 'Spring' in the first line and another after 'rocks' in the second line. These provide a 'resting-place' in the verse. This pause in the sense is referred to as the caesura. A **caesura** is often marked by punctuation, but not always. The caesura is dictated by the meaning produced through the rhythm of the language.

  Select other examples of caesura in any of the poems above, remembering that lines of poetry need not have any at all. Having identified these 'natural' pauses, discuss how these affect meaning.
- Discuss whether one single idea or image runs through each of the examples.
- The term **intertextuality** is explained in section 1.3. This term describes how we are helped in our interpretation of texts by our familiarity with other similar texts. Having read the haikus and tankas above, discuss whether familiarity with the form would help us interpret other examples of the genre. How is meaning affected by this very restricted framework in which the poets had to create their poetry?

Writing
Create your own haiku or tanka, accepting the discipline of the form. Choose any subject you like. Then write a brief commentary on the problems created by working within this restricted framework.

GLOSSARY

Caesura: the natural resting place(s) in the flow of meaning in a line of poetry. A line of poetry may have more than one caesura and a caesura need not be indicated by a punctuation mark.

6.8 Another conventional form: the ode

An ode is a lyric poem which usually has a heightened tone, a complex verse structure and is conventionally perceived as expressing deep thoughts. The ode does not have such a fixed form as the sonnet, but, as can be seen from the following example by John Keats, it is usually quite complicated and ingenious in its rhyming and metrical scheme.

Ode on Melancholy

No, no! go not to Lethe, neither twist
 Wolf'sbane, tight-rooted, for its poisonous wine;
Nor suffer thy pale forehead to be kiss'd
 By nightshade, ruby grape of Prosperine;
Make not your rosary of yew-berries,
 Nor let the beetle, or the death-moth be
  Your mournful Psyche, nor the downy owl
A partner in your sorrow's mysteries;
 For shade to shade will come too drowsily,
  And drown the wakeful anguish of the soul.

But when the melancholy fit shall fall
 Sudden from heaven like a weeping cloud,
That fosters the droop-headed flowers all,
 And hides the green hills in an April shroud;
Then glut thy sorrow on a morning rose,
 Or on the rainbow of the slat-sand wave,
  Or on the wealth of globed peonies;
Or if thy mistress some rich anger shows,
 Emprison her soft hand, and let her rave,
  And feed deep, deep upon her peerless eyes.

She dwells with beauty – Beauty that must die;
 And Joy, whose hand is ever at his lips
Bidding adieu; and aching Pleasure nigh,
 Turning to poison while the bee-mouth sips;
Aye, in the very temple of Delight
 Veil'd Melancholy has her sovrain shrine,
  Though seen of none save him whose strenuous tongue
Can burst Joy's grape against his palate fine;
His soul shall taste the sadness of her might,
 And be among her cloudy trophies hung.

Group discussion
- Consider this analysis of certain aspects of the poem above:

  The ode consists of three stanzas, each of ten lines. Within this basic structure, there is a complex sub-structure: each of the stanzas consists of an opening *quatrain* (four lines rhyming *abab*) and a *sestet* (six lines rhyming *cdecde*). The poet uses the quatrain to explore an idea about melancholy, then develops it in the following sestet. This organisation gives a coherence to the thoughts the poet wishes to explore. The use of the two rhyming schemes helps to give emphasis to the ideas.

  Working in pairs, consider each stanza of the poem, checking it in relation to the analysis of the arrangement of language given above. Then discuss these features as a group.
- Make a list of examples of poetic diction from the poem, language that you consider to be much more likely to be used in poetry than in everyday language (allowing for the fact that this poem was written a century-and-a-half ago). Discuss how any use of poetic diction affects meaning and your response to the poem.
- *Alliteration* is the repetition of initial consonants in words in close proximity to one another. 'Peter Piper picked a peck of pickled pepper' is a very obvious example of alliteration, the repetition of the initial 'p' in a succession of words. The purpose in that example is to provide a 'tongue-twister'; more often, poets use alliteration for emphasis or for the sound quality it produces, which affects meaning. Select examples of alliteration from the poem and say how the use of this figure of speech affects meaning.
- *Collocation* is the placing together of two or more words. Collocation can be familiar and expected or unfamiliar and unexpected. Select examples of predictable and unpredictable collocation from the poem and discuss how these examples affect meaning and your response to the poem.

Writing ☞ Write a critical appreciation of 'Ode on Melancholy', commenting in detail on any aspects of language use and the meaning that this produces for you.

GLOSSARY

Sestet: six lines of verse that usually follow the first eight lines of a sonnet or the quatrain of an ode.

Alliteration: the repetition of the same initial consonant in words in close proximity to one another.

7 More about the language of poetry

Poetry is often talked about as the expression of emotion by the individual poet. However, we have stated that poetry can be perceived as a particular way of arranging language. Through its 'unexpectedness' and unusual collocation that arrangement often forces us to review our perception of what we see as 'reality'. In this section, we are again concentrating on the language of poetry, or **diction**, as it is often referred to.

7.1 The language of contemporary poetry

Alison Fell is a contemporary poet, who was born in Scotland in 1944. Here she writes about growing up, and the passing of time, in a Scottish border town.

Women in the Cold War

Outside, time and famous dates passed –
Korea Suez Cuba Algeria all cannoned by
casually as a slap on the back.
In the butcher's and the grocer's,
not a word of them. No, only talk of
the sun, snow, seasons;
stillbirths, new banns posted;
the harvest, the Gala,
the Foot and Mouth which closed farm roads,
the Compensation.
As for violence, we had our own –
a thousand cattle burned in pits
a labourer, demented, raped a child
fine swimmers drowned in the loch's depths.
And most Saturdays some girl's wedding

brought the women clattering
down the High Street – they'd bang
on doors along the way and put up the cry,
then hang back respectfully and squint
at the hired cars, the ceremonial clothes.
My mother, her mother's mother
were brides like these,
country brides teetering up
the gravel-chipped path to the Kirk,
shielding their new shoes from scrapes.
By the sandstone wall, photos were posed,
against a bleak swell or lowland hills;
the photos show puckered faces
and a wind which sweeps the stiff bouquets.
The dances came and went, and fashions;
my girlfriends and I – in tight skirts
(or tiered), beads which popped and hooped net petticoats –
crushed into cars and choked
on our own close scent, and smoke, and compliments.
But soon they sobered and they planned –
knitted cardigans all summer, by January
scanned the catalogues for cottons,
drab (for work), dressy (for holidays).
I saw them smooth
and full-blown dreaming of marriage
when I was still pockmarked with envy
and a thousand wants. I became crazy:
'I'll be an artist' I said
and bristled for the skirmish; quite slowly
their eyes scaled and their good sense
bunched against me.
'That's no' for the likes of us'.
Elizabeth, Elaine, Rhoda of the long legs,
all matrons, mothering, hurrying
their men to work at 7 a.m.
Now, hunched round prams,
what landmarks of content do they stake out
as the village circles?
As tractors streak the fields with lime
and all the old women, hushed,
move to the funeral to see the flowers.

Group discussion

- Here is a section of the poem re-written in prose form:

    The dances and fashions came and went; my girlfriends and I – in tight (or tiered) skirts, beads which popped and hooped net petticoats – crushed into cars and choked on our own close scent and smoke and compliments. But soon they sobered and they planned – knitted cardigans all summer, by January scanned the catalogues for cottons, drab (for work), dressy (for holidays) (lines 30–39).

    The word order has been changed slightly in this version, but the words are the same. How the language is patterned, however, has been altered. Discuss what those changes consist of and how meaning is altered, if at all, by these alterations.

- time and famous dates passed

    These words and their use in proximity to one another could be described as an example of familiar and predictable collocation. The word 'time' and, to a lesser extent, 'dates' are often used in a combination with 'passed'. From the poem, pick out other examples of the placing together of words that are familiar and predictable.

- Korea Suez Cuba Algeria all cannoned by

    The combination of these names which, in the poem, symbolise wars that have been fought, with the words 'cannoned by' is less predictable, however. The word 'cannoned' is used metaphorically and has *connotations* of war, weapons, speed and destruction. The unfamiliar collocation here compels us to reassess the meaning of words. Working in pairs, select other examples of unpredictable collocation from the poem. Discuss how these uses of language affect the meaning produced. Then as a group try to agree what is unexpected about some of the language use and how that might affect meaning.

- Say these lines aloud:

    No, only talk of
    the sun, snow, seasons;
    stillbirths, new banns posted.

    You will have heard the repetition of 's' sounds, particularly at the beginning of successive words. This is an example of the use of two poetic devices: ***alliteration*** and ***sibilance***. Alliteration is in the use of words that start with the same initial letter in close proximity to one another. Sibilance involves the repetition of 's' sounds, which, in the above lines, occurs not only with the 's' sounds at the beginning of words, but also in the middle and end of words: 'seasons', 'stillbirths', 'banns' and 'posted'.

    Discuss what effect this alliterative and sibilant use of language has on the meaning produced. Select other examples of alliteration and sibilance from the poem.

Writing ▶ Write a critical appreciation of the poem in three sections:

1 Description: describe what the content of the poem is as expressed in the language.

2 Analysis: discuss in detail the use of language and the view of a reality that is produced.

3 Personal response: give your own personal response to the poem. What do you respond to positively? Are there any aspects of the poem that you find clichéd or uninteresting? Does it remind you of any other poetic texts or types of poems?

GLOSSARY
___

Sibilance: the repetition of 's' or 'sh'
sounds in words close to one another.

7.2 A poem from the seventeenth century

The language, or diction, that poets use can be 'simple' and close to everyday speech (as in traditional ballads and the blues), or more elaborate and 'literary' (as in the Shakespeare sonnet and the Keats ode). In the rest of this section we will analyse poems from the seventeenth century through to the present day, concentrating on how aspects of language are used by the various poets to produce meaning. Below is a poem by the seventeenth-century English poet, Anne Bradstreet.

Before the birth of one of her children
All within this fading world hath end,
Adversity doth still our joys attend,
No ties so strong, no friends so dear and sweet,
But with death's parting blow is sure to meet.
The sentence past is most irrevocable,
A common thing, yet oh, inevitable.
How soon, my dear, death may my steps attend,
How soon't may be thy lot to lose thy friend,
We both are ignorant, yet love bids me
These farewell lines to recommend to thee,
That when that knot's untied that made us one,
I may seem thine, who in effect am none.
And if I see not half my days that's due,
What nature would, God grant to yours and you;
The many faults that well you know I have
Let be interred in my oblivious grave;
If any worth or virtue were in me,

Let that live freshly in thy memory
And when thou feel'st no grief, as I no harms,
Yet love thy dead, who long lay in thine arms.
And when thy loss shall be repaid with gains
Look to my little babes, my dear remains.
And if thy love thyself, or loved'st me,
These O protect from step-dame's injury.
And if chance to thine eyes shall bring this verse,
With some sad sighs honour my absent hearse;
And kiss this paper for thy love's dear sake,
Who with salt tears this last farewell did take.

Group discussion

- Working in pairs, summarise in not more than forty words what you consider to be the themes of the poem. Then compare your summary with those of the rest of the group and agree on a consensus summary.
- The poem is structured around the use of rhyming couplets. Discuss how this arrangement of language is used to reinforce meaning.
- How would you describe the diction: is it 'simple' or elaborate?
- Make a list of words from the poem that would not have been used by a poet of this century.
- Select examples of unusual combinations of words that force you, the reader, to take a fresh view of familiar things.
- The verse could be described as an example of **euphony**, the creation of pleasing mellifluous sound. There is a good deal of **assonance,** the repetition of similar vowel sounds:

  No ties so strong, no friends so dear and sweet,
  But with death's parting blow is sure to meet.

  The repetition of the long 'o' and 'e' vowels in the first line is continued in the second line with 'blow' and 'meet'. The assonance helps to give cohesion to the lines, adds a definite euphonic quality, but also underlines the tone and meaning of the poetry: this is a reflective, gentle expression of the poet's thoughts on her own coming death. Select any other examples of assonance from the poem.

Writing ▶

Write a critical appreciation of the poem, commenting particularly on the diction, and how language and form are used to produce meaning. Make a judgement about how much the poem communicates to you.

GLOSSARY

Euphony: the creation of pleasing sounds in poetry.

Assonance: the repetition of similar vowel sounds in words in close proximity, achieving an effect of euphony.

7.3 A poem from the eighteenth century

'Standard English' is not the only language source that can be employed by poets writing in English. Robert Burns was an eighteenth-century Scottish poet who used 'Scots' vernacular, a dialect of English, to write poetry that was sometimes lyrical, sometimes reflective and often told a story. Here is the opening to one of Burns' most famous poems. 'Tam O'Shanter'.

When chapman billies leave the street,
And drouthy neebours, neebours meet,
As market-days are wearing late,
An' folk begin to tak the gate;
While we sit bousing at the nappy,
An' gettin' fou and unco happy,
We think na on the long Scots miles,
The mosses, waters, slaps, and stiles,
That lie between us and our hame,
Whare sits our sulky, sullen dame,
Gathering her brows like gathering storm,
Nursing her wrath to keep it warm.

This truth fand honest Tam O'Shanter
As he frae Ayr ae night did canter,
(Auld Ayr, wham ne'er a town surpasses,
For honest men and bonnie lasses).
O Tam! had'st thou been sae wise,
As ta'en thy ain wife Kate's advice!
She told thee well thou was a skellum,
A blethering, blustering, drunken blellum;
That frae November till October,
Ae market-day thou wasna sober;

That ilka melder wi' the miller,
Thou sat as lang as thou had siller;
That ev'ry naig was ca'd a shoe on,
The smith and thee got roaring fou on;
That at the Lord's house, ev'n on Sunday,
Thou drank with Kirton Jean till Monday.
She prophesy'd that late or soon,
Thou would be found deep drown'd in Doon;
Or catched wi' warlocks in the mirk,
By Alloway's auld haunted kirk.
Ah, gentle dames! it gars me greet,
To think how mony counsels sweet,
How mony lengthen'd sage advices,
The husband frae the wife despises!

Group discussion

- Pick out the words that are examples of Scots vernacular. Discuss whether they cause a difficulty of understanding for you and whether their use in this context still conveys meaning, even though the words themselves might be unfamiliar.
- Burns was clearly drawing on 'everyday language' for his diction. What is the overall effect of using colloquial language in a poem such as this?
- How would you describe the tone of the extract?
- Are the last four lines of the extract meant to be taken literally, or is there an underlying irony to them?
- Burns uses ***onomatopoeia*** to echo the sense of the poetry. This figure of speech uses words to imitate sounds. For example, Tam's wife's opinion of him is couched in words that imitate the sounds of complaint she would utter about her husband:

    She tauld thee well thou was a skellum,

    A blethering, blustering, drunken blellum;

    Pick out any other examples of onomatopoeia from the extract.

Writing

Write a short narrative poem, telling a simple story and written in a vernacular with which you are familiar.

Write a piece giving your response to the Burns extract and making a judgement about whether meaning is communicated, despite any difficulties you may have with the diction.

GLOSSARY
_____

Onomatopoeia: a figure of speech in which the sounds of words signal the intended meaning.

7.4 A poem from the nineteenth century

William Blake (1757-1825) was a 'visionary' poet, who sought to change the attitudes of readers and society through his poetry. At times, his vision is 'dark' and this finds its expression through the diction he uses. In this poem, poetry is employed to make some kind of social comment.

London

I wander through each chartered street
    Near where the chartered Thames does flow,
A mark in every face I meet,
    Marks of weakness, marks of woe.

In every cry of every man,
    In every infant's cry of fear,
In every voice, in every ban,
    The mind-forged manacles I hear:

How the chimney-sweeper's cry
    Every blackening church appals,
And the hapless soldier's sigh
    Runs in blood down palace-walls.

But most, through midnight streets I hear
    How the youthful harlot's curse
Blasts the new-born infant's tear,
    And blights with plague the marriage-hearse.

*Wentworth Street,
Whitechapel by Gustave
Doré*

Group discussion

- The title of the poem is 'London', but from your reading of the text, what do you think the main subject matter is?
- Select examples of unusual collocation from the poem and comment on how these examples of language use affect meaning.
- How would you describe the tone of the poem?
- How is this tone reflected in the language and images of the poem?

Writing ☞

Write an appreciation of Blake's poem, discussing what you think the poem is about, what your response to it is and how Blake produces meaning through his powerful use of language and images.

7.5 Poetry as social comment

Shelley (1792–1822) was a contemporary of Blake's and is usually classed as one of the 'Romantic' poets along with Wordsworth, Coleridge, Keats and others. However, these poets did not always write about their own private feelings, a characteristic usually attributed to the Romantics; they often looked outwards at society, rather than inwards at themselves, and expressed radical sentiments about what they saw.

England in 1819

An old, mad, blind, despised, and dying king –
    Princes, the dregs of their dull race, who flow
Through public scorn, mud from a muddy spring, –
    Rulers who neither see, nor feel, nor know,
But leech-like to their fainting country cling,
    Till they drop, blind in blood, without a blow, –
A people starved and stabbed in the untilled field, –
    An army which liberticide and prey
Makes as a two-edged sword to all who wield, –
    Golden and sanguine laws which tempt and slay;
Religion Christless, Godless, a book sealed, –
    A Senate – Time's worst statute unrepealed, –
Are graves from which a glorious Phantom may
    Burst to illumine our tempestuous day.

Group discussion

- Working in pairs, summarise in not more than forty words what, according to your reading of the text, the theme(s) of the poem is.
- List any examples from the poem of what you consider to be poetic diction and, in addition, any words that a twentieth-century poet would not have used.
- List any examples of the use of metaphor and simile and comment how their use affects meaning.
- Discuss any unusual collocation used in the poem and comment on its effectiveness.
- The poem has a 'rhetorical' aspect. It seems to be 'making a speech'; it is certainly offering a discourse on the contemporary historical situation. How would you describe the kind of language this discourse is conducted in?
- Discuss whether or not the poet seems to end the poem on a hopeful note.
- The Romantic poets are conveniently associated with the expression of private emotions and are meant to be 'inward-looking'. Discuss whether this poem by Shelley is 'inward-looking' or not.

Writing ☛

Compare the Shelley with the previous poem by Blake. What similarities and differences are there between them in terms of subject matter and aspects of language use?

7.6 Is poetry about expressing emotion?

We have already raised the point about poetry being perceived as the expression of the emotions of an individual poet. If you, as a reader, accept that description of poetry, then you might seek to emphasise with the emotions expressed by the poet. However, if you perceive poetry as a particular way of arranging language, then your emphasis as a reader might be on analysing the meaning produced by the particular use of language that the poem embodies.

Emily Dickinson (1830–1886) was an American poet, who found fame only after her death when her poems were finally published. In the poem opposite, the subject matter is the emotional issue of the death of a near relative.

The last Night that She lived
It was a Common Night
Except the Dying – this to Us
Made Nature different

We noticed smallest things –
Things overlooked before
By this great light upon our Minds
Italicized – as 'twere.

As We went out and in
Between Her final Room
And Rooms where Those to be alive
Tomorrow were, a Blame

That Others could exist
While She must finish quite
A Jealousy for Her arose
So nearly infinite –

We waited while she passed –
It was a narrow time –
Too jostled were our souls to speak
At length the notice came.

She mentioned and forgot –
Then lightly as a Reed
Bent to the Water, struggled scarce –
Consented, and was dead –

And We – We placed the Hair –
And drew the Head erect
And then an awful leisure was
Belief to regulate –

Group discussion

- The manner in which the poem is set down on the page, the word order, the fragmented flow of meaning – all these aspects of the poem are perhaps rather unusual. In pairs, discuss these aspects of the poem. Then as a group discuss what effect these elements have on the overall meaning.
- Discuss the language used by the poet. Is it close to everyday speech or full of poetic diction? Are there examples of unusual collocation or are words placed together in a conventional manner? Overall, how would you categorise the kind of language used?
- Select any examples of simile and metaphor from the poem and comment on how the use of these figures of speech affects meaning.
- Discuss whether this poem is an example of poetry as the expression of emotion. What meaning is produced for you?

Writing ☞

Analyse the subject matter of the poem and comment on how Emily Dickinson communicates ideas and feelings through her diction and the form of the poem.

7.7 Dramatising in verse

Thomas Hardy (1840–1928), in addition to being a prolific novelist, wrote eight volumes of poetry, published between the years 1898 and 1928. He aimed to use a poetic diction that was not cut off from everyday speech. Very often, too, he 'dramatised' incidents in his poems.

On the departure platform

We kissed at the barrier; and passing through
She left me, and moment by moment got
Smaller and smaller, until to my view
    She was but a spot;

A wee white spot of muslin fluff
That down the diminishing platform bore
Through hustling crowds of gentle and rough
    To the carriage door.

Under the lamplight's fitful glowers,
Behind dark groups from far and near,
Whose interests were apart from ours
    She would disappear,

Then show again, till I ceased to see
That flexible form, that nebulous white;
And she who was more than life to me
      Had vanished quite . . .

We have penned new plans since that fair fond day,
And in season she will appear again –
Perhaps in the same soft white array –
      But never as then!

And why, young man, must eternally fly
A joy you'll repeat, if you love her well?
O friend, nought happens twice thus; why,
      I cannot tell!

Group discussion
- Summarise in not more than thirty words the subject matter of the poem. Then compare your summary with those of the rest of the group.
- Consider the diction of the poem. Pick out any striking use of images (figurative use of language or literal, concrete images) and comment generally on the poet's use of language.
- The sound of the verse is an important part of the effect of this poem. What examples of alliteration and assonance are there in the poem and how do they affect meaning and tone?

Writing ▶ Compare the Hardy poem with the Emily Dickinson poem. What differences and similarities are there between them in theme, diction, tone and form? Say which of the two means more to you, stating reasons for your choice.

7.8 Poetry and history

W.B. Yeats is credited by many as one of the major poets writing in the English language in the twentieth century. In the poem on page 166, he expresses his passionate feelings about Irish nationalism, taking as his focus the 1916 Rebellion against the British.

Easter 1916

I have met them at close of day
Coming with vivid faces
From counter or desk amid grey
Eighteenth-century houses.
I have passed with nod of the head
Or polite, meaningless words,
Or have lingered awhile and said
Polite meaningless words,
And thought before I had done
Of a mocking tale or a gibe
To please a companion
Around the fire at the club,
Being certain that they and I
But lived where motley is worn:
All changed, changed utterly:
A terrible beauty is born.

That woman's days were spent
In ignorant good-will,
Her nights in argument
Until her voice grew shrill.
What voice more sweet than hers
When, young and beautiful,
She rode to harriers?
This man had kept a school
And rode our wingèd horse;
This other his helper and friend
Was coming into his force;
He might have won fame in the end,
So sensitive his nature seemed,
So daring and sweet his thought.
This other man I had dreamed
A drunken, vainglorious lout.
He had done most bitter wrong
To some who are near my heart,
Yet I number him in the song;
He, too, has resigned his part
In the casual comedy;
He, too, has been changed in his turn,
Transformed utterly:
A terrible beauty is born.

Hearts with one purpose alone
Through summer and winter seem
Enchanted to a stone
To trouble the living stream.
The horse that comes from the road,
The rider, the birds that range
From cloud to tumbling cloud,
Minute by minute they change;
A shadow of cloud on the stream
Changes minute by minute;
A horse-hoof slides on the brim,
And a horse plashes within it;
The long-legged moor-hens dive,
And hens to moor-cocks call;
Minute by minute they live:
The stone's in the midst of all.

Too long a sacrifice
Can make a stone of the heart.
O when may it suffice?
That is Heaven's part, our part
To murmur name upon name,
As a mother names her child
When sleep at last has come
On limbs that had run wild.
What is it but nightfall?
No, no, not night but death;
Was it needless death after all?
For England may keep faith
For all that is done and said.
We know their dream; enough
To know they dreamed and are dead;
And what if excess of love
Bewildered them till they died?
I write it out in a verse –
MacDonagh and MacBride
And Connolly and Pearse
Now and in time to be,
Wherever green is worn,
Are changed, changed utterly:
A terrible beauty is born.

Group discussion
- In pairs, read through the first section of the poem again. Discuss what this section means to you and then share your thoughts with the rest of the group.
- This poem was created in the midst of particular historical circumstances (the 1916 Easter Rebellion in Ireland) and the writer has a particular standpoint on these events. Select examples of language use that seems to express his feelings and thoughts about the political situation.
- Which line becomes a kind of refrain in the poem and what meaning is created by this repetition?
- *Imagery* is language use that represents objects, thoughts, feelings, ideas and experience. Images can be literal and concrete without figurative language, although these images may be used 'symbolically'. Images can also be created through figurative language. Images can be visual, or appeal to the senses of touch, smell, hearing or taste. Make a list of imagery from the poem and discuss whether each image is a literal or concrete image or is created through figurative language (metaphor or simile, for example). Discuss how imagery is an important part of the subject matter of the poem.

Writing ▶
Write a critical appreciation of the poem by Yeats, discussing the subject matter as expressed through diction and making a value judgement about what it means to you as a reader.

GLOSSARY

Imagery: a general term to describe the use of language to represent things, feelings and all types of sensory experience. Images may be literal or figurative.

7.9   First World War poetry

The horror of the trenches of World War I (1914–18) was recorded by many poets writing in English who were themselves participants in the war. Before the First World War, poetry *generally* employed a diction that was largely divorced from everyday language. The upheaval of the war, and its horror, seemed to influence poets to use the language of the everyday world, however stylised the manner of its use, rather than a more rarefied poetic diction.

As was stated in section 7.7 poets often 'dramatise' incidents, that is, they focus on a particular situation and describe what is happening and have 'characters' speak in their own voices. In the poem that follows, Wilfred Owen (1893–1918), a poet who died in the trenches of World War I, writes a 'monologue' for a particular voice.

A terre

(Being the philosophy of many soldiers)

Sit on the bed. I'm blind, and three parts shell.
Be careful; can't shake hands now; never shall.
Both arms have mutinied against me – brutes.
My fingers fidget like ten idle brats.

I tried to peg out soldierly – no use!
One dies of war like any old disease.
This bandage feels like pennies on my eyes.
I have my medals – Discs to make my eyes close.
My glorious ribbons? Ripped from my own back
In scarlet shreds. (That's for your poetry book.)

A short life and a merry one, my buck!
We used to say we'd hate to live dead-old, –
Yet now . . . I'd willingly be puffy, bald,
And patriotic. Buffers catch from boys
At least the jokes hurled at them. I suppose
Little I'd ever teach a son, but hitting,
Shooting, war, hunting, all the arts of hurting.
Well, that's what I learnt, – that, and making money.

Your fifty years ahead seem none too many?
Tell me how long I've got? God! For one year
To help myself to nothing more than air!
One Spring! Is one too good to spare, too long?
Spring air would work its own way to my lung,
And grow me legs as quick as lilac-shoots.
My servant's lamed, but listen how he shouts!
When I'm lugged out, he'll still be good for that.
Here in this mummy-case, you know, I've thought
How well I might have swept his floors for ever.
I'd ask no nights off when the bustle's over,
Enjoying so the dirt. Who's prejudiced
Against a grimed hand when his own's quite dust,
Less live than specks that in the sun-shafts turn,
Less warm than dust that mixes with arms' tan?
I'd love to be a sweep, now, black as Town,
Yes, or a muckman. Must I be his load?

O Life, Life, let me breathe – a dug-out rat!
Not worse than ours the existences rats lead –
Nosing along at night down some safe rut,
They find a shell-proof home before they rot.
Dead men may envy living mites in cheese,
Or good germs even. Microbes have their joys,
And subdivide, and never come to death.
Certainly flowers have the easiest time on earth.
'I shall be one with nature, herb, and stone',
Shelley would tell me. Shelley would be stunned:
The dullest Tommy hugs that fancy now.
'Pushing up daisies' is their creed, you know.
To grain, then, go my fat, to buds my sap,
For all the usefulness there is in soap.
D'you think the Boche will ever stew man-soup?
Some day, no doubt, if . . .

                Friend, be very sure
I shall be better off with plants that share
More peaceably the meadow and the shower.
Soft rains will touch me, – as they could touch once,
And nothing but the sun shall make me ware.
Your guns may crash around me. I'll not hear;
Or, if I wince, I shall not know I wince.
Don't take my soul's poor comfort for your jest.
Soldiers may grow a soul when turned to fronds,
But here the thing's best left at home with friends.
My soul's a little grief, grappling your chest,
To climb your throat on sobs; easily chased
On other sighs and wiped by fresher winds.

Carry my crying spirit till it's weaned
To do without what blood remained these wounds.

Group discussion
- In not more than eighty words, summarise what the poem 'says' to you.
- Identify the 'voice' of the poem.
- How would you describe the tone and the language of the poem?
- List any examples from the poem of what you would describe as poetic diction.
- Discuss how the poet uses rhyme in the poem and how this use affects meaning.

- Make a list of metaphors and similes used in the poem and discuss how their use creates meaning.
- Are there any examples of unexpected collocation in the poem?

Writing ☞ Write a critical appreciation of *'A terre'*, analysing the use of the dramatic monologue form, what ideas and feelings it expresses and the diction that is used.

7.10 Poetry and the communication of personal experience

We have already raised the issue of whether poetry is about the expression of emotion. In the sections of this book that deal with prose, the issue of how important it is to know about the author of a piece of writing and to try to gauge his or her intentions is discussed. The same 'authorship' issue arises with poetry.

Sylvia Plath (1932–63) was born in America, but published her poetry and prose in Britain. Her poems are often about extremes of suffering, but her imagery, stark and disturbing, is rooted in the day-to-day world. The poem may be autobiographical in its origins, but does this information matter to us as readers, or does any meaning the poem has for us reside totally in the text and the language that is used?

Daddy

You do not do, you do not do
Any more, black shoe
In which I have lived like a foot
For thirty years, poor and white,
Barely daring to breathe or Achoo.

Daddy, I have had to kill you,
You died before I had time –
Marble-heavy, a bag full of God,
Ghastly statue with one grey toe
Big as a Frisco seal

And a head in the freakish Atlantic
Where it pours bean green over blue
In the waters off beautiful Nauset.
I used to pray to recover you.
Ach, du.
In the German tongue, in the Polish town
Scraped flat by the roller
Of wars, wars, wars.
But the name of the town is common.
My Polack friend
Says there are a dozen or two.
So I could never tell where you
Put your foot, your root,
I never could talk to you.
The tongue stuck in my jaw.

It stuck in a barb wire snare.
Ich, ich, ich, ich,
I could hardly speak.
I thought every German was you.
And the language obscene

An engine, an engine
Chuffing me off like a Jew.
A jew to Dachau, Auschwitz, Belsen.
I began to talk like a Jew.
I think I may well be a Jew.

The snows of the Tyrol, the clear beer of Vienna
Are not very pure or true.
With my gypsy ancestress and my weird luck
And my Taroc pack and my Taroc pack
I may be a bit of a Jew.

I have always been scared of you.
With your Luftwaffe, your gobbledygoo.
And your neat moustache
And your Aryan eye, bright blue.
Panzer-man, panzer-man, O You –

Not God but a swastika
So black no sky could squeak through.
Every woman adores a Fascist,
The boot in the face, the brute
Brute heart of a brute like you.

You stand at the blackboard, daddy,
In the picture I have of you,
A cleft in your chin instead of your foot
But no less a devil for that, no not
Any less the black man who
Bit my pretty red heart in two.
I was ten when they buried you.
At twenty I tried to die
And get back, back, back to you.
I thought even the bones would do.

But they pulled me out of the sack,
And they stuck me together with glue.
And then I knew what to do.
I make a model of you,
A man in black with a Meinkampf look

And a love of the rack and the screw.
And I said, I do, I do.
So, daddy, I'm finally through.
The black telephone's off at the root,
The voices just can't worm through.

If I've killed one man, I've killed two –
The vampire who said he was you
And drank my blood for a year,
Seven years if you want to know.
Daddy, you can lie back now.

There's a stake in your fat black heart
And the villagers never liked you.
They are dancing and stamping on you.
They always knew it was you.
Daddy, daddy, you bastard, I'm through.

Group discussion

- Analyse the poem by verse and make brief notes on what it means to you. Then share your thoughts with the rest of the group.
- How would you describe the tone of the poem?
- What images does the poet use to describe her father?
- Words have connotations (see section 1.2). Make a list of words from the poem that have special connotations for you.
- Make a list of examples of unusual collocation and say how this 'unexpected' grouping of language affects meaning.

Writing ☛

Analyse the subject matter of the poem as expressed through the language. Discuss the 'autobiographical' issue arising from the text: does it matter to you as a reader whether Plath is writing about her own father? Would your reading of the text be altered in any way if you knew the poem was autobiographical?

7.11 Across cultures

All written texts inevitably reflect the cultural context from which they emerge. Poetry is not created in a cultural vacuum. Although in the end, any meaning the text has exists in the language used, that language reflects the society and culture for which the text was initially produced.

If we as readers do not share a culture with a writer, we have to attempt to interpret meaning through the signs that the text represents and cross the 'cultural gap'.

On page 174 is a poem by Flavien Ranaimo, a writer from Madagascar.

Song of a young girl

Oaf
the young man who lives down there
beside the threshing floor for rice;
like two banana-roots
on either side the village ditch,
we gaze on each other,
we are lovers,
but he won't marry me.
Jealous
his mistress I saw two days since at the wash
coming down the path against the wind.
She was proud;
was it because she wore a lamba thick
and studded with coral
or because they are newly bedded?
However it isn't the storm
that will flatten the delicate reed,
nor the great sudden shower
at the passage of a cloud
that will startle out of his wits
the blue bull.
I am amazed;
the big sterile rock
survived the rain of the flood
and it's the fire that crackles
the bad grains of maize.
Such this famous smoker
who took tobacco
when there was no more hemp to burn.
A foot of hemp?
– Sprung in Andringitra,
spent in Ankaratra,
no more than cinders to us.
False flattery
stimulates love a little
but the blade has two edges;
why change what is natural?
– If I have made you sad
look at yourself in the water of repentance,
you will decipher there a word I have left.
Good-bye, whirling puzzle,
I give you my blessing:
wrestle with the crocodile,
here are your victuals and three water-lily flowers
for the way is long.

Group discussion

- Working in pairs, summarise the subject matter of the poem in not more than fifty words. Then compare your summary with those produced by the rest of the group.
- Make a list of references from the poem that seem to you to be specific to the African cultural background from which this poem emerged.
- Discuss how the poem diverges from a 'straight' narrative line and appears 'fragmented'. How does this affect meaning?
- Make a list of unusual collocations from the poem and discuss whether this causes any difficulties of interpretation for you.
- Working in pairs, make a list of images that the poet creates through language. As a group, discuss whether these images 'symbolise' anything in particular for you.

Writing ☛

Write a poem of your own with the title of either 'Song of a young girl' or 'Song of a young boy'. You may choose to imitate the form and language use of the poem above, if you like. After writing your poem, write a brief commentary on how you completed this task.

7.12 Vernacular poems

In unit 4 of this book, we focus on the use of vernacular in narrative fiction. Poetry, too, has a 'vernacular' tradition arising from its very roots in oral performance and the ballads. The two poems below cry out to be spoken aloud. The first, 'Rites' by Edward Kamau Brathwaite, is an extract from a longer work and is in West Indian vernacular; the second, 'Owdham footbo' by Ammon Wrigley, is in Lancashire dialect.

Look wha' happen las' week at de O-
val!

At de Oval?
Wha' happen las' week at de Oval?

You mean to say that you come
in here wid dat lime-skin cone

that you callin' a hat
pun your head, an' them slip slop shoe strap

on to you foot like a touris';
you sprawl you ass

all over my chair widdout ask-
in' me please leave nor licence,

wastin' muh time when you know very well that
    uh cahn fine
enough to finish these zoot suits

'fore Christmas; an' on top
o' all this, you could wine up de nerve to stop

me cool cool cool in de middle
o' all me needle

an' t'read; make me prick me hand im me haste;
an' tell me broad an' bole to me face

THAT YOU DOAN REALLY KNOW WHA'
    HAPPEN
At Kensington Oval?

We was *only* playin' de MCC, man;
M—C—C
who come all de way out from Inglan.

We was battin', you see;
score wasn't too bad; one
hurren an' ninety-

seven fuh three.
The openers out. Tae Worrell out,
Everton Weekes jus' glide two fuh fifty

an' jack, is de GIANT to come!
Feller name Wardle
was bowlin'; tossin' it up

sweet sweet slow-medium syrup.
Firs' ball . . .
'N . . .o . . .o . . .'

back down de wicket to Wardle.
Secon' ball . . .
'N . . .o . . .o . . .'

Back down de wicket to Wardle.
Third ball comin' up
an' we know wha' goin' happen to syrup:

Clyde back pun he back
foot an' *prax!*
is through extra cover an' four red runs all de
    way.

'You see dat shot?' The people was shoutin';
'Jesus Chrise, Man, wunna see dat shot?'
All over de groun' fellers shakin' hands wid each
    other

as if was *they* wheelin' de willow
as if was *them* had the power;
one man run out pun de field wid a red fowl cock

goin' quawk quawk quawk in 'e han';
would'a give it to Clyde right then an' right
    there
if a police hadn't stop 'e!

An' in front o' where I was sittin',
one ball-headed sceptic snatch hat off he head
as if he did crazy

Spectators at a West Indies v Australia test match, Kensington Oval, Barbados

Owdham footbo'

It's run an' jump an' hop an' skip,
An' sheawt hooray, an' hip, hip, hip,
It's singin' songs an' eytin tripe,
An' suppin' pints at single swipe,
An' brass for th' wife to buy a hat,
An' th' childer brass for this an' that,
An' beauncin' gaily up an' deawn,
Yo' connut find a merrier teawn,
When Owdham's won.

Aw lost mi brass, awm crabbed an' croat,
Aw lifted th' cat eawt wi' mi boot,
Awr ne'er as mad i' o mi life,
Cleautin' th' kids an' cursin' th' wife,
Awm sure mi brains han left mi yed,
Ther's nowt to do but goh toh bed,
At six o'clock o' th' Setturdy neet,
They're o i' bed i' eawr street,
When Owdham's lost.

Group discussion

- Working in pairs, read 'Rites' aloud. Make a list of words that cause you some difficulty with interpretation and discuss whether the surrounding context helps you to interpret the language despite, perhaps, its unfamiliarity. Then compare your list of words with the rest of the group and discuss what the poem means to you.
- Carry out a similar task with the second poem. Discuss any difficulties the vernacular sets you and whether the language communicates meaning, even though perhaps it is unfamiliar.
- Discuss what the poems have in common.
- As a group, discuss whether the use of the vernacular in these two poems adds to their effectiveness. Would they have lost something had they been written in standard English?

Writing ☛

Write a poem in a vernacular with which you are familiar celebrating a sporting victory or some other achievement. Then write a commentary on how to set about this task, commenting particularly on your use of the vernacular language you have chosen.

8 Who writes poetry?

Traditionally, a poem has been perceived as the expression of an individual poet's vision, emotions or thoughts. Just as with fiction or other prose writings, the reader's 'job' seemingly has been to discover the meaning inserted into the poetic text by the poet.

Recent criticism has challenged that point of view. Not only are the poet's intentions not of any particular importance, but the poet himself or herself is also relegated to a position of comparatively minor importance: it is the poetic text itself that is the site of meaning, although that text has to be interpreted in its historical context and in relation to other poetic texts that are similar to it (intertextuality). The term ***intentional fallacy*** is used to describe the error of analysing a work of literature by trying to deduce what the writer's intentions were and whether or not s/he has fulfilled those intentions.

But what 'voice' do we hear in poetry, then, if it is not the individual poet's? Do we discard the concept of the importance of the individual 'genius' who has created a poem and substitute the idea of the supremacy of the text as the only source of meaning? Do we lose anything by giving up identifying with the 'voice' of the author?

Clearly, many readers of poetry still 'identify' with the notion of the individual poet and with his or her personality and 'point of view' as expressed in the verse. The number of literary biographies that are published is testimony to the fact that the reading public have an enduring interest in the lives and 'personas' of poets and other writers. It is difficult to discard the idea of individual authorship in favour of almost anonymously-written poetry texts. The 'death' of the individual poet has perhaps been reported rather prematurely.

8.1 Satirical poetry

Satirical poetry employs language to ridicule and attack society's hypocrisies and injustice. Since the era of classical civilisation, poets have used satire to comment on the social ills they see around them.

Wole Soyinka is a contemporary Nigerian poet and writer who spent some time studying at an English university and working in the theatre before returning to Nigeria in the early 1960s.

Telephone conversation

The price seemed reasonable, location
Indifferent. The landlady swore she lived
Off premises. Nothing remained
But self-confession. 'Madam,' I warned,
'I hate a wasted journey – I am African.'
Silence. Silenced transmission of
Pressurised good-breeding. Voice, when it came,
Lipstick coated, long gold-rolled
Cigarette-holder pipped. Caught I was, foully.
'HOW DARK?' . . . I had not misheard. . . . 'ARE YOU LIGHT
OR VERY DARK?' Button B. Button A. Stench
Of rancid breath of public hide-and-speak.
Red booth. Red pillar-box. Red double-tiered
Omnibus squelching tar. It *was* real! Shamed
By ill-mannered silence, surrender
Pushed dumbfoundment to beg simplification.
Considerate she was, varying the emphasis –
'ARE YOU DARK? OR VERY LIGHT?' Revelation came.
'You mean – like plain or milk chocolate?'
Her assent was clinical, crushing in its light
Impersonality. Rapidly, wave-length adjusted,
I chose. 'West African sepia' – and as afterthought,
'Down in my passport.' Silence for spectroscopic
Flight of fancy, till truthfulness clanged her accent
Hard on the mouthpiece. 'WHAT'S THAT?' conceding
'DON'T KNOW WHAT THAT IS.' 'Like brunette.'

'THAT'S DARK, ISN'T IT?' 'Not altogether.
Facially, I am brunette, but madam, you should see
The rest of me. Palm of my hand, soles of my feet
Are a peroxide blonde. Friction, caused –
Foolishly madam – by sitting down, has turned
My bottom raven black – One moment Madam!' – sensing
Her receiver rearing on the thunderclap
About my ears – Madam,' I pleaded, 'wouldn't you rather
See for yourself?'

- Working in pairs, summarise in not more than forty words the subject matter of the poem.
- Select any examples from the poem of unexpected collocation. Comment on how these examples affect meaning.
- Discuss what use is made of the variation of typography and whether this affects meaning at all.
- Discuss how sentence structure is used in the poem.
- This section is headed 'satirical poetry'. In your judgement, should this poem have been included under this heading? Give your reasons.
- Discuss the overall tone of the poem as expressed in the language.
- Here is a section of the poem written as prose:

  Her assent was clinical, crushing in its light impersonality. Rapidly, wave-length adjusted, I chose 'West African sepia' – and as after-thought – 'down in my passport'. Silence for spectroscopic flight of fancy, till truthfulness clanged her accent hard on the mouthpiece.

  Working in pairs, compare this rearranged section with the original. How is it different? Does this alteration in how the language is arranged affect meaning? Then as a group share your thoughts about this.
- As a group, discuss whether the brief autobiographical information about the poet helps you to interpret the poem?

Writing

Write a poem consisting of a conversation between two people. The tone has to be satirical and the subject matter a contemporary social issue.

After completing the poem, write a commentary on the writing process, commenting particularly on what you did to make the poem 'satirical'.

8.2   Poetry in a historical context

We cannot hope to 'understand' a poem or any text written in a different era in exactly the same way as people who were alive at the time. Our perspective of the text will inevitably be different.

We have discussed whether it is in the written text, the poem, that any meaning it has is located, rather than in the 'mind' of the individual poet. But any one text is similar to other texts and must also be seen against the historical context from which it emerged. A poem written in 1815 cannot be viewed as essentially the same as one produced in 1998. We have to interpret the poetry of the past in its historical context, but from our contemporary perspective.

To illustrate this point, read this canto from a long poem by the famous poet, Lord Byron (1788-1824). (A *canto* is a chapter or sub-division of a long narrative poem or epic.) *Childe Harold's Pilgrimage* was written in the years immediately following the historical event the canto describes, the Battle of Waterloo in 1815, when the French army under Napoleon was defeated by the British.

The eve of Waterloo

There was a sound of revelry by night,
And Belgium's capital had gather'd then
Her Beauty and her Chivalry, and bright
The lamps shone o'er fair women and brave men;
A thousand hearts beat happily; and when
Music arose with its voluptuous swell,
Soft eyes look'd love to eyes which spake again,
And all went merry as a marriage bell;
But hush! hark! a deep sound strikes like a rising knell!

Did ye not hear it?—No; 'twas but the wind,
Or the car rattling o'er the stony street;
On with the dance! let joy be unconfined;
No sleep till morn, when Youth and Pleasure meet
To chase the glowing Hours with flying feet—
But hark!—that heavy sound breaks in once more,
As if the clouds its echo would repeat;
And nearer, clearer, deadlier than before!
Arm! Arm! it is—it is—the cannon's opening roar!

Within a window'd niche of that high hall
Sate Brunswick's fated chieftain; he did hear
That sound the first amidst the festival,
And caught its tone with Death's prophetic ear;
And when they smiled because he deem'd it near,
His heart more truly knew that peal so well
Which stretch'd his father on a bloody bier,
And roused the vengeance blood alone could quell;
He rushed into the field, and, foremost fighting, fell.

Ah! then and there was hurrying to and fro,
And gathering tears, and tremblings of distress,
And cheeks all pale, which but an hour ago
Blush'd at the praise of their own loveliness;
And there were sudden partings, such as press

The life from out young hearts, and choking sighs
Which ne'er might be repeated; who could guess
If ever more should meet those mutual eyes,
Since upon night so sweet such awful morn could rise!

And there was mounting in hot haste: the steed,
The mustering squadron, and the clattering car,
Went pouring forward with impetuous speed,
And swiftly forming in the ranks of war;
And the deep thunder peal on peal afar;
And near, the beat of the alarming drum
Roused up the soldier ere the morning star;
While throng'd the citizens with terror dumb,
Or whispering, with white lips—The foe! They come! they come!'

And wild and high the 'Cameron's gathering' rose!
The war-note of Lochiel, which Albyn's hills
Have heard, and heard, too, have her Saxon foes:—
How in the noon of night that pibroch thrills,
Savage and shrill! But with the breath which fills
Their mountain-pipe, so fill the mountaineers
With the fierce native daring which instils
The stirring memory of a thousand years,
And Evan's, Donald's fame rings in each clansman's ears!

And Ardennes waves above them her green leaves,
Dewy with nature's tear-drops, as they pass,
Grieving, if aught inanimate e'er grieves,
Over the unreturning brave,—alas!
Ere evening to be trodden like the grass
Which now beneath them, but above shall grow
In its next verdure, when this fiery mass
Of living valour, rolling on the foe
And burning with high hope, shall moulder cold and low.

Last noon beheld them full of lusty life,
Last eve in Beauty's circle proudly gay,
The midnight brought the signal-sound of strife,
The morn the marshalling in arms,—the day
Battle's magnificently-stern array!
The thunder-clouds close o'er it, which when rent
The earth is cover'd thick with other clay,
Which her own clay shall cover, heap'd and pent,
Rider and horse,—friend, foe,—in one red burial blent!

- Each stanza follows the same rhyming scheme. Working in pairs, look at the first stanza and establish what its rhyming scheme is and then confirm that it is repeated in all the rest of the stanzas.
- As a group, discuss what effect on meaning the use of this particular rhyming scheme has.
- Working in pairs, make a list of examples of poetic diction from the poem. Then compare the list you have compiled with those of the rest of the group.
- Again working in pairs, make a list of words from the poem that would probably not be used by someone writing poetry today.
- Read through the first stanza again. Analyse how language is used to suggest the excitement of the ball. How is a contrast to that excitement created in the last line of the stanza?
- Examine how the rhythm of the language, including the use of caesura, is used in the second stanza to communicate the idea of the imminent battle breaking in on the enjoyment of the dance.
- Discuss how alliteration is used in the third and seventh stanzas and how its use affects meaning.
- Working in pairs, summarise in not more than eighty words the subject matter of the last five stanzas of the poem. Compare your summary with those of the rest of the group.
- *Childe Harold,* or this canto from it, was first published in 1818, only a few years after the battle of Waterloo. Discuss how our reading of the poem is likely to be very different from the people of that era.

Writing ▶

Write a critical appreciation of 'The eve of Waterloo', including a detailed analysis of the subject matter as expressed through its diction, a discussion of what the poem means to you and a judgement about its value to us now, reading it almost two hundred years after it was written.

8.3 Poetry and contemporary events

'The eve of Waterloo' dealt with a historical event distant in time, although it was written by an individual who was alive at the time. However, it is not only the important historical event that poetry can record in verse, but other 'smaller' events that nevertheless symbolise something significant for many people.

In the poem on page 185, Paul Durcan takes the 1979 death of Sid Vicious, lead singer with the rock group the Sex Pistols, as the starting point for a poem that may seem to you to diverge into other subject matter.

The death by heroin of Sid Vicious

There – but for the clutch of luck – go I.

At daybreak – in the arctic fog of a February
    daybreak   –
Shoulderlength helmets in the watchtowers of the
    concentration camp
Caught me out in the intersecting arcs of the
    swirling searchlights:

There were at least a zillion of us caught out there
– Like ladybirds under a boulder –
But under the microscope each of us was unique,

Unique and we broke for cover, crazily breasting
The barbed wire and some of us made it
To the forest edge, but many of us did not

Make it, although their unborn children did –
Such as you whom the camp commandant branded
Sid Vicious of the Sex Pistols. Jesus, break his fall:

There – but for the clutch of luck – go we all.

Group discussion

- As a group, discuss the meaning produced for you by the first line of the poem. What is the effect of isolating this first line from the rest of the poem?
- Working in pairs, summarise in not more than thirty words what meaning the poem has for you. Then compare your summary with those of the rest of the group.
- Make a list of examples of collocation that strike you as 'unexpected'. Compare your list with those produced by the rest of the group and discuss what exactly makes the placing together of the words you have chosen 'unexpected'.
- The last line of the poem echoes the first line. What effect on meaning does this have?

Writing ☞

Write a poem about a 'star' or stars of the entertainment industry: a rock star, a film actor, a pop group, for example. The person(s) can be living or dead. Try to express in the language you use reasons why you find the subject(s) interesting or significant in some way. Then, write a commentary on how you set about writing the poem and any difficulties you had.

☞ Write a critical appreciation of 'The death by heroin of Sid Vicious', including a comparison with 'The eve of Waterloo'.

8.4 You talking to me?

If the poet is the author of a poem, is it his or her 'voice' we detect through the language? Many poems are written in the first person: there is an 'I' of the poem with whom we, as readers, are implicitly invited to identify (see, for example, Wole Soyinka's poem 'Telephone conversation'). Often when the poem is couched in the first person, the tone established through language is intimate and colloquial. It is as if the poet, or the voice of the poem at least, is talking directly to the reader. This poem is by Sylvia Kantaris.

Lost property

I'm on this train, you see, somewhere abroad,
heading north or south perhaps. Outside it's dark.
You panic when you've lost all your effects
including passport and visas, and forget
what your name was. I study my reflection
in the glass. Is it mine or someone else's
or a ghost? And then this man in uniform
demands some document to prove that I exist?
No use protesting when it's obvious I don't
since the evidence has vanished with my face.
When he looks, he can only see himself
and says who are you kidding when I point it out.

What happens next? I have forgotten everything
except a grey, furled umbrella. Would *that* pass?
'Lost Property' the stickers indicated
in a lot of languages I couldn't read.
You don't ask questions when you're dispossessed.
So here I am, then, clinging on like death
to somebody's umbrella, but I lose my grasp.
Trains don't normally have floorboards, I thought,
as the sad old thing went down between two planks.
Funny how you kid yourself you'll 'suddenly wake up'
travelling light in a fluorescent anorak,
crossing every border on the map without a permit.

- How is language used in the first line of the poem to establish a personal tone between the 'I' of the poem and you, the reader?
- Establish where in the first stanza the first person gives way to second person. Discuss how this affects meaning.
- Summarise in not more than forty words the subject matter of the poem. Then compare your summary with those of the rest of the group.
- How formal or informal would you say the language use is? Are there any examples of language that would not normally be used in everyday speech?
- Here are a few lines from the poem rewritten as prose:

   What happens next? I have forgotten everything except a grey furled umbrella. Would that pass? 'Lost Property' the stickers indicated in a lot of languages I couldn't read. You don't ask questions when you're dispossessed.

   Compare the original lines with this prose version. What differences are there? Do these differences have any effect on meaning?
- Who is doing the 'addressing' in this poem? Who is 'being addressed'?

Writing ☞

Write a poem using an 'I' as the voice and employing colloquial, everyday language. After you have written your poem, write a commentary on how you completed the task, discussing in particular your use of the first person and everyday language.

8.5   The expression of emotion?

The 'emotional' connotations of the language of poetry are very frequently stressed when people talk about poetry. 'Poetry as a whole is somehow perceived as the expression of emotion in 'heightened language'.

Poetry is a much more 'condensed' way of arranging language than most prose is. The comparative brevity of most poems means that the language a poet chooses to use seems weighty with 'significance'. Very often that 'significance' is interpreted as deep feelings.

Yet most language use has some emotional overtones and connotations. In addition, poetry is 'not all about emotion'. It is in the language of a poem that the subject matter is born and the language may merge emotions with ideas.

John Donne (1572–1631) is often classed as one of the 'metaphysical poets' who explored in verse the nature of being, and who often merged ideas with emotions in far-fetched 'conceits' (an elaborate figure of speech which is intended to delight with its witty unexpectedness). Here is one of his poems about love.

The canonization

For Godsake hold your tongue, and let me love,
    Or chide my praise, or my gout,
My five gray haires, or ruin'd fortune flout,
    With wealth your state, your minde with Arts improve,
        Take you a course, get you a place,
        Observe his honour, or his grace,
Or the King's reall, or his stamped face
    Contemplate, what you will, approve
    So you will let me love.

Alas, alas, who's injur'd by my love?
    What merchants ships have my sighs drown'd?
Who saies my teares have overflow'd his ground?
    When did my colds a forward spring remove?
        When did the heats which my veines fill
        Adde one more to the plaguie Bill?
Soldiers finde warres, and Lawyers finde out still
    Litigious men, which quarrels move,
    Though she and I do love.

Call us what you will, wee are made such by love;
    Call her one, mee another flye,
We are Tapers too, and at our owne cost die,
    And wee in us finde the 'Eagle and the dove,
        The Phœnix ridle hath more wit
        By us, we two being one, are it.
So, to one neutrall thing both sexes fit,
    Wee dye and rise the same, and prove
    Mysterious by this love.

Wee can dye by it, if not live by love,
    And if unfit for tombes and hearse
Our legend bee, it will be fit for verse;
    And if no peece of Chronicle wee prove,
        We'll build in sonnets pretty roomes;
        As well a well wrought urne becomes
The greatest ashes, as half-acre tombes,
    And by these hymnes, all shall approve
    Us *Canoniz'd* for Love.
And thus invoke us; You whom reverend love
    Made one anothers hermitage;

You, to whom love was peace, that now is rage,
   Who did the whole worlds soule contract, and drove
      Into the glasses of your eyes
      So made such mirrors, and such spies,
  That they did all to you epitomize,
    Countries, Townes, Courts: Beg from above
    A patterne of our love.

Group discussion

- Discuss the first line of the poem. Is there anything 'unconventional' about it?
- The first stanza of the poem consists of one sentence. Trace its structure and discuss as a group what meaning it has for you.
- Identify the 'voice' of the poem and what 'argument' this voice is putting forward through the language used.
- Make a list of words that identify the poem as having been written in the seventeenth century. Then compare your list with those of the rest of the group.
- Working in pairs, make a list of unexpected collocation, or unusual 'conceits' (see the introduction above) from the poem. Compare your list with those of the rest of the group and discuss what meaning is produced by the examples you have selected.
- Discuss whether it would be accurate to say that, through the language he has chosen, the poet has merged feelings with ideas in this poem.

Writing ▶

Write a critical appreciation of 'The canonization' by John Donne, commenting in detail on the poet's language and what meaning is produced for you by this usage.

8.6 Dedicated to . . .

Sometimes the title of a poem takes the form of a dedication to a particular individual or 'kind of person'. Below is a poem with the title 'To the anxious mother'. It is by Valente Malanganata, a poet from Mozambique.

To the anxious mother

Into your arms I came
when you bore me, very anxious
you, who were so alarmed
at that monstrous moment
fearing that God might take me.
Everyone watched in silence
to see if the birth was going well
everyone washed their hands
to be able to receive the one who came from Heaven
and all the women were still and afraid.
But when I emerged
from the place where you sheltered me so long
at once I drew my first breath
at once you cried out with joy
the first kiss was my grandmother's.
And she took me at once to the place
where they kept me, hidden away
everyone was forbidden to enter my room
because everyone smelt bad
and I all fresh, fresh
breathed gently, wrapped in my napkins.
But grandmother, who seemed like a madwoman,
always looking and looking again
because the flies came at me
and the mosquitoes harried me
God who also watched over me
was my old granny's friend.

Group discussion

- Working in pairs, study the first five lines of the poem. Discuss how the arrangement of the language in these lines is different from prose. Try writing a prose version of the lines and compare them with the original. How is meaning altered when the arrangement of the language is changed?
- Decide which lines are examples of enjambement and which are end-stopped. Discuss how the use of either affects meaning.

- Again working in pairs, write a summary of the subject matter in not more than forty words. Then compare your summary with those of the rest of the group. Agree on a consensus summary.
- 'To the anxious mother' is the title of the poem. Who is this 'anxious mother'?
- Are there any examples of the use of a poetic diction in the poem?

Writing ☛ Write a poem with any of the following titles:

> To the anxious father
> To the anxious student
> To the anxious teacher
> To the anxious me

Or make up your own title along the same lines. Use the first person and address the poem to a particular individual or category of person.

8.7 A dramatic monologue

'*A terre*' by Wilfred Owen (page 168) was a dramatic monologue: the 'I' of the poem spoke in 'his' own words directly to the reader. Below is another dramatic monologue, written by Robert Browning (1812–89).

My last Duchess
Ferrara

> That's my last Duchess painted on the wall,
> Looking as if she were alive; I call
> That piece a wonder, now: Frà Pandolf's hands
> Worked busily a day, and there she stands.
> Will't please you sit and look at her? I said
> "Frà Pandolf" by design, for never read
> Strangers like you that pictured countenance,
> The depth and passion of its earnest glance,
> But to myself they turned (since none puts by
> The curtain I have drawn for you, but I)
> And seemed as they would ask me, if they durst,
> How such a glance came there; so, not the first
> Are you to turn and ask thus. Sir, 'twas not
> Her husband's presence only, called that spot
> Of joy into the Duchess' cheek: perhaps
> Frà Pandolf chanced to say "Her mantle laps
> "Over my Lady's wrist too much," or "Paint

"Must never hope to reproduce the faint
"Half-flush that dies along her throat;" such stuff
Was courtesy, she thought, and cause enough
For calling up that spot of joy. She had
A heart . . . how shall I say? . . . too soon made glad,
Too easily impressed; she liked whate'er
She looked on, and her looks went everywhere.
Sir, 'twas all one! My favour at her breast,
The drooping of the daylight in the West,
The bough of cherries some officious fool
Broke in the orchard for her, the white mule
She rode with round the terrace—all and each
Would draw from her alike the approving speech,
Or blush, at least. She thanked men,–good; but thanked
Somehow . . . I know not how . . . as if she ranked
My gift of a nine hundred years old name
With anybody's gift. Who'd stoop to blame
This sort of trifling? Even had you skill
In speech—(which I have not)—to make your will
Quite clear to such an one, and say "Just this
"Or that in you disgusts me; here you miss,
"Or there exceed the mark"—and if she let
Herself be lessoned so, nor plainly set
Her wits to yours, forsooth, and made excuse,
—E'en then would be some stooping, and I chuse
Never to stoop. Oh, Sir, she smiled, no doubt,
Whene'er I passed her; but who passed without
Much the same smile? This grew; I gave commands;
　　Then all smiles stopped together. There she stands
As if alive. Will't please you rise? We'll meet
The company below, then. I repeat,
The Count your Master's known munificence
Is ample warrant that no just pretence
Of mine for dowry will be disallowed;
Though his fair daughter's self, as I avowed
At starting, is my object. Nay, we'll go
Together down, Sir! Notice Neptune, tho',
Taming a sea-horse, thought a rarity,
Which Claus of Innsbruck cast in bronze for me.

- Working in pairs, make a summary in not more than eighty words of what the 'voice' of the poem says. Then compare your summary with those of the rest of the group and agree on a consensus summary.
- Make a list of words used in the poem that a contemporary living poet would be unlikely to use.
- The poem is written in rhyming couplets. Discuss how this affects meaning.
- Select examples of language use that are intended to give the reader an idea of what kind of man the 'voice' of the poem is.
- What does the speaker of the monologue imply through the language that 'he' is given to 'say' about the character of the Duchess? Select relevant quotes to illustrate your analysis.
- If the 'voice' of the poem is the 'speaker', whose voice lies behind this voice?

Writing ▶

Write a poem in the form of a dramatic monologue which, like 'My last Duchess', refers to one individual in particular, to events of the past and implies something sinister. When you have written your poem, write a commentary on the writing process.

8.8 A modern ballad

In section 6.3 we looked at a traditional ballad. You may wish to look back to the introduction there and check what was said about the common characteristics of the traditional ballad form.

'Literary ballads' were also mentioned in that section. Literary ballads are poems written by poets in the ballad style, but they are 'literary' in the sense that they have not emerged from a 'living' tradition of communal authorship and performance. They have usually been written by an individual poet for publication.

Eavan Boland is a contemporary poet; in the poem opposite she reminds us of the ballad inspiration in the title she gives the poem.

Group discussion

- Discuss how the first six lines of the first stanza 'lead up to' the final line. What effect does this have on the meaning produced?
- the occult house   lines of grins gaping   Strewn with cold heels
  and button-holed his smock   Slumming in my skin
  Her own museum-blind

  Discuss whether or not these words from the poem are examples of the use of unpredictable collocation and then say what the language means for you.

A ballad of beauty and time

Plainly came the time
The eucalyptus tree
Could not succour me,
Nor the honey-pot,
The sunshine vitamin,
Nor even getting thin:
I had passed my prime.

Then when bagged ash,
Scalded quarts of water,
Oil of the lime,
Cinders for the skin
And honey all had failed
I sorted out my money
And went to buy some time.
I knew the right address,
The occult house of shame
Where all the women came
Shopping for a mouth,
A new nose, an eyebrow
And entered without knocking
And stood as I did now.

A shape with a knife
Stooped away from me
Cutting something vague.
It might have been a face.
I couldn't really see.
I coughed once and said
'I want a lease of life'.
The room was full of masks,
Lines of grins gaping,
A wall of skin stretching,
A chin he had re-worked,
A face he had re-made.
He slit and cut and tucked
Then straightened from his blade.

'A tuck, a hem' he said –
'I only seam the line.
I only mend the dress.
It wouldn't do for you.

Your quarrel's with the weave.
The best I achieve
Is just a stitch in time.'

I started out again.
I knew a studio
Strewn with cold heels,
Closed in marble shock.
I saw the sculptor there
Chiselling a nose
And button-holed his smock:

'It's all very well
When you have bronzed a woman,
Pinioned her and finned
Wings on either shoulder.
Anyone can see
She won't get any older.
What good is that to me?
'See the last of youth
Slumming in my skin,
My sham pink mouth.
Here behold your critic –
The threat of your aesthetic.
I am the brute proof
Beauty is not truth.'

'Truth is in our lies'
He angrily replied:
'This woman fledged in stone
The centre of all eyes,
Her own museum-blind.
We sharpen with our skills
The arts of compromise.'

'And all I have cast
In crystal or in glass,
In lapis or in onyx
Is from my knowledge of
When from the honest flaw
To lift and stay my hand
And say "let it stand".'

- Each stanza of the poem consists of seven lines, none of which is longer than six words. There is at least one rhyme in each stanza, sometimes more. Comment on these aspects of how the language has been arranged and say whether it affects meaning or not.
- Make a summary of the subject matter of the poem in not more than sixty words. Then compare your summary with those produced by the rest of the group and agree on a consensus summary.
- The poet has used the title 'A ballad of beauty and time'. Discuss whether the use of the word 'ballad' in the title is justified.

Writing ▶ Write a critical appreciation of the poem, discussing it as an example of a 'literary ballad' and examining how the poet uses language to tell a story and create meaning.

▶ Write a contemporary ballad, dealing with some aspect of today's society. Your ballad should tell an uncomplicated story, employ 'simple' language and contemporary references.

8.9 Poetry and nature

'Nature' is conventionally seen as one of the principal subjects for the poet. Poets traditionally are meant to describe the beautiful aspects of 'nature'. However, the natural world is but one aspect of 'reality' poets may deal with. The view of nature that is created by poets is created through language. Our view of this aspect of 'reality' then is shaped by language. 'Nature poetry' that escapes cliché forces us through the unexpectedness of its use of language to reassess our perception of nature and, therefore, our concept of reality. Below is a poem about a hurricane. It is by Andrew Salkey, a West Indian poet.

> I remember the night,
> black with slack rain,
> flaccid when it first began
> but with brick drops beating later on
> like jump-Poco drumthumps,
> beating back the coming morning,
> beating with purpose,
> routine, rhythm and ritual,
> beating like the bounce of batter hide,
> hide battered on a shoemaker's block,
> batter hide, hide battered,
> pane shatter, shattered pane,
> batter hide, pane shatter through to dawn.

One bad, sneakin' breeze-blow
take time an' creep up
'pon Joe-Joe life
an' tear him shirt-tail
like bud-feather,
bruck him one-room in two
like chew-stick,
kill him common law wife,
kill him fait'ful goat
kill him layin'-hen then,
an' go 'way 'sof', sof' like tief,
like it wasn't causin' no bodders
inside the lan', at all, at all.

Group discussion

- Make a list of words from the poem that are unfamiliar to you, and in pairs discuss whether these words make the poem difficult. With the rest of the group, discuss the meaning that is created for you by the poem's language use.
- Read through the first stanza again. Discuss its use of language from these points of view: assonance, repetition, alliteration, onomatopoeia, rhyme. Say what each of these aspects of the stanza contribute to meaning.
- Working in pairs, summarise the subject matter of the second stanza in one sentence. Then compare the sentence you have produced with those produced by the rest of the group.
- Discuss the second stanza from these points of view: use of vernacular, repetition, use of simile.

Writing

Write a critical appreciation of the Andrew Salkey poem, commenting on its arrangement of language, any unexpected collocation it uses and the overall meaning the poem produces for you. Discuss what view of nature is produced through the language of the poem.

Write a poem about some aspect of nature that interests you. Try to avoid the clichés of 'nature poetry' by placing together words that are not normally seen in each other's company.

9 Poetry and genre

Just as fiction has its standard genres (detective thrillers, science fiction, romantic fiction, for example), so poetry has its recognised and conventional forms. We have already looked at examples of sonnets, ballads (traditional and literary), odes, haiku and tanka. In this chapter we will be looking at more familiar forms of poetry.

9.1 An elegy

An elegy is a poem mourning the death of an individual or a lament for some tragic event. In the poem below, Jane Elliott (1727–1805) laments the defeat of the Scottish army at the Battle of Flodden in 1415 at the hands of the English.

A lament for Flodden

I've heard them lilting at our ewe-milking,
Lasses a' lilting before dawn o' day;
But now they are moaning on ilka green *loaning*—
The Flowers of the Forest are a' wede away.

loaning: field

At *bughts*, in the morning, nae blythe lads are scorning,
Lasses are lonely and *dowie* and wae;
Nae *daffing*, nae gabbing, but sighing and sabbing,
Ilk ane lifts her *leglin* and hies her away.

bughts: folds
dowie: sad
daffing: jesting
leglin: milking-pail

In har'st, at the shearing, nae youths now are jeering,
Bandsters are *lyart*, and runkled, and gray:
At fair or at preaching, nae wooing, nae *fleeching*—
The Flowers of the Forest are a' wede away.

bandsters: sheaf-binders
lyart: grey
fleeching: coaxing

swankies: young fellows

At e'en, in the gloaming, nae *swankies* are roaming
'Bout stacks wi' the lasses at bogle to play;
But ilk ane sits eerie, lamenting her dearie—
The Flowers of the Forest are a' wede away.

Dool and wae for the order sent our lads to the Border!
The English, for ance, by guile wan the day;
The Flowers of the Forest, that fought ay the foremost,
The prime of our land, lie cauld in the clay.

We'll hear nae mair lilting at our ewe-milking;
Women and bairns are heartless and wae;
Sighing and moaning on ilka green loaning—
The Flowers of the Forest are a' wede away.

Group discussion

- In the first verse of the poem, there are two examples of ***internal rhyme:*** that is, when two or more words rhyme within a single line of verse:

  I've heard them lilting at our ewe-milking

  But now they are moaning on ilka green loaning

  Pick out other examples of internal rhyme from the poem and discuss how this technique affects meaning.

- Four of the verses end with the same line:

  The Flowers of the Forest are a' wede away.

  Discuss the effect of the repetition of this line at the end of verses.

- An explanation of some of the Scots vernacular is given in the glossary alongside the poem. Make a list of any other words that present any difficulty of interpretation and then as a group discuss how the surrounding context and connotations of other words in proximity may help you to interpret meaning.

- Discuss whether this poem shares any characteristics with the traditional ballad.

- Discuss 'A lament for Flodden' as an example of an elegy: what is it about the tone and language used that justifies calling it an elegy?

Writing 📧

Write an elegiac poem that 'laments' some sad event. Follow the arrangement of language of 'A lament for Flodden' by writing in four-line verses that rhyme *abab* and use internal rhyme as well. Keep the diction simple and direct; you may wish to employ a vernacular with which you are familiar.

After you have written the elegy, write a commentary on how you completed this task, commenting particularly on the verse form and rhyming scheme you employed.

GLOSSARY

Internal rhyme: this occurs when two or more words rhyme within the same line of verse.

9.2 Another elegy

Below is an elegy written by the Senegalese poet, Léopold Sédar Senghor. He laments the deaths of Senegalese soldiers in their fight against French colonial rule.

The dead

They are lying out there beside the captured roads, all along the roads of
   disaster
Elegant poplars, statues of sombre gods draped in their long cloaks of
   gold,
Senegalese prisoners darkly stretched on the soil of France.
In vain they have cut off your laughter, in vain the darker flower of your
   flesh,
You are the flower in its first beauty amid a naked absence of flowers
Black flower with its grave smile, diamond of immemorial ages.

You are the slime and plasma of the green spring of the world
Of the first couple you are the flesh, the ripe belly the milkiness
You are the sacred increase of the bright gardens of paradise
And the invincible forest, victorious over fire and thunder-bolt.
The great song of your blood will vanquish machines and cannons
Your throbbing speech evasions and lies.
No hate in your soul void of hatred, no cunning in your soul void of
   cunning.
O Black Martyrs immortal race, let me speak the words of pardon.

Group discussion
- Here are the first six lines of the poem written in an arrangement that would usually be called prose:

   They are lying out there beside the captured roads, all along the roads
   of disaster: elegant poplars, statues of sombre gods draped in their
   long cloaks of gold, Senegalese prisoners darkly stretched on the soil

of France. In vain they have cut off your laughter, in vain the darker flower of your flesh, you are the flower in its first beauty amid a naked absence of flowers, black flower with its grave smile, diamond of immemorial ages.

Compare this version with the original lines and discuss whether the separation into lines of verse with capital letters at the start of each line substantially affects meaning.

- Select examples of collocation that seem striking to you and comment on the meaning created by these combinations of words.
- Working in pairs, summarise in not more than forty words what meaning is produced for you by the poet's use of language. Then compare your summary with those of the rest of the group.
- As a group, discuss the poet's use of metaphor.

Writing Compare 'A lament for Flodden' with 'The dead' saying what the poems have in common in terms of subject matter, language use and tone.

9.3 An elegy and a prayer

Anne Sexton (1928–74) was an American poet who frequently took death as her subject matter. In the poem below, she laments the death of one of her own children and a child of one of her friends and offers up a prayer for the protection of their remaining children.

The child bearers

Jean, death comes close to us all,
flapping its awful wings at us
and the gluey wings crawl up our nose.
Our children tremble in their teen-age cribs,
whirling off on a thumb or a motorcycle,
mine pushed into gnawing a stilbestrol cancer
I passed on like hemophilia,
or yours in the seventh grade, with her spleen
smacked in by the balance beam.
And we, mothers, crumpled, and flyspotted
with bringing them this far
can do nothing now but pray.

Let us put your three children
and my two children,
ages ranging from eleven to twenty-one,
and send them in a large air net up to God,
with many stamps, *real* air mail,
and huge signs attached:
SPECIAL HANDLING
DO NOT STAPLE, FOLD OR MUTILATE!
And perhaps He will notice
and pass a psalm over them
for keeping safe for a whole,
for a whole God-dammed life-span.

And not even a muddled angel will
peek down at us in our foxhole.
And He will not have time
to send down an eyedropper of prayer for us,
the mothering thing of us,
as we drop into the soup
and drown
in the worry festering inside us,
lest our children
go so fast
they go.

Group discussion

- Working in pairs, make a summary of what meaning is produced for you by the language of the poem. Then compare your summary with the rest of the group.
- Pick out examples of collocation that you consider to be unusual and discuss how these unusual combinations of words affect meaning.
- Make a list of the references to everyday things the poet employs and discuss how she uses these to express her feelings.
- How would you categorise the tone of the poem and the kind of language the poet uses?
- Make a list of any examples of American English used in the poem.
- Discuss whether the poem has any characteristics of the elegy form.

Writing ▶

Write a critical appreciation of 'The child Bearers', commenting particularly on the diction employed by the poet and making a judgement about how meaningful the poem is to you.

9.4 Narrative verse

Ballads usually tell a simple story based around one incident. Often the story can be told through dialogue. In the literary ballad below, Rudyard Kipling (1865–1930) uses several of the main generic characteristics of the traditional ballad in telling a straightforward, uncomplicated story.

Danny Deever

'What are the bugles blowin' for?' said Files-on-Parade.
'To turn you out, to turn you out,' the Colour-Sergeant said.
'What makes you look so white, so white?' said Files-on-Parade.
'I'm dreadin' what I've got to watch,' the Colour-Sergeant said.
    For they're hangin' Danny Deever, you can hear the Dead March
        play,
    The Regiment's in 'ollow square—they're hangin' him today;
    They've taken of his buttons off an' cut his stripes away,
    An' they're hangin' Danny Deever in the mornin'.

'What makes the rear-rank breathe so 'ard?' said Files-on-Parade.
'It's bitter cold, it's bitter cold,' the Colour-Sergeant said.
'What makes that front-rank man fall down?' said Files-on-Parade.
'A touch o' sun, a touch o' sun,' the Colour-Sergeant said.
    They are hangin' Danny Deever, they are marchin' of 'im round,
    They 'ave 'alted Danny Deever by 'is coffin on the ground;
    An' 'e'll swing in 'arf a minute for a sneakin shootin' hound—
    O they're hangin' Danny Deever in the mornin'!
''Is cot was right-'and cot to mine,' said Files-on-Parade.
''E's sleepin' out an' far to-night,' the Colour-Sergeant said.
'I've drunk 'is beer a score o' times, said Files-on-Parade.
''E's drinkin bitter beer alone,' the Colour-Sergeant said.
    They are hangin' Danny Deever, you must mark 'im to 'is place,
    For 'e shot a comrade sleepin'—you must look 'im in the face;
    Nine 'undred of 'is county an' the Regiment's disgrace,
    While they're hangin' Danny Deever in the mornin'.

'What's that so black agin the sun?' said Files-on-Parade.
'It's Danny fightin' 'hard for life,' the Colour-Sergeant said.
'What's that that whimpers over'ead?' said Files-on-Parade.
'It's Danny's soul that's passin' now,' the Colour-Sergeant said.
    For they've done with Danny Deever, you can 'ear the quickstep
        play,
    The Regiment's in column, an' they're marchin' us away;
    Ho! the young recruits are shakin', an' they'll want their beer
        today,
    After hangin' Danny Deever in the mornin'!

- Much of the story is told through the utterances of two narrative figures: Files-on-Parade and the Colour-Sergeant. Discuss the effect of telling the story this way.
- Consider the last four lines of each stanza. They conform to the same pattern throughout the poem. Discuss what that pattern is, how repetition is used and the effect on the meaning created.
- Numerous words that usually begin with 'h' have the 'h' dropped in the poem. Several words that usually end in a 'g' are printed without the final 'g'. Discuss these features of the language and what effect they have on interpretation.
- From the poet's choice of language, can you detect what his attitude is to the 'hangin' of Danny Deever'?
- List the generic characteristics of ballads that have been used in this poem.

Writing ▶

Write a critical appreciation of the poem, commenting on its qualities as a literary ballad and on its language use.

9.5 Poetry and social issues

Poetry may use as its subject matter the expression of personal emotions, which then widens into a discourse about a social issue. Consider this poem by Ruth Fainlight and discuss whether this analysis is relevant to it.

Romance

Every time I fold the laundry
I remembered when she told me how
it took an hour to put his clothes away,
and that meant every day.

Eyes flashing, she made the list
of her duties into a metaphor.
She looked like a Minoan goddess, or Yeats'
princess bedded on straw.

She seemed to gloat on the servitude,
as if it were the fuel and source
of her obsession, and each passionate protest
a further confirmation.

My spirit shrivelled, like fingers
from harsh soap and cold water,
to see through her eyes. She frightened me,
yet I never doubted.

Fairy-tales are very specific,
almost domestic – tasks to be done,
problems to solve. They tell about bewitched
princesses, toad princes,

and the force that holds them spell-bound.
Smoothing his shirts, she dreamed
of transformation and reward, and being
happy ever after.

I'd gone down that road before,
and knew its forks and sudden twists
where one false step has mortal consequence.
But I was luckier.

Group discussion

- Discuss the 'voice' of the poem. Who is the 'I'? Who is 'she'? Who is the man referred to in the poem?
- Discuss the kind of language used in the poem, including any examples of collocation that strike you as unusual or clichéd.
- Discuss the title of the poem and its relevance to any meaning the poem has for you.
- Working in pairs, summarise in not more than forty words what meaning the poem produces for you. Then compare your summary with the rest of the group.
- What meaning does the last verse of the poem have for you?
- The poem deals specifically with the feelings of two women, but, in your judgement, does it have, through its language, wider social implications? Does it offer any kind of discourse about gender issues, for example?

Writing ☛ Write a critical appreciation of 'Romance', including a detailed analysis of the language used. Then comment on the meaning the poem has for you.

9.6 Creating a mood through word-pictures

Some poems create a 'mood' through their use of language. Often the poet creates 'word-pictures', summoning up in words images that have particular connotations. Below is a poem by Carol Ann Duffy.

I dream through a wordless, familiar place.
The small boat of the day sails into morning,
past the postman with his modest haul, the full trees
which sound like the sea, leaving my hands free
to remember. Moments of grace. *Like this.*

Shaken by first love and kissing a wall: *Of course.*
The dried ink on the palms then ran suddenly wet,
a glistening blue name in each fist. I sit now
in a kind of sly trance, hoping I will not feel me
breathing too close across time. A face to the name. *Gone.*

The chimes of mothers calling in children
at dusk. *Yes.* It seems we live in those staggering years
only to haunt them; the vanishing scents
and colours of infinite hours like a melting balloon
in earlier hands. The boredom since.
Memory's caged bird won't fly. These days
we are adjectives, nouns. In moments of grace
we were verbs, the secret of poems, talented.
A thin skin lies on the language. We stare
deep in the eyes of strangers, look for the doing words.

Now I smell you peeling an orange in the other room.
Now I take off my watch, let a minute unravel
in my hands, listen and look as I do so,
and mild loss opens my lips like No.
Passing, you kiss the back of my neck. A blessing.

Group discussion

- Read through the first stanza of the poem again. Discuss whether there are any examples of unusual collocation and, if so, what meaning is produced through them. In addition, there are two examples of metaphor in the verse. Pick those out and comment on the meaning produced.
- Discuss whether the poet uses language to create images, word-pictures that perhaps are intended to summon up a mood which the reader is meant to share.
- Make a list of unusual collocation used in the last four stanzas of the poem and comment on any meaning these create for you.
- Summarise in not more than fifty words what meaning the poem has for you. Then compare your summary with those of the rest of the group.
- Decide on an appropriate title for the poem, then share your choice with the rest of the group. Try to agree on a consensus title and then check the one you choose against the original title of the poem (see Appendix 5).

Writing ☛

Write a 'reflective' poem in which you use language to create a mood through word-pictures. Your subject matter, like the poem above, might be memories of your earlier life. Then write a commentary on how you wrote the poem, commenting particularly on how you created a mood through your use of language.

9.7 The heightened language of poetry

Poetry, as we have discussed, may force us to reassess our view of reality through language. Unfamiliar imagery and unexpected collocation can appear to demand of the reader a reassessment of what constitutes reality. If 'reality' is formed for us partly through language and its repeated use, then perhaps poetry, with its special arrangement and patterning of diction, its 'heightened' language, can cut through our accepted view of what is 'real' and ask us to see things afresh.

On page 208 is a poem by Derek Walcott, thought by many to be one of the most important living poets. Does the language he uses force us as readers to think again about familiar things and ideas?

A city's death by fire

After that hot gospeller had levelled all but the churched sky,
I wrote the tale by tallow of a city's death by fire;
Under a candle's eye, that smoked in tears, I
Wanted to tell, in more than wax, of faiths that were snapped like wire.
All day I walked abroad among the rubbled tales,
Shocked at each wall that stood on the street like a liar;

Loud was the bird-rocked sky, and all the clouds were bales
Torn open by looting, and white, in spite of the fire.
By the smoking sea, where Christ walked, I asked why
Should a man wax tears, when his wooden world fails?
In town, leaves were paper, but the hills were a flock of faiths;
To a boy who walked all day, each leaf was a green breath
Rebuilding a love I thought was dead as nails,
Blessing the death and the baptism by fire.

Group discussion

- One way poetry can ask the reader to see things in a new light is by using unexpected metaphors. 'A city's death by fire' uses a number of metaphors. Make a list of them and then discuss in the group what meaning is created by their use.

- Apart from the metaphors the poet uses, list any other examples of unexpected collocation the poet employs, and discuss in the group what meaning these create for you.

- Working in pairs, summarise in not more than fifty words what meaning the poem has for you. Then compare your summary with those of the rest of the group and try to agree a consensus summary.

- Discuss how you would describe the tone of the poem and the kind of language the poet has used.

- As a group, discuss whether the poem makes you re-examine familiar things through the force of its language.

Writing

Write a critical appreciation of 'A city's death by fire', comparing it with the poem from the previous section by Carol Ann Duffy. Say if there are any similarities between the two poems and how they differ, particularly in terms of language use and, through that, subject matter.

10 Further poems for appreciation and comparison

In this section are further pairs of poems, which you are asked to read and compare in the form of written answers.

10.1

Read the two poems below. Both are by contemporary poets; the first is by Norman MacCaig and the second by Wendy Cope.

The red and the black

We sat up late, talking —
thinking of the screams of the tortured
and the last silence of starving children,
seeing the faces of bigots and murderers.

Then sleep.

And there was the morning, smiling
in the dance of everything. The collared doves
guzzled the rowan berries and the sea
washed in, so gently, so tenderly.
Our neighbours greeted us
with humour and friendliness.

World, why do you do this to us,
giving us poison with one hand
and the bread of life with another?

And reason sits helpless at its desk,
adding accounts that never balance,
finding no excuse for anything.

The concerned adolescent

Our planet spins around the sun
in its oval-shaped orbit
like a moth circling a bright, hot, golden-yellow light bulb.

Look at this beautiful, lovely
blue and green and white jewel
shining against the dark black sky.
It is doomed.

On another planet somewhere far away in the galaxy
beings are discussing the problems of Earth.
'It is a wonderful world,' says their leader.
It has roaring oceans filled with many kinds of fishes,
It has green meadows bedecked with white and yellow flowers,
Its trees have twisting roots and fruitful, abundant branches.

But it is doomed.

'The problem with this lovely, beautiful world, you see,
Is the inhabitants, known as HUMAN BEINGS.
Human beings will not live in peace and love
and care for the little helpless creatures who share the planet with them.
They pollute the world, they kill and eat the animals.
Everywhere there is blood and the stench of death.
Human beings make war and hate one another.
They do not understand their young, they reject their ideals.
they make them come home early from the disco.
They are doomed.'

Soon a great explosion, a terrible cloud
will wipe out all the life on this planet,
including those people who do not see how important my poem is.
They are certainly doomed.

Writing ▶ Discuss any similarities of subject matter, as expressed through their language, that the two poems may have. As well as pointing out similarities, discuss any differences between the two poems and make a personal judgement about their relative value.

10.2

Read these two poems. The first is by Amy Lowell (1874–1925), an American poet; the second is by Claude McKay (1890–1948) who was born in Jamaica but lived most of his life in the USA.

From one who stays

How empty seems the town now you are gone!
  A wilderness of sad streets, where gaunt walls
  Hide nothing to desire; sunshine falls
Eery, distorted, as it long had shone
On white, dead faces tombed in halls of stone.
  The whir of motors, stricken through with calls
  Of playing boys, floats up at intervals;
But all these noises blur to one long moan.
  What quest is worth pursuing? And how strange
That other men still go accustomed ways!
I hate their interest in the things they do.
  A spectre-horde repeating without change.

My mother

Reg wished me to go with him to the field.
I paused because I did not want to go;
But in her quiet way she made me yield,
Reluctantly, for she was breathing low.
Her hand she slowly lifted from her lap
And, smiling sadly in the old sweet way,
She pointed to the nail where hung my cap.
Her eyes said: I shall last another day.
But scarcely had we reached the distant place,
When over the hills we heard a faint bell ringing.
A boy came running up with frightened face –
We knew the fatal news that he was bringing.
I heard him listlessly, without a moan,
Although the only one I loved was gone.

II
The dawn departs, the morning is begun,
The Trades come whispering from off the seas,
The fields of corn are golden in the sun,
The dark-brown tassels fluttering in the breeze;
The bell is sounding and children pass,

Frog-leaping, skipping, shouting, laughing shrill,
Down the red road, over the pasture-grass,
Up to the schoolhouse crumbling on the hill.
The older folk are at their peaceful toil,
Some pulling up the weeds, some plucking corn,
And others breaking up the sun-baked soil.
Float, faintly-scented breeze, at early morn
Over the earth where mortals sow and reap –
Beneath its breast my mother lies asleep.

Last night I heard your voice, mother,
    The words you sang to me
When I, a little barefoot boy,
    Knelt down against your knee.

And tears gushed from my heart, mother,
    And passed beyond its wall,
But though the fountain reached my throat
    The drops refused to fall.

'Tis ten years since you died, mother,
    Just ten dark years of pain,
And oh, I only wish that I
    Could weep just once again.

Writing ▷   Write a critical appreciation of the two poems, commenting on any similarities and differences of subject matter and language use.

10.3

Read the two poems below. The first is by Ruth Stone, an American poet, and the second is by Christine Evans, who is from Wales.

Room

Someone in the next apartment
Walks slowly back to a room abutting mine.
I am on this side, sitting.
It is uncomfortable trying to be quiet.
For weeks coming in here to change my clothes,
I think, are my clothes too daring?
And the sound of water rushing in

Filling a tub in the other room
Makes a loud continuity,
As though many people might be living here,
Twining their arms about me,
Passing me in the hall
Making tender jokes.
Sunlight enters the room near the ceiling.
And shadows of leaves letting go
Flash in downward slants
Falling inside the room
To sink through the floor.
And I think
Is this the way it will be?
And I listen
With my ear against the plaster.

Lighthouse keeper

Inside's gloss-painted like a hospital.
The radio stammers, blurts, then hums.
Sport or men with guns mutter on a screen
All look at, no-one watches, in an acrid haze
Of Players' Number 6 or roll-your-owns.
Nestle's Milk coffee or with white lumps floating
Is the only sign in here that you're offshore
(Formica buckling, tin teapot, pedal bin)
Till you catch reflections of the symmetry
Of nursery tale – for there are three
Of everything – three chairs with thin foam
Cushions that slide down as soon
As sat on, three tea-towels, and bookshelves;
Out in the garden, three lavatory cells
Three toolsheds, pigsties, garden plots gone wild

And three pale unfocused sedentary men
Sleeping, eating, being awake
On or off according to a roster.

Bas steps out, shirt-sleeved, to do the Met
(which numbers on the weather form he'll tick)
Acres of white foam, the air
A wide blue yawn he slams in from:
Christ! It's cold enough out there –

Their laughter drowns the throb of engines.
But sometimes, he's confided, in the small hours
Snecking the white gate close behind him
He truants, leaving light in its tower cage
Where homing seabirds grunt and scream and fall
To tread salt turf springy with old roots
And stand like a captain in the wind
Reading the dark stretch of his deck
Sensing the night miles crossed
Till his heartbeat's only a flicker
His cigarette a brave red throb
On the seabed of the floating stars.

His daylight brain thinks it forgotten
But in off-duty dreams, a hundred miles
From sea, he feels the island dip and steady;
Glimpses the dark walls building, pushed astern
Tumbling, crawling, gathering, re-gathering
Outrun, but following.

Keepers in Wolf Rock
Lighthouse

Discuss whether these two poems have any themes in common as expressed through the language. Analyse any aspects of the language used in both poems that you find striking or unusual and comment on what each poem means to you. You may wish to state a preference for one poem or the other.

10.4

Read the two poems below. The first is by Adrienne Rich; the second by James Berry.

The middle-aged

Their faces, safe as an interior
Of Holland tiles and Oriental carpet,
Where the fruit-bowl, always filled, stood in a light
Of placid afternoon – their voices' measure,
Their figures moving in the Sunday garden
To lay the tea outdoors or trim the borders,
Afflicted, haunted us. For to be young
Was always to live in other peoples' houses
Whose peace, if we sought it, had been made by others,
Was ours at second-hand and not for long.
The custom of the house, not ours, the sun
Fading the silver-blue Fortuny curtains,
The reminiscence of a Christmas party
Of fourteen years ago – all memory,
Signs of possession and of being possessed,
We tasted, tense with envy. They were so kind,
Would have given us anything; the bowl of fruit
Was filled for us, there was a room upstairs
We must call ours; but twenty years of living
They could not give. Nor did they ever speak
Of the coarse stain on that polished balustrade,
The crack in the study window, or the letters
Locked in a drawer and the key destroyed.
All to be understood by us, returning
Late, in our own time – how that peace was made,
Upon what terms, with how much left unsaid.

Lucy's letter

labrish: have a yarn

dayclean: dawn

naseberry: Caribbean
fruit

Things harness me here. I long
for we *labrish* bad. Doors
not fixed open here.
No Leela either. No Cousin
Lil, Miss Lottie or Bro'-Uncle.
Dayclean, doesn't have cockcrowin'.
Midmornin' doesn' bring
Cousin-Maa with her *naseberry* tray.
Afternoon doesn' give a ragged
Manwell, strung with fish
like bright leaves. Seven days
play same note in London, chile.
But Leela, money-rustle regular.

Me dear, I don' laugh now,
not'n' like we thunder claps
in darkness on verandah.
I turn a battery hen
in 'lectric light, day an' night.
No mood can touch one
mango season back at Yard.
At least though I did start
evening school once.
An' doctors free, chile.

London isn't like we
village dirt road, you know
Leela: it a parish

of a pasture-lan' what
grown crisscross streets,
an' they lie down to my door.
But I lock myself in.
I carry keys everywhere.
Life here's no open summer,
girl. But Sat'day mornin' don'
find me han' dry, don' find me face
a heavy cloud over the man.

An' though he still have
a weekend mind for bat'n'ball
he wash a dirty dish now, me dear.
It sweet him I on the Pill.

We get money for holidays.
But there's no sun-hot
to enjoy cool breeze.

Leela, I really a sponge
you know, for traffic noise,
for work noise, for halfway
intentions, for halfway smiles,
for clockwatching' an' col' weather.
I hope you don' think I gone
too fat when we meet.
I booked up to come an' soak
the children in daylight.

Writing ☞   Write a critical appreciation of these two poems, drawing attention to any
similarities of subject matter or tone you detect and also pointing out any
differences between the two. Make a personal judgement about the
respective merits of the two poems, saying what meaning they have for
you.

Appendices

Appendix 1

Waking is the hardest thing they ask of him.

The nurse always wakes him with the word 'morning', and the word 'morning' brings a hurting into his head which he cannot control or ameliorate or do anything about. Very often, the word 'morning' interrupts his dreams. In these dreams there was a stoat somewhere. This is all he can say about them.

The nurse opens his mouth, which tastes of seed and fills it with teeth. 'These teeth have got too big for me,' he sometimes remarks, but neither the nurse nor his wife replies to this just as neither the nurse nor his wife laughs when from some part of his ancient self he brings out a joke he did not know he could still remember. He isn't even certain they smile at his jokes because he can't see faces any longer unless they are no more and no less than two feet from his eyes. 'Aren't you even smiling?' he sometimes shouts.

'I'm smiling, Sir,' says the nurse.

'Naturally, I'm smiling,' says his wife.

His curtains are drawn back and light floods into the room. To him, light is time. Until nightfall, it lies on his skin, seeping just a little into the pores yet never penetrating inside him, neither into his brain nor his heart nor any crevice or crease of him. Light and time, time and light lie on him as weightless as the sheet. He is somewhere else. He is in the place where the jokes come from, where the dreams of stoats lie. He refuses ever to leave it except upon one condition.

That condition is so seldom satisfied, yet every morning, after his teeth are in, he asks the nurse: 'Is my son coming today?'

'Not that I know of, Sir,' she replies.

So then he takes no notice of the things he does. He eats his boiled egg. He pisses into a jar. He puts a kiss as thin as air on his wife's cheek. He tells the nurse the joke about the Talking Dog. He folds his arms across his chest. He dreams of being asleep.

But once in a while – once a fortnight perhaps, or once a month? – the nurse will say as she lifts him up onto his pillows: 'Your son's arrived, Sir.'

Then he'll reach up and try to neaten the silk scarf he wears at his throat. He will ask for his window to be opened wider. He will sniff the room and wonder whether it doesn't smell peculiarly of water-weed.

The son is a big man, balding, with kind eyes. Always and without fail he arrives in the room with a bottle of champagne and two glasses held upside down between his first and second finger.

'How are you?' he asks.

'That's a stupid question,' says the father.

The son sits by the bed and the father looks and looks for him with faded eyes and they sip the drink. Neither the nurse nor the wife disturbs them.

'Stay a bit,' says the father, 'won't you?'

'I can't stay long,' says the son.

Sometimes the father weeps without knowing it. All he knows is that with his son here, time is no longer a thing that covers him, but an element in which he floats and which fills his head and his heart until he is both brimming with it and buoyant on the current of it.

When the champagne has all been drunk, the son and the nurse carry the father downstairs and put him into the son's Jaguar and cover his knees with a rug. The father and the son drive off down the Hampshire lanes. Light falls in dapples on the old man's temples and on his folded hands.

There was a period of years that arrived as the father was beginning to get old when the son went to work in the Middle East and came home only once or twice a year, bringing presents made in Japan which the father did not trust.

It was then that the old man began his hatred of time. He couldn't bear to see anything endure. What he longed for was for things to be over. He did the *Times* crossword only to fill up the waiting spaces. He read the newspaper only to finish it and fold it and place it in the waste-paper basket. He snipped off from the rose bushes not only the dead heads but blooms that were still living. At mealtimes, he cleared the cutlery from the table before the meal was finished. He drove out with his wife to visit friends to find that he longed, upon arrival, for the moment of departure. When he made his bed in the morning, he would put on the bedcover then turn it down again, ready for the night.

His wife watched and suffered. She felt he was robbing her of life. She was his second wife, less beautiful and less loved than the first (the mother of his son) who had been a dancer and who had liked to spring into his arms from a sequence of three cartwheels. He sometimes dismayed the second wife by telling her about the day when the first wife did a cartwheel in the revolving doors of the Ritz. 'I've heard that story, darling,' she'd say politely, ashamed for him that he could tell it so proudly. And to her bridge friends she'd confide: 'It's as if he believes that by rushing through the *now* he'll get back to the *then*.'

He began a practice of adding things up. He would try to put a finite number on the oysters he had eaten since the war. He counted the cigarettes his wife smoked in a day and the number of times she mislaid her lighter. He tried to make a sum of the remembered cartwheels. Then when he had done these additions, he would draw a neat line through them, like the line a captive draws through each recorded clutch of days, and fold the paper in half and then in quarters and so on until it could not be folded any smaller and then place it carefully in the waste-paper basket next to the finished *Times*.

'Now we know,' his wife once heard him mutter. 'Now we know all about it.'

When the war ended he was still married to the dancer. His son was five years old. They lived in a manor house with an ancient tennis court and an east-facing croquet lawn. Though his head was still full of the war, he had a touching faith in the future and he usually knew, as each night descended, that he was looking forward to the day.

Very often, in the summer of 1946, he would wake when the sun came up and, leaving the dancer sleeping, would go out onto the croquet lawn wearing his dressing gown and his slippers from Simpson's of Piccadilly and stare at the dew on the grass, at the shine on the croquet hoops and at the sky, turning. He had the feeling that he and the world made a handsome pair.

One morning, he saw a stoat on the lawn. The stoat was running round the croquet hoops and then in and out of them in a strange repeated pattern, as if it were taking part in a stoat gymkhana. The man did not move, but stood and watched. Then he backed off into the house and ran up the stairs to the room where his son was sleeping.

'Wake up!' he said to the little boy. 'I've got something to show you!'

He took his son's hand and led him barefoot down the stairs and out into the garden. The stoat was still running round and through the croquet hoops and now, as the man and the boy stood watching, it decided to leap over the hoops, jumping twice its height into the air and rolling over in a somersault as it landed, then flicking its tail as it turned and ran in for another leap.

The boy, still dizzy with sleep, opened his mouth and opened wide his blue eyes. He knew he must not move so he did not even look round when his father left his side and went back into the house. He shivered a little in the dewy air. He wanted to creep forward so that he could be in the sun. He tiptoed out across the gravel that hurt his feet onto the soft wet lawn. The stoat saw him and whipped its body to a halt, head up, tail flat, regarding the boy. The boy could see its eyes. He thought how sleek and slippery it looked and how he would like to stroke its head with his finger.

The father returned. 'Don't move!' he whispered to his son, so the boy did not turn.

The father took aim with his shotgun and fired. He hit the stoat right in the head and its body flew up into the air before it fell without a sound. The man laughed with joy at the cleanness and beauty of the shot. He laughed a loud, happy laugh and then he looked down at his son to get his approval. But the boy was not there. The boy had walked back inside the house, leaving his father alone in the bright morning.

Appendix 2

The published title of the Isaac Asimov story is 'The fun they had'.

Appendix 3

The published title of the Maura Treacy story is 'A minor incident'.

Appendix 4

Instead, I said, What I have been doing lately: I was lying in bed on my back, my hands drawn up, my fingers interlaced lightly at the nape of my neck. Someone rang the doorbell. I went downstairs and opened the door but there was no one there. I stepped outside. Either it was drizzling or there was a lot of dust in the air and the dust was damp. I stuck out my tongue and the drizzle or the damp dust tasted like government school ink. I looked north and I looked south. I started walking north. While walking north, I wanted to move fast, so I removed the shoes from my feet. While walking north, I looked up and saw the planet Venus and I said, 'If the sun went out, it would be eight minutes before I would know it.' I saw a monkey sitting in a tree that had no leaves and I said, 'A monkey. Just look at that. A monkey.' I picked up a stone and threw it at the monkey. The monkey, seeing the stone, quickly moved out of its way. Three times I threw a stone at the monkey and three times it moved away. The fourth time I threw the stone, the monkey caught it and threw it back at me. The stone struck me on my forehead over my right eye, making a deep gash. The gash healed immediately but now the skin on my forehead felt false to me. I walked for I don't know how long before I came to a big body of water. I wanted to get across, so when the boat came I paid my fare. When I got to the other side, I saw a lot of people sitting on the beach and they were having a picnic. They were the most beautiful people I had ever seen. Everything about them was black and shiny. Their skin was black and shiny. Their shoes were black and shiny. Their hair was black and shiny. The clothes they wore were black and shiny. I could hear them laughing and chatting and I said, I would like to be with these people, so I started to walk toward them, but when I got up close to them I saw that they weren't at a picnic and they weren't beautiful and they weren't chatting and laughing. All around me was black mud and the people all looked as if they had been made up out of the black mud. I looked up and saw that the sky seemed far away and nothing I could stand on would make me able to touch it with my fingertips. I thought, If only I could get out of this, so I started to walk. I must have walked for a long time because my feet hurt and felt as if they would drop off. I thought, If only just around the bend I would see my house and inside my house I would find my bed, freshly made at that, and in the kitchen I would find my mother or anyone else that I loved making me a custard. I thought, If only it was a Sunday and I was sitting in church and I had just heard someone sing a psalm. I felt very sad so I sat down. I felt so sad that I rested my head on my own knees and smoothed my own head. I felt so sad I couldn't imagine feeling any other way again. I said, I don't like this. I don't want to do this anymore. And I went back to lying in bed, just before the doorbell rang.

Appendix 5

The title of the poem by Carol Ann Duffy is 'Moments of grace'.

Acknowledgements

The author and publishers wish to thank the following for permission to use copyright material:

Anvil Press Poetry Ltd for Carol Ann Duffy, 'Moments of Grace' from *Mean Time*, 1993; Carl Cowl on behalf of the Archives of Claude McKay for Claude McKay, 'My Mother'; Doubleday, a division of Bantam Doubleday Dell Publishing Group, Inc for 'Loneliness' and 'City People' from Harold G Henderson, *An Introduction to Haiku*. Copyright © 1958 by Harold G Henderson; Paul Durcan for 'The Death By Heroin of Sid Vicious' included in *The Younger Irish Poets*, ed. G Dawe, Blackstaff Press; Christine Evans for 'Lighthouse Keeper' from *Island of Dark Horses*, Seren, 1995; Faber & Faber Ltd for Wendy Cope, 'The Concerned Adolescent' from *Serious Concerns*; Garison Keillor, 'Life is Good' from *Leaving Home*, 1988; an extract from Vikram Seth, *The Golden Gate*, 1986; Jayne Anne Phillips, 'Solo Dance' from *Black Tickets*, 1980; Sylvia Plath, 'Daddy' from *Ariel*; Derek Walcott, 'A City's Death by Fire' from *Collected Poems 1948-1984*; and an extract from P D James, *An Unsuitable Job for a Woman*, 1972; Getaway Holidays for an extract from a travel brochure; Grove/Atlantic Inc for 'Princess Shikishi' from *Anthology of Japanese Literature*, trs./ed. Donald Keene, 1985; The Guardian for David Sharrock, 'Ireland is poised for peace', *The Guardian*, 31.8.94; The Harvill Press for Raymond Carver, 'Intimacy' from *Elephant and Other Stories*, Collins Harvill. Copyright © 1988 Raymond Carver; Hamish Hamilton Ltd for an extract from *Raymond Chandler Speaking*, eds. Dorothy Gardiner and Katherine Sorley Walker, 1962. Copyright © 1962 The Helga Greene Literary Agency; A M Heath on behalf of the authors for extracts from Anita Brookner, *Hotel Du Lac*, Jonathan Cape. Copyright © Anita Brookner; and George Orwell, *Collected Works, Vol.3*. Copyright © the Estate of the late Sonia Brownell Orwell and Martin Secker and Warburg Ltd; David Higham Associates on behalf of the author for Graham Greene, 'Alas, Poor Maling' from *Twenty-one Stories*, William Heinemann, 1954; International Creative Management, Inc on behalf of the author for an extract from Toni Morrison, *Jazz*, Chatto & Windus, 1992. Copyright © 1992 by Toni Morrison; International Music Publications Ltd and Warner/Chappell Music Australia for David Byrne, Chris Frantz, Jerry Harrison, Tina Weymouth and Yves N'Jock, 'Nothing But Flowers'. Copyright © 1988 Index Music Inc USA, WB Music Corp, USA, Warner Chappell Music Ltd, London; John Johnson Ltd on behalf of the author for Bessie Head, 'Heaven is not Closed' from *The Collector of Treasures*. Copyright © 1977 the Estate of Bessie Head; Sylvia Kantaris for 'Lost Property' included in *The Poetry Book Society Anthology II*, ed. Stevenson; Bill Kenwright Ltd for leaflet advertising their production of *Jane Eyre*; Norman MacCaig for 'The Red and the Black' included in *The Poetry Book Society I*, ed. Stevenson; Macmillan, London for Jamaica Kincaid, 'What I Have Been Doing Lately' from *At the Bottom of the River*, Picador, 1984; The National Magazine Company Ltd for an adapted article from Jay Andrews, 'The New Order – Become Businesslike', *Cosmopolitan*, January 1994. Copyright © 1994 National Magazine Company; New Beacon Books Ltd for James Berry, 'Lucy's Letter' from *Lucy's Letters and Loving*, 1982; Kim Newman for a review of 'Terminator 2', *Empire*, September 1991; New Statesman & Society for John Mather, 'Ripples in Time', *New Statesman & Society*, 1.3.94; W W Norton & Company, Inc and the author for Adrienne Rich, 'The Middle-aged', from *The Fact of the Doorframe: Poems Selected and New 1950-1984*. Copyright © 1975, 1978 by W W

Norton & Company, Inc. Copyright © 1981, 1984 by Adrienne Rich; Oxford University Press for an extract from Edward Kamau Brathwaite, 'Rites' from *The Arrivants*. Copyright © 1973 Edward Kamau Brathwaite; Penguin Books Ltd for an extract from Stephen Pinker, *The Language Instinct*, Allen Lane, The Penguin Press. Copyright © 1994 Stephen Pinker; Poolbeg Press for Maura Treacy 'A Minor Incident'; Presses Universitaires de France for Flavien Ranaimo, 'Song of a Young Girl' and Léopold Sédar Senghor, 'The Dead' from *Nouvelle Anthologie de la poésie negre et malgache*, ed. Léopold Sédar Senghor, 1948; Random Century UK Ltd for extracts from Isabel Allende, *Of Love and Shadows*, Jonathan Cape, 1987; Marilyn French, *Beyond Power: On Women, Men and Morals,* Jonathan Cape, 1986; Ann Tyler, *The Accidental Tourist,* Chatto & Windus, 1985; and with the Estate of the author for Bruce Chatwin, *On the Black Hill*, Jonathan Cape, 1982; Reed Consumer Books Ltd for James Kelman, 'Sunday Papers' from *Greyhound for Breakfast,* Martin Secker & Warburg Ltd, 1987; and Rose Tremain, 'Over' from *Evangelista's Fan*, Sinclair-Stevenson; and extracts from Olivia Manning, *The Great Fortune*, William Heinemann Ltd; and Elmore Leonard, *Unknown Man No. 89*, Martin Secker & Warburg Ltd, 1986; Seren for an extract from Nicholas Murray, *Bruce Chatwin*, 1993; Sterling Lord Literistic, Inc on behalf of the author for Anne Sexton, 'The Child Bearers' from *45 Mercy Street*, Houghton Mifflin Company. Copyright © 1976 by Anne Sexton; Ruth Stone for 'Room' from *Cheap: New Poems and Ballads*, Harcourt Brace & Company; Today for Paul Wilenius, 'On the Brink of a Ceasefire', *Today*, 31.8.94; Virago Press Ltd for an extract from Maya Angelou, *I Know Why the Caged Bird Sings*.

Every effort has been made to trace all the copyright holders but if any have been inadvertently overlooked the publishers will be pleased to make the necessary arrangement at the first opportunity.

Thanks are also due to the following for permission to reproduce photographs:
Patrick Eagar for page 177; Ronald Grant Archive for page 59 and page 62; Hulton Deutsch Collection for page 154 and page 160; The Hutchison Library for page 45; Redferns Music Picture Library for page 143 and page 185; Trinity House Lighthouse Service for page 214.

We have been unable to trace the photographer of the Wolf Rock Lighthouse on page 214 and would be grateful for any information which would enable us to do so.